ENRON:
ANATOMY of GREED

ARROW

ENRON:
ANATOMY of GREED

The Unshredded Truth from an Enron Insider

Brian Cruver

Foreword by Professor Steve Salbu,
McCombs School of Business,
University of Texas

ARROW

Published by Arrow Books in 2003

3 5 7 9 10 8 6 4 2

First published in 2002 in the United States by
Carroll & Graf Publishers

Arrow
The Random House Group Limited
20 Vauxhall Bridge Road, London SW1V 2SA

Random House Australia (Pty) Limited
20 Alfred Street, Milsons Point, Sydney
New South Wales 2061, Australia

Random House New Zealand Limited
18 Poland Road, Glenfield
Auckland 10, New Zealand

Random House (Pty) Limited
Endulini, 5a Jubilee Road
Parktown 2193, South Africa

The Random House Group Limited Reg. No. 954009

www.randomhouse.co.uk

A CIP catalogue record for this book
is available from the British Library

Papers used by Random House are natural, recyclable products
made from wood grown in sustainable forests. The manufacturing
processes conform to the environmental regulations
of the country of origin

Printed and bound in Great Britain by
Cox & Wyman Ltd, Reading, Berkshire

ISBN 0 09 944682 0

Author's Note

Anatomy of Greed is a factual account of my life inside Enron, covering the most catastrophic corporate collapse in American history. The events chronicled here may seem extreme, twisted, tragic, even funny—that's the way it really was, the *unshredded truth*.

The book includes my own experiences and opinions, combined with those of close associates and colleagues. Additional material was obtained from sources that included hundreds of former and current Enron employees, Enron documents and e-mails, as well as news organizations and public records (there is a list of sources on page 350).

I have altered a handful of characters' names. In some instances, this decision was made out of respect for their privacy, and in other cases it was the condition by which they elected to provide me with extremely sensitive information.

For my wife

. . . the reason this book has a Chapter Eleven

Contents

Foreword

Professor Steve Salbu, McCombs School of Business, University of Texas

T he beginning of the twenty-first century has been cataclysmic. The attacks on the World Trade Center and the spectacular demise of Enron are shaping a new era. We feel vulnerable. We are vulnerable. Truths we have always known in our minds we now feel in our guts: Bad people can obliterate the world's most massive skyscrapers; bad people can destroy the world's most powerful corporations. We muddle along as always, but at the core we are deeply shaken.

Informed Americans have read recent news stories charging some Enron executives with self-dealing, accounting irregularities, debt camouflage, insider trading, and breach of fiduciary duty. Equally disturbing are suggestions that our legal system and accounting procedures encourage activities that most people would confidently identify as unethical. The reports have been difficult to piece together, simply because the workings of any large company are so intricate. What has been missing is an insider's narrative, in the tradition of *Liar's Poker*, Michael Lewis's scalding and funny take on Wall Street in the '80s. Brian Cruver's book, *Anatomy of Greed*, is such an insider's tale. It provides a big-picture perspective on the complex workings of a corporate giant. It is the story of Enron's decline from the vantage point of a recently minted University of Texas M.B.A. who was launching his career working for "the Crooked E."

The book sheds light on questions we are all asking: How did America's seventh largest company implode? How did a company that espoused noble core values deteriorate to the point of infamy? How could the world's educated elite—professionally trained, meticulously selected, and groomed for success—make so many disastrous mistakes? Were key players in Enron's management unable to distinguish right from wrong? Were their eyes simply shut tight? Presuming they had some personal ethical grounding, did they just not care who got hurt by their actions, and at what devastating cost? These are questions that a decade of bullish markets left an optimistic nation unprepared to imagine ever having to ask, let alone answer.

Perhaps most startling is the schism between the values Enron proclaimed and the story you are about to read. We have all heard the phrase "Do as I say, not as I do." Rarely has the difference between sermon and conduct been so dramatic. The contrast between Enron's moral mantra and the behavior of some Enron executives is bone-chilling. Indeed, the Enron saga teaches us the limitations of corporate codes of ethics: how empty and ineffectual they can be. Long touted as crucial accoutrements to moral rectitude, codes are useless when the words are hollow—when executives lack either the dedication to espoused virtues or the ability to make defensible ethical decisions.

Among Enron's stated core values were respect, integrity, communication, and excellence. Recent press stories highlight the gap between corporate code and corporate conduct. Bradley K. Googins writes in *Newsday,*

> When the house of Enron came tumbling down, it exposed the worst of corporate greed, misbehavior and citizenship. Enron betrayed its employees, it betrayed its clients, and, by inflaming the public's widely perceived notion that corporations cannot be trusted to do anything other than serve their own ends and line their own pockets, Enron betrayed all of corporate America.

• • •

In a *St. Louis Post-Dispatch* column called "Board Members Need to Ask Ethical Questions," Rabbi Mark L. Shook attributes the Enron disaster to the "moral deafness" of officers and directors. *The San Francisco Chronicle*'s Mark Simon takes the criticism a step further, likening culpable Enron executives to the robber barons of yore— and quoting attorney Joe Cotchett's characterization of the culprits as "economic terrorists."

So many people—most notably investors and employees, but also society at large—have been badly hurt by the Enron debacle. How could it happen? Business schools must accept some of the responsibility. Recent survey data suggest that M.B.A. students graduate with less concern about social and ethical issues than they had when they entered business school. Sad, yes, and how can it be? Few top M.B.A. programs require students to take a class in ethics. B-school assurances that ethics are examined throughout the curriculum sound hollow, if not downright laughable, to most students and recent M.B.A. graduates. (This is not figurative. My students really do laugh at the suggestion that most or even many classes in B-school examine any ethical issues at all. Brian Cruver, while a student taking my business ethics course in the late '90s, laughed harder than anyone. Little wonder he felt compelled to write the book on Enron's demise.)

Students and alumni—from my own school and others—routinely recount stories of being rebuffed, or even ridiculed, for so much as raising ethical questions in some finance, marketing, and accounting classes. Elective work in ethics, when available, is singularly ill-equipped to address the managerial moral gap. Why? Because those students most in need of the elective courses offered by most high-quality M.B.A. programs routinely self-select out of the classes. Like it or not, business school faculty—myself included—must accept some of the responsibility for the managers we train. Too often we turn out ambitious, intelligent, driven, highly skilled over-achievers with one underdeveloped aptitude. Too many of the business leaders we graduate are hitting the ground running, but we have forgotten to help them to build their moral muscles.

I choose the phrase "moral muscles" advisedly. Doing the right thing, acting honorably, living with integrity—these are behaviors that are learned and practiced and honed, like any other skills in life. Yet the normative lesson many M.B.A.s learn in this new century continues to be the 1980s' lesson of the film *Wall Street's* Gordon Gekko: "Greed is good."

The lesson has hit home with a vengeance. *Washington Post* writer Joel Achenbach aptly describes the Enron legacy as business "newly revealed as a terrifying enterprise only lightly tethered to morality and decency." We will live with this disgraceful legacy until we demand better—until we train business leaders to be true professionals with true character.

—*Steve Salbu, J.D., Ph.D.*
Sublett Centennial Professor of Law and Ethics
University Distinguished Teaching Professor
Associate Dean, M.B.A. Program
McCombs School of Business
University of Texas at Austin

Introduction

ENRON. The very name inspired extremes of emotion in all who heard it. For the most part, it was the usual suspects: fear and greed.

Fear among competitors, suppliers, customers, and even Enron's own employees looking ahead to the next "rank and yank" performance review. Greed among those who dreamed of colossal bonuses, millions in stock options, and generous campaign contributions. Fear and greed have always played the lead role in the history of American business; but in the case of Enron, these two catalysts were radically and permanently entrenched—throughout the culture, the people, and the industries Enron touched.

And it was this same fear and greed that would ultimately destroy the company . . .

It was fear of mediocrity that sent 15 percent of employees out the door with pink slips every six months; fear of the financial truth that forced Enron executives to hide company debts and losses in a hideous web of partnership deals; fear of the future that led to hundreds of executive resignations, billions in insider stock sales, and a surge in psychiatric illness.

Greed had lifted Enron's stock price up 1,700 percent; greed had left competitors and customers, including the state of California, violently angry after dealing with Enron; greed had pushed Enron to ignore the very same risk strategies that it was preaching to the world; greed led Enron employees to madly buy stock just days before the bankruptcy; and it was greed that chose to ignore—or even punish—the messengers of bad news.

For a wildly unimaginable year of my life, I was right at the heart of it all—a witness to history as it happened all around me. In terms of job security, the Enron failure was the wrong place at the wrong time; but for experiencing the most bizarre and spectacular events in the history of business, I was very lucky to be there. If my days at Enron were "like a box of chocolates," I would have lost all my teeth.

Many books will be written about Enron: its meteoric rise and shattering fall, its impact on the global economy, and the biographies of those who started it all. Someone will write the business case, the legal case, or the accounting case; and someone will write about how *they* knew the collapse was coming.

But I want to tell you a different story. I want to show you how life really was for those of us down in the trenches; the people all around me, and how *we didn't want to see it coming*—because we didn't want to believe it was happening. I want you to see Enron through the eyes of those who lived and breathed it. I want you to walk the halls of the place we called the Death Star.

And I want you to know the *truth*. For one thing, that Enron was not about energy.

Enron, like the story I'm about to tell, is about control, risk, and greed.

ANATOMY of GREED

Welcome to the Death Star

"Where wealth accumulates, men decay."
—*Oliver Goldsmith*

Monday—March 26, 2001
ENE opening price: $61.00
ENE closing price: $61.48
ENE trading volume: 4,112,900

I wasn't dreaming.

On my first day as a new Enron employee, I could approach 1400 Smith Street as if I really belonged there. Just as you would expect from the epicenter of gas and power trading, the air and the streets were filled with high energy. The type of energy that made you walk faster. As I fell in line with the streams of Enronians heading into the main building, I suddenly realized I was marching double-time. This was it. The pace had been set, and it fit my stride perfectly.

I was built to work at Enron.

Like anyone from Houston and anyone who went to business school in Texas, I had always known that Enron was the ultimate launching pad for a business career. Highly respected, bitterly admired—if you were craving the fast track, you dreamed of working at Enron. Everyone knew it, and everybody talked about it: the people of Enron were simply "the best and the brightest" . . . and now,

I was finally one of them. On that first day, in a time that seems so long ago now, I remember trying to project the image of brilliance, sophistication, and self-control. But inside Enron's newest manager was a kid, and he was ready to scream, "This place is bad-ass!"

The excitement was mixed with a wave of relief. Finally, I would get instant respect from family, friends, business associates, and complete strangers. Finally I could just say "Enron" and not have to explain where I worked. Everyone would be impressed.

I had taken a couple of risks after B-school.

First I joined a small, babyish trading firm on the other side of downtown Houston. Even though the firm was owned by Shell, it simply couldn't compete (with Enron, that is) and quickly fell apart.

Then I wasted a year of my life creating www.startup-without-money.com. No explanation needed on that one.

With Enron, I finally felt like my days of high risk were over. It was time to get back on track and reap steady rewards from the dues I had paid—the time and money I put toward getting an M.B.A., the years of grinding away at Excel spreadsheets. Finally, I was ready to sprint down the path to my success. I had just hit the jackpot in the form of a safe, secure job at the seventh biggest company in America.

My fat head and I walked up the steps to Enron Center North—fifty stories of mirrored glass, in a shape not unlike a Speed Stick deodorant container. The mirrored glass was part of the plan—we could all glance to see how smart and successful we were as we entered our building.

The first thing I noticed when I entered Enron headquarters was the space-age environment. The lobby was surprisingly small, with simple curves and a dramatic absence of color. Only the red, green, and blue of Enron logos or the images on massive video screens distracted me from the clean, chromed shapes all around.

And if it wasn't glass or chrome, it was a soft, gray marble—imported from some distant galaxy.

Security was tight, if not intense. The checkpoints created a pair of bottlenecks, each allowing one Enronian at a time to enter the main lobby. I had heard many times that Enron Corporate Security was ex-CIA, common for large corporations with such a heavy stake in intellectual capital. I wondered if the security guards already knew me. Perhaps they had studied my picture at their last briefing. Perhaps they knew what I had eaten for breakfast that morning.

As a new employee, I was told to go wait in a special area referred to as the New Employee Waiting Area. Wow. A company growing so fast and hiring so many people that they had designated a special area for new employees. About forty of them were already gathered there on that Monday morning.

As I strolled confidently past the checkpoints, I had a telepathic exchange with one of the security guards.

He sent me a message I interpreted as, "Go ahead, buddy. Just try it."

I quickly beamed my own thoughts back at him, "Oh, I have access. . . . I'm just not quite ready to use it."

I looked up and saw a banner the size of a mobile home: FROM THE WORLD'S LEADING ENERGY COMPANY—TO THE WORLD'S LEADING COMPANY. The banner hadn't been there a week earlier during my interviews. The company was removing the word *Energy* from its mission, and the banner was declaring it to the world. Enron was now ready to take over everything.

For about two seconds, I wondered if they had changed it just for me.

As I reached the mass of new hires, I was almost clobbered by an enormous, three-dimensional "E" logo as it rotated with flashing lights. Very nice! A bit disco, but very nice.

I looked around at my new company, eating it all up as fast as I could chew and swallow. It was a constant flow of impressive people; casually dressed, moderately stressed. They all had very serious looks on their faces, but it was more of an "intellectual serious" than a "concerned serious." They were changing the world, creating new markets, and rising to the top—they had every right to be serious.

Next thing I knew—*I had turned serious.* I cleared my glazed look and tightened my upper lip.

"Cruver!" The voice was familiar.

I turned to see John Weston, an old friend from the M.B.A. program at the University of Texas. He was waiting in the same area as the other new initiates. Today was John's first day at Enron, too—our career paths had just collided.

Ordinarily, this would just be a funny coincidence, but it was more than that. You see, John had an undergraduate degree from Harvard, and he was the guy in our B-school that set the curve. Everyone thought of him as being ten times smarter than the second-smartest person they knew. Now he and I were exactly equal—in time and place—with our careers. Perhaps this meant that people would think of *me* as being ten times smarter than the second-smartest person they knew, unless they knew us both, in which case . . .

A woman with a clipboard interrupted my analysis by announcing directions on how to get to the orientation room. We were all given our first access, albeit temporary, and we formed a line.

This was the moment. I smiled at my new friend the security guard and passed through to the other side: the Enron world.

I distinctly remember my first elevator ride as an Enron employee. I had two thoughts.

Thought one: "I think it would be beneficial to my career if I could stay at Enron for at least three years."

Thought two: "I made it."

Again, I felt the energy. This time, it was flowing through my veins. We reached the orientation room to find a massive table of pastry, fruit, and other breakfast treats. The theme that day was caffeine and sugar, and we were going to need every bit of it—we had eight hours of the Human Resources department ahead of us.

"Blah" describes the day perfectly. Aside from an almost amusing introduction by an Elvis impersonator, the orientation session was pure tedium. My eyes rolled back into my head as the HR department began sucking the life right out of me. I wanted to skip it. I wanted to go upstairs to the trading floor. I wanted to start working on deals.

Handout after handout, speaker after speaker, I was being sold on the Enron values. These "core values" were being drummed into my head: Respect, Integrity, Communication, Excellence.

"Sure," I thought. "Sounds good to me."

Then something *really* got my attention. We were handed the Enron 401(k) Plan Details. Page four talked about the company matching 50 percent of whatever I put in my 401(k)—wow! Free money! At the top of that same page was a decorative headline quote: "'Lack of money is the root of all evil'—George Bernard Shaw." Okay, now we're talkin'.

After a few hours of paperwork and staring at my watch, it was time for our lunch break. All the new employees went off to grab pizza and mingle with one another, but not me. My boss showed up—was he here to rescue me from this administrative nightmare and take me up to the trading floor? No such luck.

I soon discovered that Greg McLainey was a very likeable guy, even when he wanted to rip my face off. He had a very creative business mind and a background in engineering. Everything in his brain translated to a diagram on a wall-mounted drawing board.

His hands told a story of someone who had worked extremely hard all his life—and there was no doubt he expected the same from me. He was a bit older than the average Enronian, with graying hair and a cautious smile. His personality was difficult to read, except for a constant message to the world that time was running out. Was it running out for him? Was it running out for him at Enron? I couldn't tell.

In any case, this guy was not about filler. No bullshit allowed. He would cut to the chase before you even knew he was standing over you.

He had come down during my orientation break to tell me some things before I went upstairs to join our group. McLainey disguised the meeting as "Hey, let's grab lunch," but I could sense it was more than that.

I had been hired by McLainey into one of Enron's newest start-up businesses. After some no-bullshit interviews with him and the head of the group, I was given an offer . . . and it was a great offer. A fat salary, plenty of Enron stock options, and the promise of a year-end bonus had all been handed to me; I would have taken much less to work at Enron.

The group I was joining was just a couple of years old, and its focus was on buying and selling credit risk as a commodity. The big challenge for the group was selling derivatives to customers who needed protection against third-party bankruptcies.

The concepts, products, and markets for bankruptcy protection were relatively new to the corporate world. I had been hired to join McLainey and a few others on the development team, which meant we would be responsible for polishing those concepts, creating those products, and lubricating those markets. In other words, the long-term future of this fledgling business (and the hundred or so people that worked in it) was in our hands.

They had hired me because I had started businesses before, and because I had a strategic eye for designing products and creating alliances in the market. I was young, but so was everyone else at Enron. And I had an M.B.A. I was ripe for the job.

And I was overflowing with confidence when McLainey showed up for our surprise lunch meeting.

I thought there had to be something real juicy to tell me, and I knew he wanted to just lay it on me. Instead, he began the conversation with some courtesy small talk. Then the exchange went as follows:

McLAINEY: "There's something I need to tell you about. I'm telling you because I don't want you to be caught off guard."

ME: "All right."

McLAINEY: "There was a slight mix-up in the hiring process."

ME (frozen stare): "This is a joke, right?"

McLAINEY: "No."

ME: "Uhhh . . ."

McLAINEY: "It's no big deal. We're going to keep you. I just wanted you to know because some people aren't real happy that you're here. I want you prepared because they'll probably say something to you."

ME: "Are you telling me you didn't want to hire me?"

McLAINEY: "No, I wanted to hire you. It's just that the *group* really hadn't *agreed* to hire you."

ME: "Interesting."

McLAINEY: "Just think of it like you're adopted."

At that moment I heard a "pop"—the sound of my bubble bursting. I was thinking that April Fool's Day was not for another week.

The subject quickly changed, but our conversation really didn't seem too enjoyable after that. I was stunned, to say the least.

Fortunately I had more orientation that afternoon, which gave me a few hours to simmer down.

Was this guy for real? I just kept thinking it had to be a test. One of those classic "new kid" mind games to see how thick my skin was.

It just didn't make sense. How could Enron be named the "most innovative" company seven years in a row, and then hire someone by mistake? My skin was thick, but not *that* thick.

Was I on thin ice already? If there wasn't any room for me on the payroll, would they be looking for a way to clear me off? Shit! My Enron career was four hours old and I was already losing my edge.

The afternoon was a blur; I could think about nothing but my conversation with McLainey. When the time came to head upstairs to my new desk and my new career at Enron, I had a whole new type of energy. It wasn't the "I made it" energy from before, but more of an "I'm pissed" energy. All I could do was bite my tongue and act professional.

One of the best business skills I have is the ability to hide my emotions and what I am really thinking. So when I finally met with the people in my group, I was able to smile and say "Hello," "Hi," and "Nice to meet you"—while in my head I was greeting them with "Bite me."

One of the people McLainey introduced me to that afternoon was Vic Lazarri. He was known as Vic "The Prick," a term I decided never to use. He was a deal man. More specifically, he tried to shove a variety of risk-management products down the customers' throats, whether they made financial sense or not. Lazarri was having a tough year—since his customers weren't convinced that bankruptcy risk was anything they needed to worry about.

He barely gave me a quick nod upon introduction, and then was back on the phones. Two phones, one in each hand, with six flat-screen monitors mounted in front of his face. The screens were filled with Bloomberg charts, news wires, and video feeds of other people like him from around the world. Lazarri was only about one millisecond behind every event that took place on planet Earth. Sometimes it even seemed like he got ahead of it.

Lazarri had the bushiest eyebrows I'd ever seen, and leathery skin like he went to the Caribbean four times a year. He was a bit on the midget side, barely taller than his stacked computer screens. You could actually watch him burn calories just standing there on the phones—as he constantly rearranged himself, and blinked his eyelids like a madman.

Vic was the market adviser to everyone on the trading floor, and ultimately to me as well, although oddly enough he avoided commenting on any specific stocks, with one exception: he was always following ENE (Enron's ticker symbol on the New York Stock Exchange). He seemed to know exactly where it was headed.

I relaxed at my new desk for about half a second when the phone rang.

"Cruver! Welcome to the Crooked E!" It was another friend from business school who was calling from fifteen floors above. Ron Middleton was working in the Enron group called Risk Assessment and Control, more commonly known as RAC.

The Crooked E? It *was* true: the Enron logo was the letter E tilted at forty-five degrees, though the tilt was not exactly what he was referring to. That was the first time I had heard the expression, and it made me laugh.

Soon my first e-mail arrived, from a friend at an Enron competitor across the street. He had learned the news of my Enron arrival, and figured out my new e-mail address:

Cruver! . . .
So, another Jedi goes over to the dark side . . .
—J

• • •

While the "Crooked E" nickname was new to me, I *had* heard the
many *Star Wars* references used to describe Enron. In my days at the
Shell trading firm, we often discussed Enron using these metaphors,
and of course they made perfect sense. For example:

Enron was the Dark Side or the Empire, the dominant force in
the energy universe, taking control of everything in its path, relent-
lessly gobbling up other companies and assets. The Dark Side could
manipulate anything—from politicians, to suppliers, to regulators,
to entire commodity markets. Other companies were simply help-
less against the sheer size and strength of Enron's wicked force.

Chief Executive Officer Jeff Skilling was known as Darth Vader,
a master of the energy universe who had the ability to control
people's minds. He was at the peak of his strength, and he intimi-
dated everyone. He had been lured over to the Dark Side from
McKinsey & Company in 1990.

Chairman Ken Lay, a bit past his prime, was the Emperor. He had
trained Skilling, and was now unleashing him on the rest of the energy
industry as part of a master plan. Lay had built the Empire to its current strength. Now Skilling was running the place, but the Emperor
was still the boss.

Enron headquarters in Houston was the Death Star. All of
Enron's competitors were lined up down Smith Street, watching
helplessly as the Death Star grew, and grew, and grew. Their only
hope was to destroy it while it was still under construction.

The *Star Wars* theme was actually well received by people inside
Enron. They didn't really mind being the bad guy, as long as it
meant they were all-powerful and dominant. I didn't mind joining
the Dark Side either—after all, the Empire offered great pay and
excellent benefits.

The Death Star was on the edge of downtown Houston—a city

built by the energy industry, always struggling to diversify. Companies like Continental Airlines and Compaq Computer had helped the city break away from its good ol' boy roots in oil, while companies like Enron were bringing the energy business to an ultra-modern edge.

As Enron grew at a staggering pace, so did the Death Star itself. Enron's main tower was not enough, so employees filled most of the surrounding office towers as well. Under construction was the new Enron Center South, a clone to the existing tower. Nearing completion was the new connecting ring that linked both buildings and the garage. The ring hovered about thirty feet above Smith Street.

The new ring, called the Saturn Ring, was just part of a complex system of air-conditioned passageways that connected the Death Star buildings with surrounding buildings and garages. This tunnel system was essential for Enronians from May to September, when the heat and humidity were simply unbearable. The tunnel maze went through building lobbies, up and down escalators, above and below streets, and was never the fastest way to get somewhere. It was a ridiculous maze that only a hamster could enjoy.

I sat there that first evening examining my new surroundings. It was getting late, though I had no choice but to follow one of the business rules I had developed during my career:

How to Conquer Corporate America, Rule #1: You can't go home until everyone else above you in the organization has gone home.

I simply had to stick around until Doug Waterston finally went home. He was the head of the group and the only other person left on the trading floor. Did he sleep here?

Waterston had been one of my interviewers the previous week, but I hadn't had a chance to talk to him that first day. He was too busy, and even with the janitors starting to roll in, I wasn't about to interrupt him.

He was, by everyone's definition, an absolute genius. With an intense glare, he amazed people every time he spoke. He had been at Enron for a lifetime, which was about twelve years. He knew everything there was to know about Enron, and I was determined to learn it all from him.

He had left his place within the inner circles of Enron to start our new and innovative business. It had grown to over a hundred people worldwide, and was burning through millions of dollars a month in search of profitability. This was his baby. His future and his reputation were riding on it. As he explained in my interview, trading credit risk and selling bankruptcy protection was the next big thing at Enron; and the fastest way for Waterston to reach the top at Enron was to be the man behind the next big thing.

As I looked over at him, he was hunched over his keyboard with his shoulders practically above his ears. Contracts were displayed on his computer screen, and he was visually scanning them at an alarming rate. The man seemed tense and overfocused. I noticed he had thin hair and bags under his eyes; but then again so did a lot of Enron executives.

Suddenly he checked his watch and sharply whispered "damn" under his breath. He left his computer on, left his briefcase behind, and zipped off the trading floor. He was gone, but he wasn't going home. He was headed upstairs to a meeting.

I gave up on waiting for him to leave. I stayed at my desk for just another minute, in case he had forgotten something. Then I left.

I rode down the elevator contemplating my new job, my new company, and my bright future. I gave up on trying to figure out if the hiring mix-up was real or not; I decided I didn't care. Despite that one big bump on my first day, everything was falling into place.

I was now part of "the best and the brightest." I was at the same career level as the Harvard guy. I had been hired on as an innovator, into a cutting-edge new group, at the world's most creative company. Enron was poised to take over the world, and I was going to be a part of that revolution.

I looked up at the banner as I passed through the lobby: THE WORLD'S LEADING COMPANY. Realistic, I thought.

And, the fact I was working at a place known as the Death Star—that was just cool.

In early 2001 the Empire was more powerful than ever. *Fortune* magazine came out with the Fortune 500, listing Enron as #7 for the year 2000. The ranking was based on revenues, of which Enron had over $100 billion. These revenues were 150 percent higher than in 1999, and that staggering growth was continuing.

In fact, the first quarter of 2001 put Enron on pace for $240 billion in revenues by the end of the year; which analysts were predicting would put Enron ahead of ExxonMobil by $10 billion, *making it Fortune #1 for 2001*. It was just a matter of time.

The *Fortune* lists were the pride and joy of the company. Almost every doorway in the Enron building had headline clippings stuck to them:

Ranked #31—*Fortune*'s Fastest Growing Companies
Ranked #22—*Fortune*'s Best Companies To Work For
Ranked #25—*Fortune*'s Most Admired Companies in the World
Seven Years in a Row—*Fortune*'s Most Innovative Company

That last one seemed to matter the most. *Innovation*. It was the pride and joy of the company that we were considered the most creative and inventive company year after year after year. It's all we ever talked about. The title of Most Innovative was everywhere. Being innovative was the critical aspect of our performance reviews. If we weren't innovative, we would get fired. Innovation was the key to our business, and the key to advancement within the company.

It wasn't only revenues, growth, and innovation that put Enron on top of the business world. The stock price was soaring, and Wall Street adored us. Shares had reached nearly $90 at the end of 2000, and most major investment banks were covering Enron stock with ratings like Buy, Strong Buy, Outperform, or Accumulate.

Tuesday—April 3, 2001
ENE opening price: $57.20
ENE closing price: $54.06
ENE trading volume: 3,189,500

At the beginning of April, about a week after that first day at Enron, I was invited to attend a small but prestigious energy technology conference at the Williams Tower in Houston. The conference was hosted by Williams, a major Enron competitor. The opening speaker was Ken Lay, Enron Chairman.

Lay spoke that morning of Enron's future: creating new markets, creating new technologies. He spoke about the numbers: twenty-one thousand employees in more than forty countries—with thirty thousand miles of pipeline and fifteen thousand miles of fiber-optic cable. He spoke of a future so bright and so groundbreaking that it gave me goose bumps.

When Lay's speech mentioned the start-up group I had just joined, I became an instant celebrity. The rest of my interactions at the conference seemed to center on me. It was amazing—I walked from person to person, trying to focus on their booth or their start-up or anything else, but the conversation always came back to Enron. It was all because the words from Ken Lay's mouth matched the "next big thing," the Enron division on my conference name tag. I had CEOs and bigwigs from all around the industry walking up to me and saying, "So, tell me about the group that Ken mentioned this morning."

Of course, I didn't know shit. I had only been there a week, so I had to reach back into my memory of pre-interview research. My answers were a brilliant brush of basic finance touched up with a bit of natural fertilizer.

The lunchtime speaker at the conference was David Fleischer, managing director with Goldman, Sachs & Company, and a world renowned expert on the energy industry. I had seen him around the conference all morning, mingling with the other legends in attendance. Jack Bowen, retired chairman of Transco, gave Fleischer one of his original paintings as a gift. These guys were not only business legends, they were all good friends.

According to the conference schedule, the Fleischer speech was to discuss the main topic of the conference: technology and the future of the energy industry.

Almost all he spoke about was ENE.

Fleischer spoke of Enron as the industry leader, as the best stock to own, and as a growth machine. He even threw out a dollar figure of $120 as a potential price target for ENE stock in 2001. I was blown away. I wanted to call my broker right after lunch to load up on ENE. When the speech was finished he sat back down at his table that included Enron's top brass.

I was convinced. If Fleischer loved ENE, if Goldman loved ENE, and if investors loved ENE, then Enron was on top of the world. The Empire was running the show, just like we ran the conference that day in a competitor's building. I left the conference feeling like I had won the lottery.

It took me a while to drive back to Enron. Houston was about thirty years behind in road construction, so traffic was eternally constipated.

My mobile phone started vibrating in my pocket—earlier, at the conference, I had switched it to mute. I sat and enjoyed the sensation for a few seconds, and then answered. It was one of my closest friends, Bernie Bickers.

BICKERS: "Cruver!"
ME: "What's up, Bickers?"

Bernie Bickers and I had worked together at the other trading firm, and shared a passion for sailing. He was going to be a groomsman in my wedding in a few months. He was calling me from New York.

BICKERS: "Dude. Your office said you haven't been there all day. Did they fire you already?"
ME: "Not yet. . . . So what's up?"
BICKERS: "Dude. I just pulled an all-nighter going over Enron crap."
ME: "Anything interesting?"
BICKERS: "Actually, there's somethi . . . hold on a second . . ."
I was suddenly listening to Wall Street's finest cheesy hold music. Five seconds later . . .
BICKERS: "Dude. It's about Enron. I'll call you back . . ."

That was pretty much a typical conversation with Bickers. He was a purebred New Yorker, and he was very excitable. The only thing working faster than his brain was his mouth. Fortunately, he was one of the funniest people this side of Connecticut. I always thought he should do stand up. Instead, he was a Wall Street geek.

He had left the old trading firm right after I did. Houston just didn't agree with him, and from the moment he got there he was trying to get back to New York. He landed a job as an equity research analyst with a top banking firm, covering the energy industry. He loved his job and he loved New York City. His biggest thrill was when he was quoted in the papers or on CNBC. Ironically, the companies he researched were all in Houston, the city he so desperately tried to escape.

Mostly he spent his time analyzing Enron.

I reached the Death Star parking garage and began the dizzying journey to the top. That late in the day, the only available spaces would be on the roof level, thirteen spirals up.

It was a hypnotic left-hand turn that seemed truly infinite. As you drove past an impressive collection of SUVs, Porches, Mercedes, and BMWs, the subject of money would naturally come into your head. These people had money. Lots of money. Soon, I would have lots of money, too. Let's see, I want that one in black, and that one in green, and . . .

As if to distract you from the car shopping, management had made a sincere attempt to steer your mind back to the true meaning of life at Enron. The walls on each level of the parking garage were covered in colorful, billboard-size messages. For a few minutes, as I fought my way to the top, Enron took control of my brain . . .

Level 1—"BOLD . . . enough to see the right answers and look for the right questions."

Level 2—"INNOVATIVE . . . both in our quest for ideas and our creation of new businesses."

Level 3—"SMART . . . enough to see a new solution, wise enough to judge its merits."

Level 4—"UNITED . . . internally to reach our goals and with our clients to exceed their expectations."

Level 5—"AMBITIOUS . . . to succeed because we know our work has purpose and consequence."

Level 6—"ACCOMPLISHED . . . because for us, ambition is only a measure of our ability to succeed."

Level 7—"RESOURCEFUL . . . because the leader of the pack is usually the one that got to the front first."

Level 8—"CREATIVE . . . because we believe if you're not in a box, you don't have to think outside of it."

Level 9—"CONFIDENT . . . by blazing our own trail and showing the competition a better way to get there."

Level 10—"ADVENTUROUS . . . because we've established a reputation for excellence and excellence means outdoing ourselves every day."

Level 11—"ADAPTABLE . . . because we pride ourselves on the unity of our efforts, while resisting predictability in our actions."

Level 12—"UNDAUNTED . . . because we take pride in our accomplishments and even greater pride in our potential to exceed them."

By the thirteenth level, I was ready to puke from my tornadic ascent. Fortunately I was resourceful, confident, and adaptable— so I was able to hold back the wave of bile rising in my throat.

I arrived at my desk to a ringing phone. My voice-mail message light was blinking, and my e-mail inbox had a dozen messages from McLainey. Almost a full day had been used up at the conference, and I was running on fumes. I was starving.

Lazarri was telling a customer to "eat shit and die" for holding out on a deal. Waterston had a huge coffee stain on the front of his shirt, and his sleeves looked like he had rolled them up in a hurry. McLainey was peeking out of the corner of his eye, as if to say, "I'm watching you . . . so get to those e-mails."

I answered the phone call just in time.

"Enron," I answered, with a been-there-done-that tone. I'm sure I sounded like I had answered it that way a thousand times before.

It was Bickers again, calling me back from New York. He had just finished his earlier phone call concerning Enron.

"Dude . . . Your company is in *deep shit*."

Somehow, after just a few days at the company, I took it personally. "What are you talking about?" I asked with a tone like I didn't really care.

"Let's see," he began. I sensed he would be giving me a list. "India, Broadband, Azurix . . . "

I faded him out. He was listing everything and anything negative about Enron that the world already knew. Whatever! With $100 billion in revenues there had to be a few bumps and bruises. Anything that went south and incurred a loss would just be absorbed by the massive gains.

I tried to argue a few points but Bickers was being his usual stubborn self. He started going off about "page 48" from the 2001 Annual Report—something about related-party transactions. I suddenly lost track of what language he was speaking. I ended the conversation there; I didn't have time to discuss big-picture ENE when I had to focus on my new job in a small start-up business.

Bickers was new at this. He just wasn't thinking of Enron the way everyone else did.

Enron should be thought of in terms of the future.

2

A Risk e-Business

> "If everything seems under control, you're just not going fast enough."
> —*Mario Andretti, automobile racing legend*

For over a decade, the people of Enron were telling me about the future. Even before I studied Enron as a business student, my friends and associates that worked at the Houston-based pipeline company were preaching to me about market making and empire building. It didn't mean much then, but it sounded exciting and it sounded like it was happening fast.

By the time I arrived at business school in Austin in 1997, Enron had become the model for strategic growth. Enron was a common case-study for concepts such as commoditization, deregulation, and globalization. We studied Enron furiously, knowing that by the end of each semester the Enron story would have already changed.

Believe it or not, the history of what many people later called the most innovative company goes all the way back to the 1920s, when a pair of Houston pipeline companies each formed to carry gas along the coast of the Gulf of Mexico. In 1956 these companies merged under the name Houston Natural Gas (HNG).

While these companies were working the coast, another company was building a pipeline network between the Texas Panhandle and the midwestern United States. Northern Natural Gas, which would ultimately call itself InterNorth, went public on the New York Stock Exchange (NYSE) in 1947.

HNG joined InterNorth on the exchange in 1968, and they continued to expand their network of pipes through both new construction and acquisitions. In 1985, these two companies merged to create a pipeline system that touched every coast and border of the continental United States. The fun was just beginning.

Ken Lay became CEO of the new company, which took on the new name "Enron" in an attempt to sound more modern. In 1987, the new company and its new leader would state the first company vision: "To become the premier natural gas pipeline company in North America."

Lay took Enron global in the late '80s and early '90s, beginning with the monster Teesside power plant in England. Back in North America, Enron had increased its natural-gas market share enough to be the biggest in the hemisphere. It was time to change the company vision in 1990: "To become the world's first natural gas major."

With completion of the Teesside plant in England, Enron had begun a mad rush of international expansion. Central and South America, the Caribbean, India, and the Philippines became major development or acquisition sites for pipelines and plants. Back in the States, Enron was the dominant force in marketing both natural gas and electricity. In 1995, it was again time for a new vision: "To become the world's leading energy company."

For an energy company, there wasn't much more than that. But Enron was becoming much more than an energy company, even as it was announcing that goal in 1995. The second half of the '90s saw Enron creating new markets in water, metals, coal, paper, Internet bandwidth, weather, and anything else that could be "commoditized." The business model was simple: Control the assets that are needed to control the commodity, create a standard platform or "hub" for that commodity, and establish a network of trading partners to deal in that commodity. The rapid expansion of this strategy, beyond just dominating the world's energy markets, led Enron to the new vision that appeared the week I arrived in 2001: "To become the world's leading company."

It wasn't just about energy anymore. And it wasn't about Ken Lay anymore. Lay had stepped down as company CEO at the end of 2000, allowing his sidekick Jeff Skilling to take his place at the controls for the new vision and the new millennium. It made perfect sense. After all, it was Skilling in the '90s who had taken Enron's vision beyond energy in the first place.

Dr. Kenneth Lee Lay was a politician. As he passed by my desk in the middle of his biggest trading floor, it was like he was garnering votes. Before I looked up to see him, the regular floor noises had stopped and been replaced by a buzz of excitement. When I did look up, he was gliding by as if he owned the place. He did own the place. He was the man who started it all. He was a hometown hero.

Ken Lay dreamed of being a business giant even as a kid, sitting atop a tractor in rural Missouri and dreaming about the legends of American industry. He was a consistent crusader for free enterprise, who established himself both academically and professionally as a believer in the benefits of the open market. And he knew how to talk about it—this son of a Baptist minister could really talk about it.

Ken and his sister Sharon attended the University of Missouri. In 1965, Ken received both a master's degree in economics from Missouri and a doctorate in economics from the University of Houston. After some time in the navy, Lay wound up working for the Federal Energy Regulatory Commission (FERC). One of the companies he regulated, Florida Gas, was run by Jack Bowen. Bowen hired Lay as his vice president of new energy ventures. Ultimately Lay would end up in Houston when Bowen became chairman of Transco in 1981. Four years later, Ken Lay was ready to run his own show.

Over the next fifteen years, Lay built the Enron Empire—from a Texas pipeline company to Fortune #7—and built his own fortune as well. He and his wife, Linda, lived in a $7 million penthouse apartment in River Oaks, the tight-faced core of mega-money Houston. They owned several other properties as well, including several multimillion-dollar estates in Colorado and along the Texas coast. A friend of mine who knew Lay in the early days of Enron quotes him as saying, "I don't want to be rich, I want to be world-class rich." As one of the highest-paid executives in the country, he had certainly achieved that goal.

The Lay family was also very generous with their millions. It seemed as if every other charity in Houston had the Lay or Enron name attached to it. Most Houstonians recognized Lay for his contribution to Houston sports. After the Houston Oilers NFL franchise had left Houston and moved to Tennessee (becoming the Titans), the baseball and basketball teams were hinting at similar exit strategies. Lay took center stage, in public debate and with some corporate money.

Soon the Houston Astros were hitting home runs in sparkling new Enron Field, and Dr. Ken Lay himself was throwing out the first pitch on opening day. He helped save the NBA franchise as well, pushing a referendum to build a new downtown arena. He was Houston's father figure. He was trustworthy. You could sit on his lap and tell him what you wanted for Christmas.

Many people believe that Ken Lay passed the controls to Skilling in late 2000 so the good doctor could start his political career. The rumors circled mostly around Lay as Houston's next mayor. As I watched him pass by my desk that first time, there was no doubt in my mind: "He's got my vote."

Expansion, innovation, and shareholder wealth were the

driving forces that pushed Ken Lay and Enron to the edge of global dominance with startling ease. The strategy had not only put Enron on the world map, but it allowed Lay to pick up a brilliant supporting cast along the way. First and foremost was Skilling, who became glued to Lay's side—first as a consultant to Enron (with McKinsey), and then as a permanent part of Enron leadership.

Skilling was known to himself and others as the smartest human being ever to walk the face of the earth. He never lost, and he never failed. He was arrogant and ultracompetitive. He was known for taking fellow executives on dangerous, extreme-sports junkets around the world; he loved to take risks.

Jeffrey Keith Skilling was the perfect partner for Ken Lay. It wasn't just the Harvard M.B.A., or the fact that they shared the Beta Theta Pi secret handshake; but the fact that together they were a perfect one-two punch for representing Enron. Lay on the outside, Skilling on the inside.

Lay, again the politician, would be the faceman on the street telling investors, analysts, employees, and regulators the story of Enron's future. Lay would publicly preach about markets and mission statements, while Skilling was deep inside the Enron core, masterminding the company's clean and mean culture and its strategy for changing the world. It was a strategy of controlling markets through trading, while being light on assets.

A new employee at Enron was expected to hit the ground running. My first few days, I was running as fast as I could. Not only was I being bombarded with assignments from McLainey and Waterston, but I had a pile of reading material that was hitting my chin. It was not critical that I read it all, but was more along the lines of, "Hey, you should look this over when you get a chance." Everyone had something to donate to the pile. The stack included training manuals, magazine articles, investor propaganda, and recent presentation slides. It was all Enron—and I was expected to know Enron.

I found a few spare minutes late one afternoon, and decided to dive in. The most obvious starting point: the Enron Annual Report for 2000. Like most annual reports, this one began with a letter to shareholders from the company leaders.

Inside that letter, Skilling and Lay told me all about the growth Enron had realized the year before. Growth in each of the company's four "service" groups: Wholesale, Energy, Broadband, and Transportation. They spoke in terms of volume, delivery, and transactions—and everything had increased from the year before.

But forget the year-over-year increase; their message was about the future. As I read it, I sat back in my chair and visualized Enron's blue ink spilling across a map of the world, until every continent was covered:

> *We believe wholesale gas and power in North America, Europe, and Japan will grow from a $660 billion market to a $1.7 trillion market over the next several years. Retail energy services in the United States and Europe have the potential to grow from $180 billion to $765 billion in the not-so-distant future. Broadband's prospective global growth is huge—it should increase from just $17 billion today to $1.4 trillion within five years. Taken together, these markets present a $3.9 trillion opportunity for Enron, and we have just scratched the surface.*

Scratched the surface! One hundred billion dollars in revenue, and we had just scratched the surface. It was the kind of business poetry that brought a joyful tear to an investor's eye. No wonder Enron had Wall Street's undivided attention and investors' affection.

And that future growth potential didn't even include the weird stuff. Enron was making new markets in recycled newsprint, advertising space, freight, and bottled beer. Okay, maybe not bottled beer—but it seemed like that was just around the corner. Everything was just around the corner.

And how did all of these new markets come about? Innovation! There's that word again. Enron rewarded people . . . that is, Skilling rewarded people, for coming up with new ideas that applied the Enron business model. If you were stuck in the middle of an established group, like gas or power, then your fast track to success was to break free from that group and make headlines with your new idea. If you could sell the new idea to Skilling, you had yourself a new business unit and a mention in the next year's annual report. If you could prove the market potential, and get Skilling and Lay to pass the message to their Wall Street friends, then suddenly your new idea was increasing the stock price . . . long before that new idea was off the ground, let alone showing and/or making a profit.

Once you had your new business unit dealing in the next big thing, you had to quickly ramp the business up and start proving your idea. The goal at that stage was very clear: volume, volume, volume. The truth is, margins on commodity-related deals are microscopic. So the only way to make $1 million in profit was to transact on $1 billion's worth of the commodity. It took time to build volumes; therefore, it took time to build a successful idea into a money-making business.

So how did Enron build volumes? One way was by selling the transactions to customers as "services" or "solutions." Enron was a service company, just as the annual report said. The service Enron provided could be described as certainty, reliability, or predictability, and it was all true. Enron customers would transact with Enron to protect themselves from uncertainty or risk. If the customer was worried about rising gas prices, then Enron would sell them a contract that "fixed" their price. Whatever the risk Enron could structure a deal that eliminated the customer's risk and transferred the risk to Enron.

How to Conquer Corporate America, Rule #2: Never talk about the weather.

Of course, gas and power were the bread and butter of Enron, but it was innovation that put Enron on the map. There's no finer example of such revolutionary creativity than a weather derivative.

Let's say you own a company in Atlantic City, New Jersey, that sells snow shovels. In November, you suddenly find yourself glued to the Weather Channel day in and day out, hoping for snow. Why? Because having snow on the ground will help you sell your shovels. In any given year, a lack of snow can seriously depress your sales volumes, and you might go out of business. On the other hand, record snowfall or a lengthy snowfall season will have you dancing in the salted streets.

What you and your business are facing is *uncertainty,* or risk. In this case, it's weather risk creating what Enron would call earnings volatility.

So in order to sleep at night, and so you can watch NASCAR instead of the Weather Channel, you decide to call Enron for some risk-management solutions. Enron will sell you a financial product called a weather derivative, which will cost you a premium. You end up paying Enron a steady, predictable premium; or in some cases you only pay Enron when the snowfall is extremely heavy and your increased sales allow for it.

If the worst happens—no snowfall—then the payment conditions in the contract are triggered, based on some established standard for weather (most commonly "heating degree days" or HDDs). Enron will then pay you the full amount of protection your premium had covered. Yes, it *is* like insurance—except that there is nothing physical being insured: There won't be any claim investigation or partial payout. You don't sell any snow shovels that year, but Enron's payment from the weather derivative keeps you in business. The earnings volatility is eliminated.

Now let's say you own the casino across the street from the snow shovel store. You watch the Weather Channel, too; except you are hoping for a brief, dry winter. You want people off the ski slopes and on the beach, staying at your hotel and pulling the cranks on your slot machines. For you, a cold and nasty winter means fewer people come to Atlantic City. You buy the same type of weather risk-management product from Enron, only your payout is triggered by the opposite event from the snow shovel deal.

The net effect for Enron is deals on each side of the weather uncertainty coin. No matter what the winter brings, Enron collects premiums from customers—it hopes hundreds or thousands of customers—like the snow shovel business and the casino, but pays out on only a fraction of those deals (whichever deals are triggered). If Enron prices the deals correctly, Enron will make money regardless of the weather.

This is an *extremely* simplified example. In reality, derivatives have names like *caps, floors, swaps,* and *costless collars,* and can be structured to create multiple triggers (resulting in "bands" or ranges of protection), or be linked to a commodity such as power.

Whatever the structure, these transactions usually result in a hedge—meaning they create offsetting positions in related commodities. If the uncertainty is completely eliminated, it's a perfect hedge. If the transaction stands alone and doesn't offset anything— then the position is naked, and is nothing more than a speculative bet.

Back at the Death Star, the weather trading-floor is buzzing with originators (deal makers who interact with the customers), traders (who price and transact in the weather markets), and a team of meteorologists who are analyzing the weather. Marketing people are there as well, putting together the next press release or glossy brochure introducing "weather risk-management" to the world. The brochure targets all types of industries where earnings could be affected by the weather—from farming to soft drinks to swimsuits to electricity suppliers. The potential market is huge: the U.S. Department of Commerce estimates that more than 70 percent of businesses are facing weather risk.

It's creative, it's market-making, and ever since Enron transacted the first weather derivative in September 1997, it's been growing very fast.

Now apply this weather example to any commodity, any price uncertainty, or any risk that a customer may worry about. For gas and power, these deals are happening constantly across very well established markets—gas and power volumes are what make Enron the world's leading energy company. But across the trading floor, the same concepts and strategies are being applied to credit risk, interest-rate risk, currency-exchange risk, steel prices, coal prices, plastics, pulp, recycled newsprint, and on and on and on.

Now multiply all these commodity types times thousands of deals times thousands of customers. Now globalize it. Now build an automated, web-based trading exchange (EnronOnline) where more than twelve hundred types and billions of dollars' worth of seamless transactions occur each day. Enron is making pennies on the dollar, but volumes are doubling and tripling year after year. Like the railroads built Wall Street in the 1800s, the businesses that Enron create are now building new markets. Other companies in Houston and around the world are forced to get in the game—and play in those same markets—just to keep up with Enron.

• • •

Information was the key, and the ability to manage these markets was behind the locked door. Enron was forced to adopt a strategy of *ruthless automation* to help control Enron deal flows, risk portfolios, and pricing structures. Suddenly the business was running on a platform of *intellectual capital,* and even the oldest Enron businesses—the pipelines—were managed using some crafty new technology.

With Skilling in charge, Enron was becoming the model of the new economy. He termed his strategy as one of virtual assets—meaning Enron could rule a market by dominating the marketplace, without owning a ton of physical assets. The Enron business was no longer about energy; it was all about risk and control of risk. It was expanding into new markets, it was *commoditizing* everything, and it was starting to move at the speed of electrons.

It was a risk e-business.

It took a few days to absorb the trading-floor atmosphere. There I was, smack in the middle of it. The floor was brand-new; in fact, the floors above and below us were not yet completed. The ceilings were at least thirty feet above us on a wide-open floor the size of two football fields. A handful of huge, ten-foot-diameter columns stood along the middle; they were covered with a dry-erase surface so McLainey could draw his diagrams all around them.

The desks were in long rows, with a person seated every four feet on either side. The only thing that kept you from staring at the person across from you was the eye-level mounted flat-screen computer monitors. They were like a status symbol. The more flat screens you had, the more critical your need for information. I had two. Waterston had three. Some traders had four, five or six.

The place was noisy. Aside from hundreds of people talking,

yelling, and laughing, there was construction going on to finish the building, and a set of department-store-style escalators nearby. Along the ceiling were more than one hundred flat-screen televisions, each of the seventy-two-inch variety, displaying everything from commodity prices to news channels to the occasional baseball game.

The noise was something your brain learned to accept. After a while, the lack of noise was more disturbing. If for some reason the escalator stopped and the humming disappeared, everyone on the floor would pop their heads up to see what the new "noise" was.

The open area of the floor was surrounded by a ring of glass offices. You could see across the floor, into the office, and out to the Texas sunshine. These offices were occupied by the top executives, or at least the ones who chose to have an office. Waterston, like the other VPs, had been given a choice between one of those offices and a space on the trading floor.

Waterston chose to have his small section of desk in the middle of our group, with a space the same size as mine, his assistant, and everyone else. It's not that he couldn't appreciate the big, fancy office along the windows—he just wanted to be where the action was. He had to be.

There we were—the fledgling Enron business trying to commoditize bankruptcy risk. Like the weather example, we sought customers who faced earnings volatility—in our case as it related to the uncertainty of unpaid bills. For example, the snow shovel business might sell a hundred thousand snow shovels to Home Depot each year. If Home Depot were to ever go bankrupt, then the snow shovel business has a huge problem—especially if an unpaid invoice is still hanging out there. How can Enron help the snow shovel business? By selling them a bankruptcy swap (a form of credit derivative) on Home Depot.

Again like the weather derivative, the snow shovel guy pays

Enron a premium (the price based on the probability that Home Depot will file for bankruptcy), and would be paid by Enron if the trigger event occurs. In this case, if Home Depot files for bankruptcy, then Enron pays the snow shovel business enough money to cover the lost revenue that was at risk.

Again, a simplified example—but the point is still the same. With every type of risk that an Enron customer was facing, there was a financial instrument that Enron could structure to eliminate the uncertainty. With our group, that uncertainty was the possibility that any one of thousands of companies worldwide could suddenly go bust.

But who would believe that? It was a tough sell: the idea that well-established, smoothly operating, financially stable companies could suddenly plunge into bankruptcy. And that became our strategic focus—doing everything we could to convince the world that bankruptcy risk was a risk they should consider. The American Bankruptcy Institute estimated that about fifty-thousand companies went bankrupt every year. Unfortunately for our group, most companies didn't worry about (or recognize) bankruptcy risk until it was too late—when the market price of bankruptcy protection had already skyrocketed.

Our credit group sat along half a dozen rows, marked by a plastic flag sticking up in the air that read CREDIT. Looking around the trading floor, a dozen other flags marked other areas, like STEEL or PULP or ENRONONLINE.

The people in my group could all see each other, and we could all hear each other. If I wanted to talk to the people thirty feet behind me, I had a few options: I could call them on the phone, I could e-mail them, I could send them an electronic instant message, or I could turn around and just yell at them.

If there was a meeting scheduled, we usually didn't worry about the location. We would just spin around in our chairs and start talking. McLainey was right behind me. In fact, there were a few unfortunate times when he and I both reclined at the same moment, crashing the backs of our skulls together.

Usually I met with McLainey and a guy named Jim Duffy, who was a deal man specializing in relationships. He was a smooth talker who looked like a seven-foot-tall version of *Baywatch* lifeguard David Hasselhoff—but with silver hair. Duffy was situated just next to McLainey, so if the three of us wanted to meet, all we had to do was whirl around and face each other. Whatever the scheduled start time for the meeting, it didn't really get started until the first person spun around and said, "You guys ready?" Then the others would spin around, and we would all take notes in our laps while we were careful not to touch one another's feet. I was especially concerned about Duffy's feet. For some reason he was always taking off his shoes, and his socks in my face just weirded me out.

Monday—April 9, 2001
ENE opening price: $54.55
ENE closing price: $55.96
ENE trading volume: 2,478,200

It was a groggy Monday morning and I was late to work. I had been flying down Louisiana Street when a Houston police officer nabbed me for doing 60 mph in a whatever zone. He was a friendly HPD officer, driving his baby blue Camaro and aiming his handheld radar gun at me like a pissed-off Dirty Harry. He was friendly enough to write the ticket quickly. Now I would be late for my meeting, when at 60 mph I would have been right on time.

I arrived at the parking garage from Hell and parked on the "Adaptable" level eleven. I raced from my car to the entrance by the Saturn Ring, and my heart sank as I fumbled through my pockets. I had forgotten my employee identification badge.

The Enron guard at the Saturn Ring checkpoint was not going to accept my bullshit. Now I was screwed. The Death Star had rules about people without their stinkin' badges.

I was sent down and out and around to the main lobby where I had first come on my first day. Somewhere beyond the new employee waiting area was a desk where I could prove my existence, sign my life away, and acquire a temporary sticker for my chest. It was more like a dunce cap than a security measure.

Once I had my temporary ID, I made the long journey through the main lobby checkpoint, back through the Saturn Ring checkpoint, and then finally past the checkpoint on the trading floor. Whew!

I reached my desk about thirty minutes late for my meeting with McLainey and Duffy. "Sorry I'm late," I said without catching my breath. I was ready to pull out the speeding ticket, and I had the dunce sticker to prove I hadn't overslept.

No response. I sat at my desk with the computer still on from the night before. The phone-message light was blinking, but I could deal with that later. I spun around in my chair to see the backs of McLainey and Duffy.

"You guys ready?" I asked with unruffled confidence.

Without spinning around, McLainey responded, "Did we have a meeting?"

I was still catching my breath. "Yeah. At eight o'clock to prep for our meeting with RAC."

McLainey, still with his back to me, "RAC canceled on us, so there's nothing to prep."

"Cool." I wasn't late. I spun back around and started the morning ritual of sorting through e-mails and voice mails.

My dashboard, as we called it, was running wild. I had a phone, which I called the Beast, festooned with display buttons for thirty different phone lines. As if thirty lines weren't enough, it had scrolling buttons up and down to reveal a total of fifteen pages of phone lines—which made 450 phone lines total. The phone had two separate handsets, a long, flexible microphone sticking out of it, and several buttons whose purpose I could never figure out. I taught myself the minimum skills required to use the damn thing.

The best thing about the phone was that I could pick up anyone else's line and join the conversation. There was no transferring or conferencing; I could just hit the button for McLainey's line and I was instantly part of his conversation. Or at least I could listen to it. This feature also allowed me to answer my own calls even when I was on the other side of the trading floor.

But perhaps the highlight of the Beast was that it had a set of phone lines wired to the huge flat-screen televisions hanging above the trading floor. The phone buttons were conveniently labeled: CNN, CNBC, Fox News, MSNBC, Bloomberg, ESPN, and many more. If something caught your eye, such as a news report about Enron, you could pick up that line and hear every word on your phone, as you watched the action on the TV monitor above. If you were tired of doing real work, you could pick up the ESPN line for an hour and pretend it was business-related, while you were actually listening to SportsCenter.

At one point a car chase broke out in Los Angeles. Enron-related work came to a screeching halt on the trading floor, as everyone picked up the TV audio phone lines. We all leaned back in our chairs as if we were having a relaxing conversation; instead we were listening to the play-by-play of news helicopters and the California Highway Patrol updates. Every news channel was covering the chase, and every monitor hanging from the trading-floor ceiling was showing the action. The car thief finally ran out of gas, at which point we went back to work. Amazingly, some schmuck had stolen a car and simultaneously shut down the seventh largest corporation in America; he wasn't charged for the latter crime.

Work on the Enron trading floor was easily divided into three categories. Either you were doing deals (Origination), making trades (Trading), or spinning a message (Marketing). Obviously, there were other people doing strategic work, analytical support, or managing the teams—but for the most part this was the three-headed monster that made Enron tick.

And that three-headed monster was constantly biting its own ears.

Originators wanted to do deals, plain and simple. When a deal was ready to be done, they went to the trader for execution. The trader often resisted the deal because he was responsible for the "book," or the entire portfolio of Enron positions on that commodity. A trader wanted deals, too, but only if they fit nicely into the book. For a trader, the worst nightmare was a situation in which the book "blew up." He protected his book wisely and carefully, and this often meant telling the originator, "No deal." It wasn't that the trader was being overly cautious with his positions—it was more like an attempt to ensure that the book made more money (or lost less money).

Meanwhile, the marketing team was busy creating a consistent message for the market, a message filled with promises of what Enron could do for them. The trader-originator conflict had everything to do with the details of that message, and marketing had to carefully please both groups. If the marketing materials matched what originators told customers, but the traders were unwilling to make the trades, then the business would fall flat on its face. Such was the case with many Enron trading groups.

Traders had a special chip on their shoulder, like they were the reason Enron existed in the first place. For one thing, they knew more than the rest of us—or at least they knew it before the rest of us. They talked about how smart they were in terms of age of information and timing, not by traditional measures such as IQ. They had little time to deal with you. If you distracted them for five seconds, then they lost their edge for five seconds. They were moody, uninterruptible, and heavily bonded with one another. When markets were slow and spirits were high, it was commonplace for a football to fly from one end of the trading floor to another. Sometimes late on a Friday, you could see several footballs whizzing through the air. Sometimes early on a Wednesday, you could see several billion dollars whizzing through the air.

The first thing I noticed about Enron traders is that they all looked very similar. A goatee was fairly common; otherwise they maintained a clean-cut yet outdoorsy look; and if they didn't wear some version of a blue shirt every day, then it was like they weren't on the team.

I recall the first time I showed up to work in a green button-down, only to realize I was *completely surrounded* by a dozen guys wearing the same blue shirt. Not just blue shirts—but the *same* blue shirt. I asked the group, "When did they hand those out?" I said it with a smile, but no one laughed.

Lazarri and the traders had a unique language all their own. I needed a glossary just to keep up with the scattered conversations and sound bytes that rattled around the trading floor. In addition to the lingo surrounding the "book" and the threat of that book being "blown up," there was a constant mix of unique terms and four-letter expletives. Across the room was a senior trader yelling to another that it was time to "puke," which meant to sell and take a loss on their trading position. Transactions were made and discussed in terms of "bucks"—one "buck" being $1 million.

Everything was an inside joke, and the jokes would build and change and live for years. If you didn't get the joke, you laughed anyway, because that was the only way you could ever get "invited" to the joke.

"August!" barked Lazarri across a room of five hundred people. I was sure this had something to do with a future price or some other financial structure he was trying to pimp. Something to do with a deal related to the month of August. I was wrong.

Once I finally got invited to that joke, I learned about the "Women of Enron Calendar." Over time, the traders on the floor had argued and negotiated and finally determined which twelve Enron women belonged in the pages of the imaginary Enron calendar of sexy babes. When Lazarri yelled out "August," he was telling the others on the floor that Miss August had just appeared. Another executive was known for keeping a list called the "Hottie Board," which basically served the same purpose as the calendar. I suspected there had to be other versions of female indexing throughout the Death Star.

And there was certainly quite a collection of supermodels and strippers to choose from. Enron was known for it—scattered throughout the two Enron buildings were hundreds of women who could easily take the cover of *Vogue* or *Cosmo;* hundreds of other women were more of the "dancing around a pole" type (but for some guys that was more their taste). In any case, these women must have been lured away from their "modeling" careers to become Enron employees. No one really knew what the calendar women did at Enron, or who they worked for; but none of the guys on the trading floor really cared.

The good-looking people of Enron had somehow escaped the Houston stereotype. In 2001, Houston was given the distinct honor of "Fattest City" in America by *Men's Fitness* magazine—a title Houston had successfully defended from the year before. I could only theorize how the Fattest City title came to be. I assumed the restaurants, of which there were zillions, had something to do with it: they were mostly steak, barbeque, and Mexican food. It was hard to order anything in this town without getting a question like:

"Which type of cheese would you like that smothered with?" Fat and grease were included with everything. Nothing came "on the side."

But I saw little evidence of obesity at Enron. This company, either by stress or by exercise or by unwritten hiring rules, had avoided the Houston heaviness and built a workforce of athletes. The Enron gym, known as the Body Shop, was crowded all throughout the day. It was perfectly acceptable at Enron to take time for a workout in the middle of the day. McLainey was one of those who hit the Body Shop in the mid-afternoon. Even Duffy and his socks were in shape, thanks to his daily dose of "protein salad."

The only thing saladlike about Duffy's lunch every day was the fact that it came from the salad bar. He would appear at his desk with a Styrofoam container.

"Duffy, what-cha got today?" I would ask.

Duffy would spin around with a smile. He knew I had to give him a hard time. "Let's see . . ." He would point to each tiny pile with his fork. "I've got some grated cheddar, some bacon bits, some hard-boiled egg chunks, and some other kind of meat . . ."

Enron, like most modern corporations, had an emphasis on employee wellness. It was not only effective for managing health costs, but also for attracting and retaining employees. Plus it was hip. And Enron was the hippest of the hip.

So Duffy ate his salads, McLainey went to the gym, and I watched as Miss August of the Women of Enron Calendar strolled by. Who says Silicon Valley is in California? Houston, in addition to being Fattest City, was also the birthplace of the breast implant. Not only were implants invented here, but it's also where they became a flourishing industry—thanks in part to another Houston factoid: there are about as many topless bars in Houston as there are McDonald's restaurants. Just like any good city along the Bible Belt, every other mile had a "Gentleman's Club" offering the finest in nude or seminude entertainment. These establishments were known for catering to the Houston businessman. Most of them had reputations for excellent food, especially the lunch specials. It was exactly what the stressed-out Enron executive needed on a Tuesday afternoon: a dimly lit bar with a $5.99 all-you-can-eat steak buffet, ESPN on the big-screen TV, and a naked nineteen-year-old bouncing across the stage.

And if *Playboy* magazine ever saw the trading floor, they would no doubt call for a Women of Enron issue.

I was just a couple weeks into Enron, and I was already up to my ears with Enron customers, Enron partner companies, and the Enron culture. Almost as important as learning the business itself was learning how to talk about it. The reality, as I quickly found, was that perception led the way. It was the classic case of the self-fulfilling prophecy, multiplied times a hundred for Enron. If we said we could do something over and over again, eventually the world would start believing it and it would start to happen.

No one played this perception game better than Elizabeth Perry. She was marketing, sales, public relations, and the queen of perception for our start-up business. Liz was in front of everything we said, everyone we said it to, and how we should say it. She was continuously defining not *what we were,* but instead *what we wanted to be.* We would be perceived as a leader in credit risk management and bankruptcy protection *long before* that reality was actually formed. Such was the Enron PR machine—not just for our group, but for *every* group.

Liz snuck up behind my desk and tapped me on the shoulder. "You ready to meet?"

She didn't sit near the rest of us, so there were no spin-around meetings with her. She suggested we go downstairs to grab some coffee. We were meeting to discuss the Enron marketing spin; I felt I was long overdue for a briefing on the Enron branding game.

We had two choices: the Starbuck's in the Enron lobby, or the Enron cafeteria, called the Energizer. She chose Starbuck's. I really didn't care because I didn't drink coffee or anything else with caffeine—doctor's orders.

"How long have you been at Enron?" I started the conversation off with the obvious.

"Wow. It seems like forever." Her eyes went up to indicate deep thought. "About a year."

I was beginning to sense that a year *was* forever at Enron. "Where were you before that?"

She listed just about every other oil and gas company in Houston. It seemed she had plenty of experience with the energy industry. She had studied Enron in her M.B.A. program as well, specifically the marketing success story. She had tried to get a job with Enron for almost a year before joining our group.

I asked her to compare Enron to the other energy companies she had worked for.

"Enron clearly has a much more futuristic view of the world . . . so much faster and more high-tech." She wasn't telling me anything new.

"You're talking about the business. What about the people?" I guess I was digging for something.

"It's definitely the youngest company I've been a part of. Very fraternity-like." She paused, then added, "Borderline immature."

Okay. Now we're getting somewhere. Like myself, Liz was a graduate of the University of Texas, and she knew fraternity behavior. She was the classic college-girl-gone-corporate. She had long blond hair, a laid-back business demeanor, and she even wore glasses—not for her eyesight, but because she wanted no part of . . .

"Like that calendar thing."

"You know about that?" I wanted to hear her take on it.

"Of course," she said, with an expression like she knew every bit of gossip Enron had to offer. "I even thought we should go ahead and make an actual calendar and give it away at conferences and trade shows."

"No kidding!" I was a bit confused. "So you're cool with the fraternity-like behavior?"

"If it's harmless like that, just boys being boys. As long as it's not directed toward me."

I didn't quite know where to take the conversation after that. I decided to change the subject.

"So." She beat me to it. "What did you want to talk about?"

"Well, I'm dealing with a lot of people on the outside. I thought you could give me a quick overview of Enron marketing rules."

"Are you lying to them?"

"No, of course not." I was caught off guard.

Her question brought up the subject of the Enron "core values." I already knew them—they had been drummed into my head during the first day's orientation, and they were printed at the bottom of my Enron stationery:

Respect—We treat others as we would like to be treated ourselves. We do not tolerate abusive or disrespectful treatment. Ruthlessness, callousness, and arrogance don't belong here.

Integrity—We work with customers and prospects openly, honestly and sincerely. When we say we will do something, we will do it; when we say we cannot or will not do something, then we won't do it.

Communication—We have an obligation to communicate. Here, we take the time to talk with one another . . . and to listen. We believe that information is meant to move and that information moves people.

Excellence—We are satisfied with nothing less than the very best in everything we do. We will continue to raise the bar for everyone. The great fun here will be for all of us to discover just how good we can really be.

Most people inside Enron just referred to the core values as RICE, which I thought was pretty lame. The people at Enron who hailed from Rice University in Houston were proud of that fact. But then, people at Enron named Eric believed that Excellence should have been the value listed first.

"All you really need to know is to be careful when using the Enron logo. There are a lot of rules about the logo." She took another sip of coffee.

"The logo?" I started to doodle the logo on a napkin as the subject turned to it. "You mean the Crooked E?"

She pulled the coffee down with a jerk. "Ooh . . . don't call it that." She was wiping some of her grande non-fat latte off her chin as she said it.

The logo had special rules for size, color, placement, and surroundings. In fact, there was an entire website on the company intranet dedicated to it. Liz briefed me on how I could use the logo.

"So what if I want the Enron logo tattooed on my chest?" I had to ask—the conversation was getting too stale and serious.

"That's acceptable, as long as you get the colors right." She almost said it with a straight face, until a grin crept over her.

The use of the logo and the Enron brand was a critical issue for Enron. At the beginning of 1997, in anticipation of a growing retail energy market, Enron decided it was time to become a household name. The goal, as the Enron press release stated, was to take Enron from being one of the least-known big companies to "joining McDonald's, Coca-Cola, and American Express as one of the most recognized names in the world." Enron unveiled the new logo and launched a massive advertising campaign.

The logo itself was designed by Paul Rand, known for developing the logos of ABC, IBM, and UPS. The Crooked E was the last logo Rand created before he died in 1996. The logo has held its magnum opus status ever since.

Perhaps the logo paranoia that was running rampant within the company stemmed from past mistakes. Liz explained that when the tilted E logo was first introduced, it was just as it looked today, except that the red-green-blue combo was originally red-yellow-blue. It wasn't until Enron had already spent millions of dollars on the release of the new logo that they realized the mistake: Yellow didn't copy or fax correctly, so letterhead and documents were appearing with a partial E. The change was made to green, and the rest is history. I wondered if the person who agreed on the color yellow was history, too.

Liz and I finished our coffee break, me without the coffee, and headed back to the trading floor. I arrived at my desk, and the Beast was flashing and ringing and I dashed to grab my line . . .

"Enron!" I answered, as if the call was an inconvenience.

"Hello, Brian." Nobody called me Brian, not even my own parents.

"Yes, sir. How are you?" I knew immediately who it was, and he knew I knew. I straightened up my posture.

"How are things going down there? You've been there, what, a few weeks now?" His voice was rugged. I remembered his face was rugged, too.

"Five and a half, sir." I felt like an ass as soon as I said it.

"Good . . . good. Why don't you and I grab lunch one of these days and catch up." It wasn't a question. "Call my secretary to schedule it." He was calling from a wireless phone. I guessed he was somewhere on the other side of the globe.

"Yes, sir. Looking forward to it . . . Thank you."

As soon as he hung up, I started breathing again. This voice from my past was a senior Enron executive, calling from somewhere upstairs in an elite corner of the Death Star. I thought of him as a friend and mentor, but that might have been a stretch. He had written a few letters of recommendation back when I applied to business schools, and I always listed him as a reference, but we hadn't spoken in about a year.

I was a full generation younger than he was, and almost an entire career behind him. We met originally through family and family business dealings—now we were both at Enron. I probably could have used him to land an Enron job out of business school, or to land this Enron job, but I had some kind of mental block against such exploitation. I always thought it better to earn my way into a job. It was a *career karma* thing. And now that I was at Enron by my own doing, I felt I could lean on this personal connection all I wanted. That strategy included calling him "sir" until he told me otherwise.

He had been everywhere and done everything, including rise to the top of Enron. He had been with the company since the mid '80s. He was rich and powerful, and he was everything I dreamed of becoming at Enron. Just hearing his voice brought back hundreds of wild stories he had told me about the early days of Enron—especially his Indiana Jones–like adventures around the world. The new global Enron was on the way to being the world's leading company, and he was one of the reasons Enron had come this far.

I looked his assistant up on the Enron Intranet and dialed her extension. She was cold and callous with me, but in the nicest way. It wasn't about my schedule at all; it was about his.

I remembered he had *blue* eyes, and he always wore a *blue* shirt—maybe he had started that trend among the traders. Last I knew he was driving a midnight *blue* Mercedes-Benz SL600 convertible. His cocktail of choice: a double shot of Johnnie Walker *Blue* Label.

His assistant booked the meeting and sent me a confirmation e-mail almost instantly.

It had been set. The following week I had a meeting with an Enron legend—Mr. "Blue."

The elevator that went to the top floors of Enron Center North had a different feel than the elevators for the lower floors. I noticed a different smell: like it was cleaner, and was used by cleaner people. As I took the ear-popping ride to Enron's fiftieth floor, I thought about what I wanted to discuss with Mr. Blue.

I decided that I hadn't been at Enron long enough to ask for a spot on the board of directors. In fact, his card was one I didn't plan on playing for a while. At Enron, it was important to build a network of support within the company. It was critical for upward mobility, and as a safety for when you needed to move somewhere else in the company.

The fiftieth floor was like a museum. Fine art, including a spectacular collection of rugs and vases, made the floor look more like a palace than a corporate office. The floor was very quiet, with a pair of Enron receptionists the only visible life-forms.

Past the reception area was a stairway—which I was surprised to see—leading to a *fifty-first floor*. Much of the fifty-first floor was open to the area where I was standing. I could easily imagine the two floors playing host to some sort of black-tie corporate function.

I told the receptionist I was there to meet with Mr. Blue. She explained that he was expecting me but running a little late. She allowed me to wait in his office.

The office was spotless and organized; not a single paper was on his enormous desk. The wood from the desk to the chairs to the shelves was a perfect match, and the room was larger than my apartment. I took a seat on the couch and ran my eyes along the walls and bookcases. The room was filled with Enron trophies.

The bookshelves displayed pictures of his three kids, absent any sign of their mother since he had been divorced for several years. In addition to photos, the shelves were filled with trophies representing major deals and company milestones. Framed on the walls were diplomas, sailboat paintings, and an artist's rendition of the new Enron Field baseball stadium.

A brass rack held a dozen hardhats, which represented Mr. Blue's history of international power and pipeline projects. From England to India to the Caribbean to the Philippines—this was the stuff of Enron's globalization. And Mr. Blue had been there every step of the way.

I flashed back to his stories of adventure around the world. Mr. Blue had flown through militarized jungles at the mercy of crusty old Cessna airplanes. He had raced along mud-slicked roads through angry crowds and busy intersections to avoid getting shot. He said that in India he would have starved to death if not for the granola bars he packed. He had built a career at Enron from off the trading floor and outside the cubicle—his typical "day at the office" included a military escort and a run-in with a water buffalo.

Company names like Enron International (EI), Enron Power & Pipeline (EP&P), Enron Engineering & Construction (EE&C), and Enron Global Services (EGS) were displayed on the trophies around his office. It was a confusing structure of subsidiaries and joint ventures, but it all went toward the same purpose of dominating the world's energy assets.

He had brushed elbows with so many other Enron greats.

Rebecca Mark, a Harvard M.B.A. with Enron from 1982 to August 2000, was well known as Hell in High Heels when it came to her role as chairwoman of Enron International and later as head of Azurix. She was thought to be next in line to be Enron CEO, until Azurix tanked and she was sent packing.

Tom White, who was also part of the ex-military crowd running EE&C and Enron Energy Services (EES), had an epic career in the U.S. Army that took him to the rank of brigadier general. In early 2001, George W. Bush would name Tom White the new secretary of the army, ending his eleven-year Enron career.

Joe Sutton, who had left Enron at the end of 2000, was CEO of EI before becoming Enron's vice chairman in 1999. The position of vice chairman became known as the "ejection seat"—as it seemed to be the last stop for executives on their way out the door. Sutton exited Enron from his position of vice chairman, as did Rebecca Mark, and as did Cliff Baxter in early 2001.

Mark, White, and Sutton—these were the legends that put Enron on track to become the world's leading company.

And the Enron projects Mr. Blue had taken part in were legendary as well: the Puerto Plata power facility in the Dominican Republic, the twenty-mile San Juan Gas pipeline in Puerto Rico, the Subic Bay power project on the island of Luzon in the Philippines, and the massive 2,184-megawatt Dabhol power plant in India.

I stood up from Mr. Blue's sofa and stepped over to the window at the top of Enron Center North. I could see the top of the slightly shorter Enron Center South as construction crews completed the rooftop helipad.

Beyond the shiny new Enron south tower was an entire city

under construction: a new retractable-roof football stadium for the soon-to-arrive Houston Texans; a new basketball arena to keep the Houston Rockets and Comets in the city for a few more decades; and Houston's first attempt at a city rail system, connecting downtown with the museum district and medical center.

Not to mention construction on what seemed like every Houston road.

I was staring out the window like a tourist when Mr. Blue's assistant poked her head in the door. "Pick up line one," she demanded.

"Enron . . ." I answered in my usual way, mostly because I didn't know how else to answer someone else's phone.

"Brian." It was Mr. Blue. "Sorry but I'm stuck and won't be able to make it. Have my secretary reschedule. I hear you're engaged. Who's the lucky girl? Congratulations. Let's talk soon. Take care."

My brain was still on the word *reschedule* when he hung up.

3

The Millionaire Factory

"Because that's where the money is."
—*Willie Sutton's response when asked why he robbed banks*

Tuesday—April 17, 2001
ENE opening price: $60.00
ENE closing price: $60.00
ENE trading volume: 4,715,300

After trying dozens of different combinations, I settled on the best route for getting to work. The commute would take me almost exactly an hour in the morning, from driveway to desk, and could be broken into two parts: half an hour to drive to Enron, and another half hour to ride up the elevators.

Ahhh, the Enron elevators. Just the memory of them sends a chill down my spine. Each morning the Enron faithful would arrive at the Death Star, fresh and clean and recently caffeinated—then spend a preposterous amount of time waiting for an elevator. Each elevator bank had six elevators, shiny and chromed like the rest of the lobby, and a crowd of a hundred people waiting to pile in. There was no method or order to it, especially since the arrival of the next open door was so unpredictable. Some would wait patiently for a certain elevator to open, while others rudely pushed their way past the masses and squeezed their way in. The whole thing was a mess, but it was fun to watch—like an adaptation of a B. F. Skinner experiment involving cages full of stressed rats.

The elevators were a clear symptom of Enron's overcrowded headquarters. Again, Enron was constructing a new south tower, and was occupying much of the space in the surrounding office buildings. I remembered my orientation session with around forty new employees, and heard from Liz and Duffy that their orientations had similar numbers. With fifty orientations each year, Enron was hiring people at a rate faster than they could create new office space (or elevator space).

Once you were lucky enough to get into an elevator, it was time for Enron TV (known as ETV) to massage your sleepy brain back to life. Each elevator had two video screens facing the passengers that played a series of Enron infomercials—each quick enough to get the point across before you reached your floor. Some showed employees receiving awards from Ken Lay for representing the core values. Others told us when and where we could sign up for this and that, including the next fund-raising walk or the next wireless e-mail gadget.

And then there was the "Building Guy." Our chunky friend with a hard hat and a smile greeted us more often than the other ads; and it was a new episode every couple of weeks. He was there to inform us about Enron headquarters, both new and old, answering common questions about the evolving state of our surroundings. Each of the Building Guy episodes ended with a corny joke and a catchy jingle that would take hours to shake from our heads. For a while I had thought the Building Guy was a real Enron employee who worked in building maintenance or something. I found out later he was an actor named John Swasey, hired by Enron to entertain us in the elevators.

If we were lucky, ETV wouldn't have any commercials or

Building Guy episodes to show us—so instead we might get a live feed from CNBC or, on rare occasions, a baseball game.

If you chose not to stare at the video monitors, you had only one other choice: stare at yourself. The insides of the elevator doors were perfectly mirrored, and so we all watched ourselves standing there, like a pack of sardines awaiting our fate. The mirrors were useful if you suspected you might have spinach in your teeth, and even more useful if you wanted to see who was standing behind you.

On that April morning, just a few weeks into my Enron career, the building was abuzz. Enron was about to deliver its first-quarter earnings report for the fiscal year 2001, and everyone raced to get their breakfast and e-mails out of the way before the 9:00 A.M. conference call.

The earnings-report conference call has evolved over the years into a quarterly tradition representing the very best in corporate disclosure and shareholder sharing. Four times a year, the top execs from all publicly traded firms hit the airwaves, spinning the numbers and predicting the future in the most conservative and indisputable manner possible. The quarterly conference call coincided with a press release and some pressing questions from Wall Street analysts. Conference calls were gaining in popularity, especially as technology allowed for more universal delivery, and as investors became more in tune with their own portfolios. For most calls, any investor, employee, reporter, or barnyard animal with a phone or Internet connection could listen in. For the big companies, like Enron, the call was joined by thousands of interested parties.

As 9:00 A.M. arrived on the trading floor, business as usual slowed to a soft whisper, and the speaker phones and computer webcasts all began echoing the call across every floor in the building. It was my first time hearing an Enron call from inside Enron, and it was awesome. It just sounded cool, like a surround-sound system on steroids that included hundreds of speakers all *slightly* off from one another. Multiple technology lines and multiple communication systems fed the Enron voices into my ears from out of nowhere—like the Enron gods were speaking to me from another dimension.

And Enron, which had gone several years without a negative earnings report, had nothing but good news again.

As I listened to our fearless CEO, Jeff Skilling, and the others run through the numbers, I also scanned the newswire:

- An 18 percent increase in earnings per share for the quarter, compared to the same quarter last year
- A 281 percent increase in quarterly revenues to $50 billion
- A 20 percent increase in net income to $400 million
- Energy volumes increased 65 percent to 69 trillion British thermal units per day
- $5.9 billion in retail energy services deals, a 59 percent increase
- A "sevenfold increase" in broadband services delivered

In addition to these impressive first-quarter results, Enron was officially raising expectations for the future—raising the earnings target for the fiscal year 2001 from $1.75 to $1.80 per share. Skilling threw in another nugget: "In addition, our retail energy services and broadband intermediation activities are rapidly accelerating."

After running through the State of the Business address, the call switched gears and opened up to a question-and-answer session. I remember yawning at the seemingly canned questions, as the Enron leadership picked through the inquiries from top Wall Street firms.

Then Richard Grubman, managing director of Highfields Capital Management in Boston, began to get a bit surly with Mr.

Skilling. Grubman wanted to see Enron's balance sheet, but Enron was not going to provide a balance sheet until it was filed with the SEC a few weeks later. Enron wasn't required to deliver it along with the call, and so the world would wait as usual.

Grubman then switched from asking a question about the balance sheet to making a statement about it: "You're the only financial institution that can't come up with a balance sheet or cash-flow statement after earnings."

Skilling responded, "Well, thank you very much. We appreciate that, asshole."

Everyone froze. Did he just say what we think he said? Liz Perry thought he must not have known the microphone was on. Waterston disagreed. "Oh, he knew it was on. That's just Skilling."

In a later interview, Skilling explained that he was indeed fully aware that the microphone was on and that he likes to let people know "when he is exasperated." Skilling added that Grubman was a "short seller in the market" and he shouldn't be using the call as a platform for his personal interest.

We were all annoyed with Grubman, and for the most part we found the incident very amusing. Skilling kind of chuckled when he said the word, and we all chuckled when we thought about the thousands of people listening in.

The details of the "asshole" incident hit the news wires almost immediately. The CEO said a bad word and it completely overshadowed the company's great numbers. Forget the three-digit percentage increases or the rapid acceleration—the big news was that Skilling said something that would have made Beavis and Butthead very proud. Did Grubman have a point about the financial statements? Who cares? Skilling said "asshole."

Within an hour I got an e-mail from Bickers. There was no message, just an attachment. I opened it to find a Bernie Bickers original creation: an exact replica of the Enron logo, only instead of ENRON in block letters down the back of the E, the logo had the word ASSHOLE. It was flawless, and it would have looked magnificent spinning around in the lobby downstairs.

Bickers's new logo was displayed on my computer screen for only a few seconds, but it was enough to get a giggle out of someone behind me. McLainey was looking over my shoulder and laughing out loud.

"Where did you get that? Did you make it?" He scooted in for a closer look at the masterpiece.

"No no. A friend of mine who was on the conference call just e-mailed it to me."

"You have *got* to send that over to me," McLainey insisted. "Waterston would love to see that, too."

At first I was a bit nervous about it—my first few weeks at Enron, and they hired me accidentally? I didn't think the new logo was appropriate to be sending around the group—but then I realized that Skilling's expletive was fast becoming the joke of the week. Besides, what a great way to bond with McLainey, right?

I forwarded the e-mail to McLainey and a few others. McLainey forwarded it to Waterston and a few others. Waterston forwarded it to . . .

Wait a minute! My name is on that e-mail, and now the VPs were sending this thing around the company! Oh, well—at least the e-mail attachment itself didn't have my name on it.

At that thought the phone rang.

"Dude . . . can you believe it?" He was out of breath like he had been scrambling all morning.

"What? You mean the sevenfold increase in broadband?" I pretended I didn't know what he was talking about.

He skipped right over my sarcasm. "Whatever. Did you get the e-mail?"

"Yes—another Bernie Bickers classic. It's hysterical."

Bernie switched his tone. "Dude . . . promise me you won't send that around to anyone. I'm afraid it might come back to haunt me."

He should have thought of that a whole lot sooner, and I didn't want the guy to go bananas, so I took the path of least resistance. "Oh, yeah . . . no problem."

Later that afternoon I passed by Waterston.

"Nice e-mail," he said with a grin.

"Not mine," I was quick to point out. "Hey if you don't mind keeping that e-mail inside the group, my friend is a bit . . ." He interrupted my sheepish request by turning his grin into a big smile.

I just had to ask: "Skilling?"

His big smile turned into a laugh, and he walked off. By now the entire building had the Bickers logo, and I wondered if by tomorrow Skilling would have it mounted on a wall in his office.

Bickers and all the other Wall Street analysts covering Enron went into crunch mode during earnings season. Enron wasn't an easy company to analyze, as it stretched beyond energy into the world of heavy finance . . . not to mention all the strange new worlds Enron was creating.

As if broadband intermediation, weather derivatives, and trillions of British thermal units weren't enough, Bickers had to sort through the mountain of information in a matter of days.

From quarter to quarter, Bickers and his Wall Street firm would update a sophisticated financial model that was used to put a price target on ENE stock. The model was increasingly complex with each Enron innovation, but fortunately for Bickers it was somewhat reusable every three months.

A few days before Skilling's classy "a-word" incident, Bickers was plugging away at the Enron financial model, preparing to update the inputs as soon as he got Enron's new numbers. The resulting outputs would then be put into his firm's "note" about Enron, which Bickers was also preparing. For the wording of this new note, Bickers would also recycle the verbiage from the previous quarter.

About ten minutes before the Enron conference call began, Bickers would dial in and set up the recording system to tape the call. After ten minutes of Wall Street's cheesiest hold music (a symphony orchestra version of Led Zeppelin), the Enron execs would begin the disclosure process. Bickers would scribble down the important points while making sure the tape was recording; someone else from his firm would get into the queue to ask a question of Enron. It wouldn't be a spectacular question; it would just be something related to the firm's outlook.

After the call, Bickers would do a rough update of the financial model based on the new numbers. In the case of Enron, with a 10:00 A.M. EST conference call, the goal would be to get the firm's note out before the market close the same day. The note would include the conference call highlights, the firm's projections for the stock price, and the firm's rating on the stock. Bickers's firm had always kept ENE in the firm's highest rating category, which equated to a "strong buy."

When Bickers was finished editing and proofing the note, it went out by e-mail and fax to a list of clients and media outlets; most important was Thomson Financial/First Call, the cornerstone of worldwide financial information.

After the conference call was over and the firm's note had been released, Bickers had anywhere from a day to a week to prepare for the analyst meeting—when the top Enron execs would arrive in New York City to meet with the top firms and disclose details. The event was a supplement to the earnings call, and for Bickers it also meant another stack of information to sort through. What he looked for would be something new or different from the conference call, something worth sending out to clients in a separate note.

After the torrent of Enron quarterly info, Bickers would go back to the financial model and clean it up from the first rough update.

Then, in the case of Enron, the actual quarterly filing with financial statements (called the 10-Q) wouldn't go to the SEC until even later (as Richard Grubman so bluntly pointed out). Enron actually filed its 10-Q for the first quarter of 2001 on May 15, about a month after the conference call.

Tuesday—May 22, 2001
ENE opening price: $55.60
ENE closing price: $54.95
ENE trading volume 3,879,600

The Beast started ringing, and it was Bickers.

"Dude . . . your company is making me want to shoot myself," he said, sounding exhausted.

"Now what?" I didn't have time for this. I was feeling exhausted myself, especially with Bickers and his badgering.

"You guys filed your 10-Q and all I can think to do is wipe my ass with it."

"Thanks for the visual." I was ready to hang up.

He continued. "There's all kinds of high-quality dogshit in here about limited partnerships and 'related party transactions.' Maybe you can explain it."

"Or maybe I can't. Maybe that's your job . . . you're the equity analyst. Maybe you should call our CFO instead of harassing me about it." I put my finger on the button to drop the call.

"It's the same crap you guys put in your annual report last year." Someone at his firm interrupted him. "Dude . . . I gotta run."

He hung up and I was relieved. I had a meeting with McLainey and Waterston in a few minutes and needed to do some prep. As I was digging around the piles on my desk, I found the Enron Annual Report for 2000. Bickers had chewed on my face enough to get me looking at it.

And there it was—way back behind all that good news, on page 48, was note 16 regarding "related party transactions." Annual reports and SEC filings are the public's access point to a company's consolidated financial statements. These statements—income statement, balance sheet, statement of cash flows—are accompanied by a series of notes that explain policies, activities, and other supplementary data. The notes include anything that Enron and its auditor, Arthur Andersen, are required to disclose along with the financials.

The 2000 Annual Report for Enron had, again on page 48, the following information for shareholders:

16. RELATED PARTY TRANSACTIONS
In 2000 and 1999, Enron entered into transactions with limited

partnerships (the Related Party) whose general partner's managing member is a senior officer of Enron. The limited partners of the Related Party are unrelated to Enron. Management believes that the terms of the transactions with the Related Party were reasonable compared to those which could have been negotiated with unrelated third parties . . .

The opening paragraph was followed by a summary of the transactions, with a hundred million here and a billion there, which just made my eyes hurt. The section kept referring to those transactions as being with the Related Party. I remember thinking, "Does this party have a name?" I looked up the recent 10-Q that Bickers was pissy about. The section was nearly identical, except in the 10-Q it was tied to a separate note about JEDI. I remember thinking that JEDI was a funny coincidence with all of the *Star Wars* terminology floating around. I also remember wondering, "Who's the Enron senior officer?"

A migraine headache was creeping up on me. I had no time for the supersleuth mess that Bickers was obviously wrapped up in. In any case, this was between Arthur Andersen, the Enron finance group, and Wall Street. It wasn't my job. I had smaller fish to fry.

McLainey's voice then poked me in the back of the head. "You ready?" I wasn't, but that hardly mattered.

The meeting was above the sensitivity level of the trading floor, so we took it into a glass conference room. We talked about non-Enron subject matters while we waited for Waterston to join us. Greg discussed how his wife and kids were adjusting to Houston after being relocated from California. His decision to join Enron was based on several factors, not the least of which was Houston's low cost of living.

We decided that $300,000 in Northern California could buy a two-bedroom house without a roof. That same amount in Houston could fetch a new five-bedroom, with a pool and detached garage in a gated community—roof included. Just as we were doing the mortgage math, Waterston entered.

The subject of the meeting was the Peer Review Committee (PRC). The PRC was Enron's semiannual weeding-out process that most people referred to as "rank and yank." I had asked Waterston and McLainey to enlighten me a bit on how the process worked. Even though I had only been at Enron for a couple months, it was mandatory that I participate in the PRC—and I was nervous enough about it to ask them to clarify exactly how it would work.

The PRC, as Waterston explained, was a 360-degree review process. This meant that coworkers above and below and to the side of you would provide feedback. Their opinions were broken down into easily defined and measurable categories, like "innovation" and "communication." Gulp.

The entire process was managed through the company intranet. I would select five people that I wanted to provide feedback on me. Others would select me to provide feedback on them. Perfect! It was the ideal situation for negotiating a trade. Unfortunately, anyone could provide *unsolicited feedback* to McLainey about me as well. If someone absolutely despised me, I could avoid them when choosing my five reviewers—but that didn't stop them from delivering a vicious message to my boss anyway.

McLainey was a mandatory reviewer, since he was my boss. It was easy to pick Duffy, Perry, Lazarri, and Waterston as the others. In addition to my peers, I would also review myself (no need to cut a deal on that one). Once the feedback was gathered, McLainey would take it all to one of the infamous PRC meetings.

The PRC meeting would rank me, from 1 to 5, among all the other Enron employees at my level in the organization. My picture would be displayed on a wall as part of a slide show; and McLainey,

Waterston, and others would then discuss me. The rankings were on a forced curve. For example, the rank of 5, the worst performing category, would be given to 15 percent of those reviewed. The bottom 15 percent could be great performers, but it only mattered relative to the other employees.

After a few minutes of discussing the PRC, Waterston had to excuse himself and head off to a media interview. We were both happy to get some of Waterston's time, since McLainey had never been on the management end of the PRC and I didn't have a clue what to expect. All I knew was that everyone at Enron was very nervous about it. As the PRC time grew closer, it seemed like a cloud of suspicion was forming throughout the building.

After our meeting, I decided it was time to tune in to the Gossip Channel—Liz Perry. I knew she was frantically putting together the conference schedule for the fall, but she answered the phone anyway.

"Liz, you got a minute?"

"Hey, what's up? How's the wedding planning?" She was bubbly as usual.

"It's great." It was great because my fiancée and future mother-in-law were handling most of it. "How's the conference planning going?"

She answered with a huff. "Good. It's months away, but it's never too early to panic."

"Well, sorry to interrupt that—but I was wondering if you had a few minutes to talk some PRC."

"Why—you want to cut a deal?" She was one step ahead of me.

"Done," I said—and just like that we cut our deal. That was easy. I would give her a good review, she would give me a good review, and we would both have one less reviewer to worry about. Then I asked, "So what happens to the people who get 5s anyway?"

"They get redeployed," she answered with artificial cheerfulness.

"Re-duh-what?"

"It means that you get sent off to find another job within Enron. It means that you end up in Siberia looking for a new position with a number five on your file." She saw the dazed look on my face. "It means you get fired, only in a really slow and painful way."

"And fifteen percent of us get hit with this every six months?" I found it difficult to believe.

"It's a Jeff Skilling thing. It's his baby that he created to keep us on our toes . . . or on edge, anyway."

Redeployment was the big bad word at Enron. If you fell into that bottom 15 percent and got redeployed, you literally picked up your things and headed off to redeployment land (or what Liz called Siberia). This was an area of desks—complete with phones and computers—where the 5s had a few weeks to get another Enron job. They could use their new desks for job searching—on the Web or on the phone—both inside and outside Enron. They could also go on interviews, which included interviews for positions within Enron.

It had me on edge. Without having gone through my first PRC, I had no idea where I stood. I decided that if I could just get through the first one without too many bruises, then the next time I could be less worried.

Liz continued on about what it was like inside a PRC meeting. Some of the meetings would get downright nasty; people were either fighting for you or against you as you smiled on the slide-show screen. There was no statute of limitations, either. You could dig up any old dirt you wanted and fling it across the table at the target employee.

As for the rankings, if you ended up being ranked a 1, 2 or a 3, then life was pretty good. If you got a 4, then you could expect to sweat for the next six months. If you got a 5, then you had *big* problems—and there was no getting around the fact that 15 percent of the employees would get 5s.

Liz explained that often a group of managers would begin horse trading in the PRC. If one manager wanted to give 5s to 30 percent of his or her team, and another manager wanted that rank for 0 percent, then they could cut a deal to reach the combined 15 percent. It sounded ridiculous and somehow realistic at the same time.

At one point I was asked to hire a new analyst into the group. The position was to support McLainey, Duffy, and myself. When the request was sent in to find new talent from within Enron, what I got was a stack of résumés of the recently redeployed. Each résumé had a huge 5 written at the top of it. Why didn't they just tattoo it on their foreheads?

When I interviewed the 5s, they were automatically defensive. They walked into the interview room knowing their days were numbered and knowing that *I knew* they got a 5.

We ultimately hired someone from outside the redeployment pool.

Then, a few weeks later, Liz Perry would rescue one of the 5s we had rejected and hired her to support the marketing team. "Tina" sat just a few awkward feet from me. What was I supposed to say? "Sorry, and I'm glad you made it out of Siberia anyway?"

Then, about ten days after Tina showed up, a budget problem in our group sent her packing again—back to Siberia, back to redeployment.

The whole thing just made me sick. The whole "rank and yank" process seemed more like "displace and disgrace."

Once again, it all came down to innovation. It was part of the PRC review process—you had to be innovative or your performance would get slapped with a lower rank. I wondered how innovation was measured in the accounting and legal departments.

"Who is Waterston talking to today?" I asked Liz if she could fill me in on the latest media contact.

"Some risk magazine or something," she replied. "They're asking him how he started the group."

"How *did* he start the group?" It seemed a logical question at the moment.

Liz went on to answer exactly what I expected her to answer. It was the same old formula—if you were futzing along in a stagnant area within Enron, then the fastest way to break out and make zillions was to start a new group. Waterston had done just that, pitching our credit-risk idea to Skilling and getting a green light. Waterston knew that such an all-or-nothing strategy would be high risk and that such adventures had a 95 percent failure rate, but hey, he was in his late thirties so this was his time.

Part of the strategy for getting our group off the ground was hitting the financial media, which had always *loved* Enron! Every week I saw a new article or case study that referred to our innovative products. Waterston had a whole team of people to manage his media relations, and they were the best.

But of course they were the best—they *had to be the best,* because if they ever fell to the bottom 15 percent they would lose their jobs.

How to Conquer Corporate America, Rule #3: If you want to be really successful, you'll need a good psychiatrist.

It was late on a Tuesday evening, and I had entered an empty visitor parking garage next to an unfamiliar building. I found an unmarked door with a small button, which made no sound when I pressed it. Moments later the door rattled and buzzed, allowing me to enter.

The building was cold and lifeless, with only the sound of a vacuum cleaner in the distance. An elevator was open without a light inside—too spooky, so I took the stairs.

I reached the third floor out of breath, thinking it was time to stop eating ice cream late at night before I went to bed. I reached the door to Dr. Muckenberger's office, thinking this was a waste of time.

I sat in the empty waiting area for a few minutes until he appeared.

"Mr. Cru-vay . . . right this way." He had spiky gray hair and a thin gray goatee.

Normally I would correct someone who mispronounced my name, but I didn't plan to stay long, and I didn't plan to ever come back—so what was the point?

I walked into an office filled with the smell of new leather furniture. As I looked around at all the seating options, I asked, "So where should I sit?"

"Wherever you like, Mr. Cru-vay."

This was my first test. I examined the room and looked for the best angle to have conversation without discomfort. I slipped into a slick seat, facing a Monet print of some boats tied to a dock. I had seen the print somewhere before.

"So," he began slowly, with a blank notepad resting in his lap. "Tell me why you are here."

"I have no idea."

My insolence didn't seem to faze him. "Okay then . . . tell me what inspired you to come here today."

"My fiancée." I waited, but he didn't follow up the question. As he started writing notes, I realized I was supposed to keep talking. "She thinks I'm stressed out. She thinks that with our wedding a few weeks away, and with the stress of my job, I need to chill out or something."

"Do *you* think you need to chill out?"

Great question.

"No." Even better answer.

He looked up from his notes. "Are you nervous about the wedding?"

I *was* nervous about the wedding, but not about being married. The thought of spending forever with my fiancée was a piece of white cake compared to the thought of the ceremony itself. I wanted to go to Las Vegas; I wanted to keep it simple. Instead we would be exchanging vows in front of hundreds of people.

"No, not *too* nervous."

He scribbled excitedly. "And you mentioned job stress. Tell me about that."

"I work for Enron." I waited. That was to be my full answer, until we just stared at each other for a long five seconds. "It's *very* stressful, but it's definitely worth it. Most people would love to be in my shoes . . . I mean . . . the place is a millionaire factory."

Tuesday—June 12, 2001
ENE opening price: $51.37
ENE closing price: $50.37
ENE trading volume 3,262,000

The Enron millionaire factory was in full force through the '90s and into the new millennium. Shiny new M.B.A.'s from the top schools, former consultants from McKinsey and Andersen, and military geniuses making the transition to private industry—they all came to Enron seeking a fortune. If they could survive the culture, the PRC, and the demands of meeting growth targets from quarter to quarter—then they believed they had won something much more valuable than a lottery ticket.

It wasn't the salary, although many executives took home a few million a year. It was the bonuses and the stock options. The bonus was the reward for meeting targets from quarter to quarter. It was paid at the beginning of the new year based on the prior year's performance. The size of the bonus often dwarfed the employee's salary. There was literally no cap on the bonus.

During bonus week, the car dealerships around Houston would park their finest new Mercedes, Porsche, and BMW models on the grassy mound next to Enron Center North. The employee with a fresh seven-digit deposit in the bank could then conveniently browse and test-drive the latest in automotive extravagance, even on a short lunch break.

The stock options were a longer-term incentive, although it didn't take ENE stock very long to leave the option price in the rearview mirror. A typical executive would accumulate options by the tens or hundreds of thousands. By the time the options were vested and could be cashed out, they would be worth millions.

Lou Pai, the Enron Energy Services (EES) executive who left Enron in May 2001, cashed out with more than $350 million in Enron stock. Of course, much of this went to pay for his divorce; but in the end, he found a new wife with different talents at the Men's Club in Houston—one of the city's most popular topless bars. His new wife, Melanie, loved horses, so Pai retired to seventy-seven thousand acres in Colorado and a horse-breeding ranch in suburban Houston.

Ken Rice, who made his fortune in Enron Broadband, was a car freak. He loved his Porches, Ferraris, BMWs, motorcycles, and more. His vision for creating bandwidth markets that mirrored energy markets was worth billions; and Rice took that intellectual capital and transformed it into, among other things, a *truck full* of Ferraris that he once brought to an Enron race in the Texas hill country.

Tom White, who was also with EES before his new job as

secretary of the army, didn't leave the company empty-handed. Yes, he had to kiss his $5 million salary good-bye—but he was able to salvage $14 million in severance and stock payments before he left. With just over a decade served at Enron, White moved into a $5 million Washington penthouse, with a pair of $5 million properties in Colorado and Florida as backups. Not too shabby for a guy that used to serve coffee to Colin Powell.

Andy Fastow, Enron chief financial officer, was upgrading his art collection at the same time he was upgrading his home. He and friends Skilling and Michael Kopper were all moved or moving from upscale Southampton Place to superscale River Oaks—the neighborhood where Ken Lay lived.

Skilling loved the adventures almost as much as the money. It was typical for Skilling and his top money-making Enron boys to head off to Colorado or Australia or to some mountain or some high-risk motorcycle race. Like Lou Pai, Skilling also upgraded his marriage after a messy divorce, hooking up with Enron corporate secretary Rebecca Carter. CEO Skilling and fiancée Carter shacked up in a monster multimillion-dollar estate—again in River Oaks.

Carter, who others had nicknamed Va-voom, was promoted under Skilling to a salary of $600,000 per year.

And then there was Ken Lay—"world-class rich." Also divorced from his first wife, and married to his former secretary, Linda Phillips, he had a passion for real estate. Aside from a $7 million penthouse apartment in River Oaks, Lay had nearly a dozen other properties. Four of those properties were in Aspen, Colorado, each worth several million dollars each.

The lifestyles of the rich and powerful trickled down throughout the company. It showed in everything Enron built, sponsored, or displayed—from the baseball stadium to BMW giveaways to . . . the Enron cow?

The world-famous CowParade came to Houston in 2001, just as it had graced the streets of Chicago and New York in prior years. Hundreds of the life-size cow statues were displayed all around the city, each specially designed and painted in creativity and color. Every cow had a sponsor and would later be sold to the highest bidder. All proceeds from the CowParade auctions were used to support a local Houston hospital.

The Enron cow was proudly displayed just in front of Enron Center North and was covered from horn to hoof in mirrored glass—to match the building. The cow was named Moost Immoovative, and from a distance it could have been a cow-cut diamond.

At Enron's office building in London, a banana-yellow BMW Z3 sat in the lobby for someone to win. The car was an incentive for people to refer potential new employees to Enron, a way to bring much-needed talent into the company. In addition to the regular referral bonus of a few thousand dollars, an employee would also get one chance in the drawing for the BMW.

It was a simple raffle, until people started buying and selling each other's "chances" for thousands of dollars. Each week a name would be drawn as a loser, making the value of the remaining names increase. If, for example, I owned two of the five chances left in the hat—I could peg the value of those chances at 40 percent of the "value" of the car. I could try to win it, or I could sell those chances to a BMW-hungry gambler more willing to take the risk. Sound familiar?

Some Enron events were highlighted by live elephants or by executives on Harley-Davidson motorcycles. When the stock passed $50 in 1998, each employee had a $100 bill waiting on his or her desk. Everything was over the top. Sometimes the opulence had a reason behind it, like the BMW raffle; other times it was pure pomposity. In either case, Enron knew that the estates, the cars, the glitter, the parties, and the global adventures would add to the lure of Enron. The most talented recruits from around the world would eat it all up, so Enron made a habit of flaunting it.

It wasn't unusual for recruits to attend special "happy hour" parties with ice sculptures, mariachi bands, to-and-from car service, and a $50,000 bar tab. In 1998, recruits attended a party at trader Kevin Hannon's multimillion-dollar home in Piney Oaks Estates. Skilling and Ken Rice were also there, and it looked like a car show. Rice had zoomed up on his new BMW motorcycle. All the hot toys were on display for the potential Enron hires. They could check out the cars, the house, and if they were really lucky get a handshake from Skilling.

These and hundreds of other stories were well known to both Enron employees and business school students across the country. It was a Wall Street recruiting atmosphere deep in the heart of low-cost Texas, where a million bucks went three times farther than it did in Manhattan. This was an important point—as Enron and Wall Street were competing head-to-head for the best talent in finance and trading.

It was top-down sports cars and top-off dancers. It was river-rafting trips and River Oaks Country Club. It was the American dream to an extreme. Even Ken Lay, when asked about the fleet of private jets known as Enron Airlines, said, "It's something my top people can aspire to."

It was early in my Enron career, but it wasn't too early to dream. There was a charity auction on the Enron Intranet website; I placed a bid of $100 to have Ken Lay's parking space for a week—complete with security cameras. I didn't win the auction, but I felt like it made me somehow close to being him for five days.

Soon after, an e-mail arrived from Skilling and Lay.

——Original Message——
From: Enron Announcements/Corp/Enron@ENRON on behalf of Ken Lay
and Jeff Skilling@ENRON
Sent: Tue 6/12/2001 2:06 PM
To: All Enron Worldwide@ENRON
Subject: Business-Wide Cost Saving Opportunities

At Enron, we're good at a lot of things: making markets, commoditizing
products, managing risk, offering innovative energy solutions to customers—the list goes on and on. However, one of the things we could do a
lot better is watching our expenses. We're all shareholders in this company,
and we need to spend our company's dollars as wisely as we spend our own.

There are some simple, yet significant measures each of us can
take to make sure we're careful with Enron's money. The Policy Committee has approved and recommended the following:

• Professional Services—This is our largest area of discretionary
spending, at more than $600 million last year. "Professional Services"
includes our contracts with outside law and accounting firms, contrac-
tors and other consulting groups. . . . We are requiring all future professional service contracts and those up for renewal to be negotiated
through or in consultation with Global Strategic Sourcing (GSS), effective
July 1. . . .

• Enterprise wide portal—We currently have 122 internal websites
across the company. . . . It makes sense to have one Enron portal so you
can efficiently access content and services through a single, personal-
ized channel that will make it easier for you to find information and per-
form basic tasks online. . . .

Another significant area where we can be more diligent in our
spending is travel and entertainment. Enron has long had travel policies
in place. As we have grown, we have not done as well as we should have
in communicating those policies to new employees and reminding all
employees to take advantage of the discounts we have negotiated. . . .

Any regular deviations from these travel policy recommendations will be reviewed by each business unit leader.

• Air travel—Employees are requested to use . . . Travel Agency in the Park (TAP) . . . we strongly encourage all employees to purchase non-refundable domestic coach tickets when possible.

. . . Each of us has a responsibility to make sure we do our part to ensure Enron retains its competitive edge . . . If you have an idea or a suggestion you would like to share with us, please e-mail us at recommendationsforcostsavings@enron.com.

. . . If you have additional questions, Policy Committee member Kevin Hannon will host an eSpeak on Tuesday, June 19 at 10 a.m. Houston time to discuss these cost saving recommendations.

What struck me the most was the four-inch-long e-mail address where I could send ideas. Were they serious? Other than that, I thought it was nice to see a plug for the Travel Agency in the Park, which was 50 percent owned by Ken Lay's sister, Sharon Lay. I also thought it was funny to see Hannon's name as the cost-savings contact, after hearing about the recruiting party at his luxurious estate.

The e-mail also seemed an odd change of tune for the Enron we all knew; but it made sense as the stock had just trickled down into the $40s for the first time in nearly eighteen months. I figured it was a good public-relations move, but I don't think anyone took it seriously. They weren't selling Enron Airlines, stopping the $200 million construction of Enron Center South, or taking away our laptops. Personally, I continued taking business-related trips, staying in the best hotels and eating in the best restaurants. These were the perks that the majority of Enron employees enjoyed—and it was a fair trade for being on the road, for being away from families, and for working fourteen-hour days. We considered it part of our compensation.

• • •

The next day we received another e-mail from Skilling and Lay. I would have glanced at it and forgotten about it, but I was still feeling the weird vibe from the cost-savings e-mail the day before:

——Original Message——
From: Enron Announcements/Corp/Enron@ENRON on behalf of Ken Lay and Jeff Skilling@ENRON
Sent: Wed 6/13/2001 7:49 PM
To: All Enron Worldwide@ENRON
Subject: Organizational changes
We are pleased to announce the following organizational changes:
Enron Global Assets and Services
In order to increase senior management focus on our international businesses, we are creating a new business unit, Enron Global Assets and Services (EGAS). EGAS will be led by Kevin Hannon, Chief Executive Officer, and Jim Hughes, Chief Operating Officer. Kevin will report to the Enron Corp. Office of the Chairman. With the exception of the Wessex Water Company (which will remain in the Enron Transportation Services organization) and Enron India (discussed below), EGAS will include all of the assets and activities of the former Enron Global Assets group and the Azurix organization. EGAS will include Enron's assets and merchant activities in South America. . . .
Enron India
Enron's significant interests in India are commanding increased attention from Enron's senior management. We are pleased to announce that Rebecca McDonald will focus exclusively on Enron's business in India, as Chief Executive Officer of Enron India, reporting to the Enron Corp. Office of the Chairman.
Enron Broadband Services
With Kevin's departure from Enron Broadband Services (EBS), we are also making a number of changes in the EBS organization. Jim Fallon

will now be President and Chief Operating Officer of EBS . . . Dave Cox will continue as Chief Commercial Officer of EBS and will also join Ken Rice and Jim Fallon in the EBS Office of the Chairman. . . .

Enron Corporate Development

In order to improve coordination of Enron's corporate development activities, we are consolidating these activities under Andy Fastow, Executive Vice President and Chief Financial Officer. . . .

One of Enron's most compelling challenges is the sale of certain assets or businesses that are no longer core operations. Mark Metts, Executive Vice President of Enron Corp., will head up a new Special Projects group to specifically focus on the completion of some of these more challenging transactions.

Please join us in congratulating all of these individuals on their new responsibilities.

Azurix, India, and Broadband—these were the same three I remembered Bickers pointing out. Broadband had brought ENE stock down with the unraveling of a deal with Blockbuster, Inc., to offer videos for rent over the Internet. The Dabhol plant in India was only partially completed and facing serious political and environmental obstacles. Azurix had a wimpy IPO in 1998, followed by several months of lackluster performance, which ended Rebecca Mark's Enron career.

Everyone knew that those three groups had big problems, but I had always assumed the problems were just a drop in Enron's hugely profitable bucket.

What conclusions could I draw from this? On these two days in a row in mid-June, Skilling and Lay sent us messages that spoke of the need to cut costs and to reorganize Enron's failing companies. ENE stock was bouncing around in the 40s after being in the high 80s just eight months earlier. Was there a reason to be concerned?

I asked Liz Perry what she thought.

After she responded with, "What e-mails?" I explained my question in greater detail. "I think they are starting to realize Enron has problems," she said. "Maybe Skilling is getting itchy about the stock price."

In June 2001, we could only speculate about what Enron's real problems were and how Skilling was feeling about the drop in ENE stock. But whatever the answers might be, that summer was not about Enron's problems. For me, it was about getting married, going on a long honeymoon, and buying a new home. June and July of 2001 weren't about a falling Enron stock price, but about the Houston Astros rising in the baseball standings at Enron Field. Our company was just going through some ups and downs like any other monster corporation, except that the future for Enron was so much brighter than all of the others.

Friday—August 10, 2001
ENE opening price: $42.75
ENE closing price: $42.81
ENE trading volume 1,400,700

The offices of Risk Assessment and Control (RAC) were being overhauled. Black sheets hung down to cover areas being rebuilt. Construction noise echoed through the dusty halls.

As part of a commercial group that was supposed to be making a market with external customers, McLainey, Duffy, and I didn't have much clout there. People in RAC were suspicious of any commercial group stepping into the middle of their system of risk controls.

We were there to propose a more efficient technology for monitoring Enron's credit risk internally (for which RAC was responsible). It was a technology that had spun off of our development activities; certainly if it was good enough for customers, it was good enough for Enron.

They greeted us with cold disregard. It wasn't necessarily resistance to change, but more a resistance to people outside of RAC. The meeting was short. The senior RAC executive didn't have much to say to us.

RAC people had built up a tough outer shell—and it was a shell that would be tough to crack. It was like Risk Assessment and Control believed they already had everything *under control*.

The three of us left the meeting with a sort of "back to the drawing board" feeling. McLainey and Duffy headed back to the trading floor. I stopped by to visit Ron Middleton, who was clearly going to be my only RAC friend that day.

"Middleton." I walked up behind him as he leaned in toward his computer screen.

"Hey, Cruver. What's happening?"

"Whoa! What happened to you?" His eyes were barely open, and what I could see of them was dry and red.

"Lots of late nights. This place is wrecking me," he said in short, painful bursts.

I convinced him it was time to take a break. We headed over to grab some coffee; again, just bottled water for me. The conversation went straight to why he was so burned up.

"RAC just doesn't have the time to do the right amount of due diligence on a deal. We see four hundred major deals a year. It's a joke." He was trying hard not to sound too frustrated, which came across as just sounding tired.

RAC was essentially the control group within Enron—a cost center—that was responsible for approving deals and managing Enron's overall risk. Deals would come to guys like Middleton in the form of a Deal Approval Sheet, commonly known as a DASH.

The DASH was pretty straightforward from a financial perspective and it included the following:

- A description of the deal
- Origination information
- Economic data
- A cash-flow model, which included sources and uses of cash as well as the deal's value (internal rate of return, net present value, etc.)
- Risk components
- Financial Approval Sheet (FASH)
- Authorization page

The DASH would be originally put together and submitted by a business unit. An analyst within RAC then did an independent assessment of the deal's value.

Middleton explained that more often than not, he found that his RAC value didn't match the value submitted by the business unit, in which case they had a problem.

"Where does the gap between the two values come from?"

Middleton explained, "From anywhere they can get it . . . economic assumptions, price curves, or just out of thin air. They usually aren't trying to come up with the real value of the deal; they are trying to meet their individual bonus targets."

"Okay, so that's what the head of the business unit is doing. What about the authorization page? It's not like these deals get through the system." I was still trying to grasp what he was telling me. "Doesn't RAC and Legal and Finance and everyone else have to sign off on the thing?"

"Yes . . . and they do. Andersen, Legal . . . No one is going to resist these guys when their bonuses—and the Enron stock price—

are riding on it. They justify it as working for the shareholder; you know, increasing shareholder wealth." He paused to catch his breath. "If I had a dime for each time someone chewed my ass to push an overvalued deal through . . . I mean, I've gotten phone calls like 'bleep bleep bleep Skilling bleep bleep bleep Skilling.' "

It sounded like he was saying that the "S" word was dropped by people from Skilling's inner circle, almost like a threat.

"You're saying that Skilling is pushing inflated deals?"

"He's standing behind the guy ripping me a new one . . . at least figuratively speaking. They like to drop his name, not just to me but to Andersen." He paused as if he was about to discover the meaning of life. Then he delivered the whole truth:

"Everything that happens inside Enron is driven by two things: the PRC process and earnings per share." It wasn't the meaning of life, but it was starting to dawn on me that it was the meaning of life at Enron.

What Middleton dumped on me that day was the systemic reality of the magnificent Enron—that if the people in the business units wanted to survive the PRC process and meet their personal bonus targets, then they often needed to inflate the deal value (which was the estimated value of future cash flows from a deal). With inflated deal value they could deliver bigger earnings. More specifically, they could deliver bigger earnings to senior management—who in turn would deliver them to Wall Street and investors.

Fortunately for those involved, the accounting system *allowed* RAC and the business units a lot of flexibility in valuing deals. Enron and other energy companies used a relatively unregulated form of mark-to-market accounting—which enabled them to put the full value of a long-term contract on the books immediately, based on commodity prices that were pulled from someone's ass.

The reason the prices were pulled from this place is because there was nowhere else to get them! Enron, more than any other "energy" company, dealt in commodities and derivative structures and deal terms that were far too unusual to have an established price. It was an issue of liquidity: if the deal required a price on something that was rarely bought and sold (making it illiquid), and there wasn't much of an established market, then the price had to be made up. For example, if the deal involved the delivery of a million tons of thong underwear each year for ten years, then the trader would have to rely on instinct and *expertise* to make up a price. The traders' expertise on a commodity was difficult for someone from RAC or Arthur Andersen to credibly question—so the fact that the price would favor higher bonuses and higher Enron earnings makes perfect sense.

And the deals involving the future delivery of commodities up to three, five, or even ten years in the future could be booked in the current quarter. Energy companies develop price curves as predictions of the long-term price outlook and use those curves in valuing the deals.

This is mark-to-market accounting, and Enron linked individual bonuses to this mark-to-market value. As a result, the strategy was less about booking profitable deals or controlling the risk of deals—and more about booking as many of the biggest deals possible.

Middleton continued with the gruesome details. "When Lou Pai left EES and took his $350 million with him, Delainey [Pai's replacement] had to fix the curves," Middleton explained. "When Delainey fixed the curves, we found that the deals Pai had built EES on were losing money."

On that note I was holding my bottled water like a Sippy Cup and about to curl into the fetal position. Forget about broadband, water, and international assets. EES was supposed to be Enron's big future. EES was the big bet on deregulation of energy.

Middleton went on to tell me about the "Friday Night Special," which was the nickname given to a DASH sent to RAC just hours before the end of the quarter. RAC would have no time to evaluate the deal's merits, some of which looked like a bad joke.

Our conversation ended with an agreement to have lunch sometime, *without* bringing up Enron business.

I was blown away. I wanted to understand the forces that were at work and how big the problem really was. As I walked back to my desk, I thought about what I knew of the DASH authorization page. Signatures were usually all over this page, including legal, origination, accounting, finance, and RAC; and on top of that was an approval hierarchy that took the big deals to the Office of the Chairman, which in 2001 meant Skilling and Lay. Some deals were big enough to require additional approval, even from the board of directors.

When I reached my desk I pulled up the Enron press releases for the big EES deals. I remembered in 1998 when Enron signed one of the coolest deals imaginable. It was the deal that first ignited my fascination with Enron and the deal that first shaped my eagerness to work there.

I pulled up the Enron press release from December 3, 1998:

ENRON AND SAN FRANCISCO GIANTS SIGN LONG-TERM COMMODITY, FACILITIES MANAGEMENT AGREEMENTS FOR PACIFIC BELL PARK

HOUSTON——*Enron Energy Services, Inc., a subsidiary of Enron Corp., announced today it will become the exclusive provider of electricity and energy and facilities management services for the San Francisco Giants through a 10-year energy commodity agreement and a 15-year management contract for Pacific Bell Park. Through these two contracts, totaling more than $60 million,*

Enron Energy Services will provide the electricity to operate Pacific Bell Park, as well as services for heating, ventilation and air conditioning and administration of various subcontracts for maintenance of all mechanical and electrical equipment.

"These agreements capture our core competency—the integration of commodity, capital and energy and facilities management services—and exemplify the tremendous value we can bring to sports facilities as their full-service energy and facility management provider," said Lou L. Pai, chairman and CEO of Enron Energy Services. "This comprehensive relationship with the Giants further confirms our commitment to the California market and is the first to take advantage of our full range of capabilities, including facility management services which we have been building as part of our overall strategy for Enron Energy Services."

After spending a painful twenty minutes with a frustrated Middleton, and after I reread the details of the Pacific Bell Park deal, I started to feel sick. From the Enron building and the Enron cow, I knew about the mirrors. Now I was starting to see the smoke.

4

The Beginning of the End

> "When you are the CEO and you are on the Board of Directors, you are
> supposed to know what's going on with the rest of the company."
> —*Betty Skilling, mother of former Enron CEO Jeff Skilling,*
> *in February 2002*

Tuesday—August 14, 2001
ENE opening price: $42.25
ENE closing price: $42.93
ENE trading volume: 2,013,200

The summer of 2001 was winding down, and Houston was glad to see it go. The city was still in recovery after tropical storm Allison dumped thirty-five inches of rain in two days, chasing seventeen thousand people from their waterlogged homes. It was a disaster of biblical proportions, and even the hundred-degree days of August couldn't dry out the city fast enough.

The Death Star was chugging along, trading as usual. There was even a day in which Darth Vader himself greeted me at the office. Enron was sponsoring an exhibit at the Museum of Fine Arts called "*Star Wars:* The Magic of Myth." The promotion in the Enron lobby that morning included a herd of people dressed in black Darth Vader outfits and white storm-trooper costumes. It would have made sense for Enron security to wear those uniforms year-round.

I almost felt guilty for having a great summer; heck, I was having a great *year!* The wedding went off without a hitch, the honeymoon was perfect, and our new house had survived the flood.

The wife, the dog, the cat, and the new furniture all fit together nicely. Even my job at Enron was coming together with accelerating responsibilities and challenges.

I was still a bit nauseated from my meeting the week before with Middleton. I had to assume he was right about the underlying cause of the inflated deals, but I wasn't so sure about the effect. Maybe people were trying to push these deals past *him,* but surely someone in charge within RAC or at Arthur Andersen had control of the overall situation. This company was profitable, and you can't just pull profits out of thin air. If the problem really was as bad as Middleton made it seem, then surely the actual deal values—and the actual losses—would have caught up with Enron a long time ago. If the bonus-driven problems he described were real, then where were the resulting losses?

I had a 9:30 meeting on the other side of Enron headquarters, so I took one last glance at my e-mail before heading out.

——Original Message——
From: Ken Lay and Jeff Skilling@ENRON
Sent: Tue 8/14/2001 9:17 AM
To: All Enron Worldwide@ENRON
Subject: Enron All-Employee Meeting
To: All Enron Employees:
    Please join us at an all-employee meeting at 10 a.m. Houston time, Thursday, Aug. 16 in the Hyatt Regency Houston's Imperial Ballroom. We will review Enron's second quarter financial and operating highlights and update you on key issues affecting the company. We welcome your questions. . . . We look forward to seeing you there.
    Ken and Jeff

I put the meeting into my calendar and dashed away from my desk. I was looking forward to seeing "Ken and Jeff" in person.

• • •

It was a Wednesday, just two weeks before Christmas 2000, and the press release was no surprise. It announced that effective February 12, 2001, Jeff Skilling would become the new Enron CEO, and Ken Lay would remain as Chairman of the Board. The effective date was almost laughable. Skilling had actually been running Enron for years.

"The best time for succession is when the successor is ready and when the company is well positioned for the future" were the words of Ken Lay. "Jeff is a big part of Enron's success and is clearly ready to lead the company."

Skilling was now officially in charge, which was a huge change from being *unofficially* in charge. Skilling would now become the outside guy—his would now be the top name attached to Enron's performance. He could no longer hide in the background while Ken Lay made appearances around the world as Enron's public face. As the new CEO, Skilling would have to represent the company— Skilling had just been named Enron's *new* public face.

The December 13 press release announcing that Jeff Skilling would be the new Enron CEO came five years and a day after Enron first dropped the hint. It was a Tuesday in December 1996 when Skilling was announced as new president and chief operating officer—a fancy title that really meant "the man behind the man." That 1996 promotion put Skilling in line for CEO; all he needed was five years to make the adjustment from finance type to manager type.

From the beginning of his career Skilling displayed pure genius. He had an extraordinary gift for producing new ideas within the framework of old philosophies. He went from the top 5 percent of his Harvard M.B.A. class straight to McKinsey & Co. in 1979. He made such an impression on Ken Lay—as he rose to the top of McKinsey's energy and chemical practice during the '80s—that when Skilling was finally lured over to Enron in 1990, a new division was created just for him. The group was called Enron Finance, and Skilling quickly began implementing his vision of Enron as more of an investment bank than an energy company. Initially, he was Enron Finance's only official employee. From there he took Enron on a mission of growth. The strategy was simple: to take the money that was outside the building and move it inside the building.

His rise to Enron CEO at age forty-eight was no surprise to those who knew him. They describe a hyperactive personality— always on the go, can't sit still, very curious, never slows down. "Rocky," as he was known, loved to push the envelope and take risks.

Being CEO of Enron was Skilling's dream-come-true. At age forty-eight, he was leading a revolution.

McLainey and I were sketching out the future of our business on a dry-erase wall. It had been a long day of planning, as we struggled to organize our group's new strategy for selling bankruptcy protection. For the third time in as many months, management had sent Waterston a new set of objectives, and he was putting it on us to make it happen. We were a start-up group that was starting up over and over and over without getting anywhere. Meanwhile, our new market was starting to get mixed messages about what we could offer. The confusion added to the difficulty of convincing customers that bankruptcy risk was a reality; most customers just didn't believe it.

Waterston was heading quickly toward our glass room, where people had been going in and out of the all-day meeting.

He swung the door open. "Skilling just resigned!"

I saw all the life in McLainey's body spill out through his shoes. He flopped into a chair. "No."

I flipped my pen across the table. It went too far and dropped onto the floor. The three of us just sat there for several seconds, all staring at one another. Waterston still hung leaning forward with one hand on the outside door handle.

Finally, McLainey broke the silence with a barely audible "Why?"

Waterston answered, "I don't know . . . there should be a formal announcement later today."

The next few moments involved squirming in our chairs and rubbing our faces in our hands. With the wind out of our sails, we called the rest of the meeting off. We headed back to our desks where we could watch the newswires and monitor our e-mail.

CEOs don't just resign—they hit retirement age, they find a better company, or the board *tells* them to resign. They don't just resign! Particularly CEOs like Skilling, not at forty-eight years old, and not when he's been CEO for just six months!

The rest of the day untangled like a hairball. We waited and waited as if Skilling himself would appear to explain it all. Waterston was on the phone all day; in my wildest dreams he was talking Skilling out of it. McLainey was looking for news. He needed to see it to believe it. Everyone agreed, regardless of the explanation, that Skilling's exit was a sign, a very *bad* sign.

Once again, it was time to tune in to the Gossip Channel. When I reached Liz's desk she was already on the case. She was ready to roll through her dozens of Skilling resignation theories, so we found an empty meeting room.

Right off the bat: "Skilling hates being CEO." She said it to the tune of "I told you so."

"Don't you mean *hated* . . . being CEO."

"He was never cut out for it. He's a geek," she added.

"He's a brilliant geek. Maybe now is a brilliant time to leave Enron." As I said it we both stared into space for a few seconds, as if our careers were flashing before our eyes. Then we decided to explore more realistic answers.

Liz began to focus on the marketing perspective: "He has always been a public relations nightmare."

"Example?"

"A while back he had his little road-rage incident in the parking garage, where he impatiently raced around a line of cars."

"So, we all have our moments." I wasn't exactly a model driver myself.

"And he stuck his hand out the window giving them the finger! He is the leader of our company and he's giving his employees the finger!" She was exasperated.

"*Was* the leader." I felt I needed to keep pointing that out. "I do remember the question about Enron's vision." Liz gave me a look like I needed to explain. "Skilling was asked about Enron becoming 'the World's Leading Company' . . . the question was how he defined that. How would we know when Enron had reached that goal?"

"And . . . "

"Skilling answered, 'It's like pornography—you know it when you see it.'" I felt like I was telling the punch line of a joke.

"See! That's what I'm saying. They couldn't afford to have him as the company spokesman anymore. They asked him to leave!" Liz was trying to solve the mystery. "He calls some guy an 'asshole' on the conference call, he gives employees the finger, and he compares our company mission to pornography."

I didn't buy it. Skilling and others acknowledged that it was just his personality. The attitude just wasn't a big deal to most people at Enron. They liked his boldness. It matched *their* personality; it matched Enron's personality.

"Maybe he's bored? Maybe he's just ready to move on to something else?" I thought for a second that if Jeff Skilling started a new company after leaving Enron, I'd be the first one sending him a résumé.

We picked over Skilling resignation theories for a few more minutes, when Vic Lazarri came in the room.

"The wire says it's for personal reasons," he said.

Liz jumped on it. "What kind of personal reasons?"

"Don't know." Vic closed the door and returned to his desk.

Liz ran through everything she knew about Jeff Skilling personally. She knew he was engaged to Rebecca "Va-voom" Carter, she knew he had kids and an ex-wife, she knew he lived in a *palace* in River Oaks.

"Teesside?"

"Oh, yeah. He was there last week."

Liz and I went back to our desks, not sure if we would ever really know why Skilling was leaving. The newswire said personal reasons. McLainey, Waterston, Lazarri, and everyone else on the trade floor thought that was just public-relations spin.

I thought it was spin, too. Then I read the Teesside e-mails from just a week before.

——Original Message——
From: Jeff Skilling—President and CEO@ENRON
Sent: Thu 8/9/2001 11:46 AM
To: All Enron Worldwide@ENRON
Subject: Teesside Update
Dear Enron Employees:

I'm sorry to report that a third Enron employee has died in the hospital as a result of injuries from yesterday's explosion and fire at Teesside Power Station. To lose another employee is a devastating blow to all of us. A fourth employee remains in the hospital and is in stable condition. Please keep these employees and their families in your thoughts and prayers. We will release their names as soon as all family members and relatives have been notified.

I'm in the U.K. now and will be visiting with the employees and families who've been affected by this tragic accident. I will also visit the site and will meet with authorities in order to determine the cause of the explosion. I will keep you posted on any new developments.

Personal reasons? I can't explain it, but by some irrational spark of logic I believed it. Jeff Skilling wasn't a machine, but human like the rest of us. Why *couldn't* he make a decision like this for personal reasons? Not everything has to be done in the name of business, does it?

I decided to give Mr. Blue a call. We had never rescheduled our lunch, and I was dying to hear his view of the Skilling departure. His assistant explained that he was unavailable, so I left him a voice mail requesting a return call.

Seconds later, my phone rang.

"Enron." My tone was soft, as this was now a day of mourning.

"Dude! . . . Whyyyyyy? What the . . . "

"Bickers. Chill out. It's just for personal reasons." I knew it was going to be one of those classic Bickers disputes, so I threw my position up early in hopes of his surrender.

"Whatever . . . all I know is ENE will be rockin' tomorrow."

He let the Skilling question slide. Then we started talking volume. ENE stock typically traded at a volume between 2 million and 3 million shares per day. Bickers guessed that the post-Skilling-resignation session would hit 20 million. I bet him $1 and took the "under."

Then, less than seven hours after the last e-mail from "Ken and Jeff," the following message popped up in my Inbox:

• • •

——Original Message——
From: Ken Lay@ENRON
Sent: Tue 8/14/2001 3:59 PM
To: All Enron Worldwide@ENRON
Subject: Organizational Announcement

It is with regret that I have to announce that Jeff Skilling is leaving Enron. Today, the Board of Directors accepted his resignation as President and CEO of Enron. Jeff is resigning for personal reasons and his decision is voluntary. I regret his decision, but I accept and understand it. I have worked closely with Jeff for more than 15 years, including 11 here at Enron, and have had few, if any, professional relationships that I value more. I am pleased to say that he has agreed to enter into a consulting arrangement with the company to advise me and the Board of Directors.

Now it's time to look forward.

With Jeff leaving, the Board has asked me to resume the responsibilities of President and CEO in addition to my role as Chairman of the Board. I have agreed. I want to assure you that I have never felt better about the prospects for the company. All of you know that our stock price has suffered substantially over the last few months. One of my top priorities will be to restore a significant amount of the stock value we have lost as soon as possible. Our performance has never been stronger; our business model has never been more robust; our growth has never been more certain; and most importantly, we have never had a better nor deeper pool of talent throughout the company. We have the finest organization in American business today. Together, we will make Enron the world's leading company.

On Thursday at 10:00 a.m. Houston time, we will hold an all employee meeting at the Hyatt. We will broadcast the meeting to our employees around the world where technically available, and I look forward to seeing many of you there.

• • •

And just like that, we all felt better. Ken Lay was back at the tiller; and Ken Lay believed in Enron.

I read it again: *"Our performance has never been stronger; our business model has never been more robust; our growth has never been more certain."*

Wednesday—August 15, 2001
ENE opening price: $40.00
ENE closing price: $40.25
ENE trading volume: 29,748,400

I lost the dollar to Bickers, as trading volume hit close to 30 million shares. The stock closed above $40, but during the day had dipped into the $30s for the first time since 1999.

Meanwhile, an anonymous one-page memo arrived at Ken Lay's office. He had requested that employees submit questions or concerns following the Skilling resignation. A drop box outside of his office could be used by those who preferred to remain anonymous.

"Has Enron become a risky place to work?" the memo began. "For those of us who didn't get rich over last few years, can we afford to stay?"

The memo was detailed and volatile. The person who wrote it was obviously an accountant close to Raptor and LJM transactions. The memo spoke of aggressive accounting, pointing to international assets and the mark-to-market issues of EES.

"We enjoyed a wonderfully high stock price, many executives sold stock, we then try and reverse or fix the deals in 2001 and it's a bit like robbing the bank in one year and then trying to pay it back two years later.

"What do we do? I know this question cannot be answered in an all-employee meeting, but can you give some assurances that you and [Rick] Causey will sit down and take a good hard objective look at what is going to happen . . . in 2002 and 2003?"

Thursday—August 16, 2001
ENE opening price: $39.50
ENE closing price: $36.85
ENE trading volume: 13,428,800

Many of us were too busy to head over to the Hyatt for the all-employee meeting, but it was being broadcast through the Enron intranet. As 10:00 A.M. rolled around, I tried desperately to connect to the video feed. It didn't work. I missed the pep rally.

Liz returned from the meeting.

"Anything interesting?" I asked, knowing that all-employee meetings were never newsworthy.

"Actually," she began with a look of pleasant surprise, "it was really cool."

"Cool?" It wasn't the adjective I expected.

"Linda Lay was there, and he introduced her. He's amazing. He's so sincere, and you can really trust him that everything is going to be fine. He's a family man." She smiled. "We gave him a huge standing ovation."

Two days after Skilling had resigned, Ken Lay was soothing the minds of Enronians everywhere. Just hearing about the meeting secondhand from Liz put my mind at ease.

On that same day, the market took ENE stock to a closing price just under $37.

Enron stock would never again reach the $40 level. If only we

had known that. If only we had known about the memo to Ken Lay
from the day before.

Monday—August 20, 2001
ENE opening price: $36.80
ENE closing price: $36.25
ENE trading volume: 4,895,100

"If you liked it at $80, you *love* it under $40," announced Lazarri
across the trading floor. The guy who always thought simple equities
were beneath him—the guy who was more likely to drop a few grand
into beef jerky futures than a three-letter ticker—had just decided
that ENE was oversold and it was time to start paying attention to it.

The dust was starting to settle after Skilling's bombshell. The
stock had stabilized in the mid-$30s and volume was coming back
down to earth. Ken Lay was on the campaign trail, and the polls
were looking better every day.

In an interview that day with *Businessweek,* Lay told the world,
"There are no accounting issues, no trading issues, no reserve issues, no
previously unknown problem issues. . . . There is no other shoe to fall."

Wednesday—August 22, 2001
ENE opening price: $37.30
ENE closing price: $37.26
ENE trading volume: 6,472,300

Another memo arrived, this time for Sharon Butcher, Enron
attorney. The memo was a response from Vinson & Elkins,
Enron's outside lawyers, to Butcher's request for information on

the "possible risks associated with discharging (or constructively discharging) employees who report allegations of improper accounting practices."

The V&E response included the possibility of a wrongful discharge claim, as well as the damaging effects of a report to the SEC and IRS.

On the same day, a meeting was scheduled between Ken Lay and Sherron Watkins.

Sherron Watkins was a C.P.A., and had an M.P.A. from the University of Texas. She had twenty years of accounting experience, including eight years with Enron. She was the author of the anonymous, one-page memo dropped in Ken Lay's suggestion box just a week earlier, on the fifteenth.

She wasn't comfortable bringing these issues to her boss, Andy Fastow, so she decided it was Ken Lay that needed to be made aware of the issues. She wanted him to know before it was too late, while something could still be done to avert disaster. Skilling had just resigned, and the Wall Street microscope was focusing on Enron, which she believed made discovery of Enron's accounting practices a surefire scandal.

The meeting between Lay and Watkins lasted just over half an hour. This time, in addition to the one-page memo, Watkins had several pages of backup. She believed the notes to the financial statements did not adequately explain the structures. Enron was booking income with transactions backed by its own devalued stock.

Lay asked Watkins if she was certain something was wrong with these accounting structures. Watkins insisted that something *was* wrong—especially when Enron "was owed $700 million, which it had already booked on its income statement, and that the $700 million was going to be paid by an entity cashing in on Enron's own stock."

Lay told Watkins he would look into it. In addition, she asked to be transferred because she was no longer comfortable working where she was.

The meeting with Lay and Watkins came to an end.

Lay had settled things down with employees and investors; in fact the stock began to rise again. Lay brought Greg Whalley and Mark Frevert into the Office of the Chairman to replace Skilling. Later, in an all-employee meeting in front of five thousand people, Ken Lay would introduce Greg Whalley as "Jeff," but few noticed or commented on the slip.

Skilling was gone, the summer was over, and Sherron Watkins got her transfer.

And no one—outside the Death Star, across the city of Houston, up and down Wall Street, or in Washington, D.C.—had heard any whistles blowing.

Tuesday—September 11, 2001
ENE price: $32.76
ENE trading volume: 0

Enron, like most modern companies, invested a great deal of money in professional education. On that Tuesday morning, I was signed up to take an advanced derivatives training class. Liz Perry was taking the class as well. For the most part, I was annoyed—I had already had the same coursework a few years earlier, but McLainey insisted that I soak in the Enron version of the material. I was in for two days of hedging and mitigating.

The class was set to begin at 8:00 A.M. in Enron Center North, and I had a pile of work on my desk that couldn't wait. I arrived at the office early and scrambled to get as much done as possible before class began.

At some point, while people were still trickling onto the

trading floor, I glanced at the big screens above my head. Every channel was showing one of the World Trade Center towers. There was smoke pouring out of a massive hole near the top.

I looked over at McLainey. At this point we were all standing and staring at the different screens and their different camera angles. Someone put one of the channels on speaker phone so we could hear the story unfold.

I had been on the top floor of that tower just two weeks earlier. McLainey had been there just five days ago. Lower Manhattan was the heart of all our group's business dealings, and we traveled there monthly. We both had the building fresh in our memories. We just looked at each other and shook our heads.

The reports and wires began to explain that a plane had hit the building. We were all floored by the news of such a horrible accident. I picked up the phone to call my wife. She didn't work at a company with a hundred televisions all around her, and this was major news. I looked at my watch; the training class was about to begin. I left the trading floor hoping that the fire would be put out by the time I came back to my desk.

Liz and I sat in the class for about an hour. We were in the midst of a discussion—how a department store owner in West Texas could benefit from a hedge against falling oil prices—when we were all startled. A building speaker system, that we didn't even know existed, began blasting a message:

"We have no reason to believe Enron is in any danger."

Everyone looked at each other. The "no danger" message was extremely alarming. In a moment each person in the class was on his or her cell phone. People began announcing headlines to the class from bits and pieces of conversation:

" . . . towers collapsed . . . "

" . . . the Pentagon is hit . . . "

I suggested to the instructor that the class take a break, and he agreed. Liz and I left the training room. We opened the stairwell to find a steady stream of Enron employees rushing down the stairs. It was quiet, except for a few whispers.

I asked a stranger, "What's going on?"

"I don't know—but a lot of people hate Enron, so we're leaving."

Liz and I were sick to our stomachs. We waited outside the building and began calling people we knew. I tried calling Bickers, but couldn't get through to New York. I called my wife to tell her I loved her and was going home. I called McLainey, who was still up on the trading floor.

I asked, "What the hell is going on?"

He didn't have an answer and sounded crushed. We agreed that we should all be with our families, and he told me to go home.

Enron was completely evacuated, the first of just a few buildings in Houston. The whole world was turned upside down. Nothing seemed real. It was horror and terror and darkness all wrapped into one.

The events of that day had a staggering effect on the entire planet, and Enron was no exception: an executive from Enron Wind was aboard one of the flights. Another Enron employee was missing—actually, he was one of hundreds of suspects being pursued by the FBI.

A conference being hosted by the Risk Waters Group was on the 106th floor of the North Tower that morning. We were all desperately trying to find out which of our business partners, customers, and media contacts were among the eighty-seven attendees.

McLainey and I could hardly believe our eyes as we looked at the conference invitation on his desk.

The rest of the week was a blur. Nothing Enron really mattered; all that mattered was trying to get to a new definition of "normal." When the stock market opened again on September 17, no one cared about ENE. We cared about the market as a whole. For Enron stock to stabilize in the mid-$20s was great news—except that no one really noticed. It just wasn't important.

Wednesday—September 26, 2001
ENE opening price: $26.75
ENE closing price: $25.15
ENE trading volume: 10,033,700

Bickers and I didn't talk much about Enron or ENE stock during September. We talked more about philosophical issues—the future of humanity, the future of capitalism, and how he and other New Yorkers were getting back to some new version of reality.

The third quarter of Enron's fiscal year was coming to an end, and there were three weeks until another Enron earnings report. Bickers did offer me an opinion on that:

"Dude, all I can say," said Bickers, with an almost sinister tone, "is you guys better give us some answers this time."

Wall Street wanted to know the whole truth and nothing but the truth about Enron's financial statements. The obscure references to "related parties" and "a senior Enron officer" buried in the back of the notes were no longer going to cut it, especially now that Skilling had made his surprise exit. Bickers was warning me that he was fed up. He was tired of telling his clients that Enron was a sure thing, all the way from $80 to $25 per share in a matter of ten months.

I told Bickers what I always told him: that it wasn't my problem. Our start-up group was still on track with our business plan. We had grown to about a hundred people, and we had some exciting things brewing on the horizon. Unfortunately, we were still less than a blip on Enron's income statement—so Bickers was barking up a tree stump by complaining to me about the bigger picture. I could only hope that the right people within Enron were getting the Bickers message as well: "More disclosure!"

Every Enron employee was required to attend the "sexual harassment training." Was the training about *prevention*? Or did they want us all to become better harassers?

We were given a few choices of sessions. Liz Perry and I happened to sign up for the same one.

As we walked over to the Doubletree Hotel, Liz brought up the subject of sex at Enron. She found it ironic that Enron would be requiring such training, especially with the company's history.

Again—the Gossip Channel . . .

"Some of the execs had their own harems."

"Harems?" I knew the word, but was surprised to hear it in the context of Enron.

She continued, "They would have a whole group of young women around them, like when they traveled . . . mostly analysts and secretaries."

"Hmmm," I said with forced detachment.

I had already heard similar stories and didn't request more details.

We arrived at the sexual harassment training and grabbed our handouts, drinks, and cookies. The class was packed with a few hundred Enronians, and a projection screen displayed the Crooked E logo.

A local law firm had been hired to do the session, and we all listened to the dos and don'ts of sexual harassment. The instructors focused on legal implications and how an incident could hurt your career. "Right and wrong" was not on the agenda.

I was almost asleep in my chair when the instructor broke into a story. It was a tragic tale of female coworkers at a bar discussing sex and "power tools," which had resulted in lawsuits and terminations and emotional scarring. I took a bite of my cookie and tried to pretend I wasn't amused.

The instructors gave us a few rules to take away from the session, such as "No touching, especially back rubs" and "Try to avoid talking about sex."

Liz and I walked out of the session.

"So all the sex at Enron . . . " I began, noticing a few nearby heads turning, "is it sex for the sake of sex, or is it a power thing?"

"Just sex, I think. I don't know . . . I've heard a few things about climbing the corporate ladder the old-fashioned way." And with that, Liz and I implicitly agreed that two coworkers could talk about sex without suing each other.

"How do you feel about Rebecca Mark?" I was wondering what Liz thought of the former Enron executive. Mr. Blue had once described Mark as "so sexy she makes it difficult to think."

"I think she's brilliant, beautiful . . . and she got screwed by Enron."

Rebecca Mark, who earned the nickname "Mark the Shark," was no longer with Enron because of her failed attempt at Azurix. She was put in charge of the water company in 1999, which sought to commoditize and trade H_2O via the classic Enron formula. Mark led Azurix to a $700 million IPO, but then its new stock quickly trickled from $20 down to $4.

Before Azurix, Mark was climbing through the ranks of Enron at a rocket pace. She roared around the planet like Wonder Woman. With jet-powered high heels and her blond hair blowing in the wind, she developed international power projects from Bombay to the Philippines.

She was Enron's version of sexy and smart, and she knew it. She had blasted through the glass ceiling without conforming to a prescribed set of gender-neutral rules; there were no unisex outfits or tearful complaints about a male-dominated culture. She instead *used* that culture to her advantage, flaunting her sexuality and making men drool—as they stared at her across boardroom tables.

She had learned her ass-kicking skills from John Wing, another ex-military turned Enron executive. Although they were both married to other people at the time, several published sources reported that Wing and Mark had an affair. However, in a 1996 *Fortune* article called "Women, Sex and Power," when asked to comment on rumors that she'd had relationships with other Enron colleagues, Mark said, "Of course they're not true, but it's terribly flattering that people think my life is so exciting. I think all I do is work, travel, and take care of my eleven-year-old twins." When Wing left Enron, Mark had his job. She was suddenly considered one of the most powerful women in American business and rumored to be next in line for Ken Lay's job.

But with the dreary performance of Azurix, Enron began to distance itself. Rebecca Mark was fired from Azurix in 2000, and she left her position on the Enron board as well. Mark had gone from the Enron superheroine, raking in a couple million dollars in bonus each year, to the ex-leader of a failed Enron venture.

"She should have had Skilling's job," added Liz Perry. "She should be the CEO of Enron."

I hadn't heard from Mr. Blue since leaving him that voice-mail message. I couldn't believe that after six months at Enron, I still hadn't had lunch or a meeting with him. He wasn't just an Enron contact; he was a family friend I had known for years.

I figured he must be ass-deep in alligators with recent events and let it go.

The conversation with Middleton about RAC was still on my mind, when I remembered the Harvard guy. It had been months since I had spoken to John Weston, the one from my M.B.A. program who joined Enron the same day I did. I remembered he was going to work in EES. He would have been there long enough to at least get a feel for the situation, so I decided to give him a call.

I looked Weston up in the Enron intranet directory, and couldn't find his name. I tried pulling his contact info through the e-mail system, and couldn't get it there either. It was like he had fallen off the face of the earth.

I called a dozen business-school classmates to find out his number, until someone finally clarified the situation:

"He left Enron."

I was told he had gone to an Enron competitor just a few buildings down Smith Street. I got his new number and gave him a call.

"What's going on, Weston?" The curiosity was killing me.

"Oh, hey Cruver. I was going to send all you guys my new contact info when things got settled."

"What happened? I didn't realize Enron fired people from Harvard."

"No, I quit—and I got a better deal over here."

"Wow. It seems like last week we were sitting through orientation together. Explain, please!"

"I just didn't think EES had its act together. I was working on a dead-end product, and there's just more upside over here."

I had a lot of respect for Weston's opinion. To hear him say that there was *any* company, let alone a competitor, with more upside than Enron, made me squirm in my chair.

"I also think the accounting is too aggressive. Not illegal or intentionally deceptive, just aggressive. But, everyone thinks that."

The conversation didn't go any deeper into Enron than that. We talked a bit about his wife and new baby, and agreed to have lunch soon.

Then it suddenly hit me: Rebecca Mark, Jeff Skilling, and now my friend Weston were all gone from Enron, and all three had graduated from Harvard.

For a moment, I wondered if there was some insider news about Enron in the Harvard alumni newsletter.

In business classrooms around the world, more than a dozen Harvard Business School case studies and articles (some I studied while at the University of Texas) have hyped and praised the innovation of Enron and the Enron business model. But Enron was more than just a subject of academic discussion—it was a placement opportunity. Every year, more than 1,800 Harvard MBA students consider which company will help them recoup their investment—over $30,000 in tuition per year—with the best job offer. Enron was just one of a zillion options for a Harvard MBA, whose average starting salary and signing bonus for 2001 was around $122,000 (not including stock options or performance bonus).

And it wasn't just Jeff Skilling and Rebecca Mark that made the Enron-Harvard connection solid as an iron chain.

For sixteen years, Herbert "Pug" Winokur had been on Enron's Board of Directors. Pug was also a Harvard grad, with three Harvard degrees, and in 2001 he was one of seven members of the university's governing body called the Harvard Corporation. Back at Enron, Pug's board duties included chairmanship of the Finance Committee—approving major financial transactions such as off-balance sheet partnerships and the thousands of special entities Enron was creating.

In 2001, the Harvard Corporation selected Lawrence H. Summers as the twenty-seventh president of Harvard University. Two years earlier, as the Secretary of the Treasury under President Clinton, Larry Summers wrote a personal note to Ken Lay. "I'll keep my eye on power deregulation and energy-market infrastructure issues," said the May 25, 1999 note to Lay, written in response to Ken's letter congratulating Summers on succeeding Robert Rubin. Before Summers replaced him, Harvard grad Robert Rubin was offered a spot on Enron's board by Lay. Rubin declined the offer, but did become chairman of the executive committee of Citigroup—one of several major banks that would invest in Enron partnerships and lend Enron hundreds of millions of dollars as the company began to fail.

In the end, Rubin would be appointed to the Harvard Corporation as a replacement for Winokur when he resigned. "[Harvard is] replacing Enron's finance director with its banker," said one Harvard student.

Spring and fall were the convention seasons, and the fall of 2001 was a packed schedule. Liz Perry would endure the most of it, spending weeks at a time flying from city to city for trade shows. I was lucky to draw only one conference, in Northern California, where I was scheduled to speak about our innovative bankruptcy-related products.

The speaking engagement was a welcome change for me. I had become exhausted with calling potential customers and product partners via the Beast, and looked forward to keeping a whole auditorium full of people captive for thirty minutes. Like the phone calls, I would gain instant respect because I was Enron. And at the conference, I would *not* have to worry about if or when they would return my cold call.

A week or so before the California conference, Liz informed me that she and I were meeting with Enron's public relations people to prepare for the trip. I was not surprised that a prep session had been called. Tensions between Enron and California were high.

California and Enron had a special relationship in 2001—the whole state hated us. Even my own relatives living in California were upset that I had gone to work for such an "evil" company.

The story of California's power crisis is hardly a simple one. It begins with a century of government-regulated power, in which utility companies were guaranteed profits. Consumers in California, especially big industrial consumers, became tired of the high prices in their state—an average of 50 percent higher than the rest of the country.

Huge companies threatened to move their operations out of California, unless they were given the right to buy cheaper power from nonregulated producers. It was time to change the system, and so lobbying efforts in the form of millions of dollars began to flow—between politicians, regulators, utilities, consumers, and Enron. The push was on for deregulation.

In 1996, Governor Pete Wilson signed California into history, making it the first state in the nation to deregulate electricity. The law was passed unanimously by both houses of the state legislature. It seemed like a deal that would benefit everyone:

- Utility companies would be forced to sell their power-generating assets, a sacrifice in exchange for the opportunity of new business and unrestricted profits. It was worth giving up the guaranteed profits, and it was worth the risk of paying deregulated wholesale energy prices—prices that could fluctuate on the open market.
- Consumer prices would be frozen until the dust settled and the utilities had completed the sale of their assets. Once the market opened up to competition, consumers saw an opportunity to pay less for energy.

- The marketplace itself would become free, and energy prices would be driven by supply and demand—instead of by the government.

In 1997, Enron entered the California market with an aggressive campaign. Lou Pai was heading up EES that year: "The message is simple: We are here to do business. Enron has been fighting for deregulation for over a decade and now we're offering low rates and more innovative products to as many Californians as possible."

Deregulation in California worked well until the spring of 2000, when the so-called perfect storm hit the California energy market.

There was a lack of new power plants, a drought that dried up hydroelectric supply, and weak supply from generators outside the state. These supply issues collided with a California heat wave, and wholesale power prices began to soar. Unfortunately for some utilities, they began paying the high wholesale prices to generators while the prices they charged consumers were still frozen.

Pacific Gas & Electric filed for bankruptcy protection. Lawsuits began to fly across the country. Angry Californians experienced rolling blackouts and higher utility bills. California began kicking and screaming and looking for someone to blame for the mess. Enron was included in the wave of accusations.

"I would love to personally escort [Ken] Lay to an eight by ten cell that he could share with a tattooed dude who says, 'Hi my name is Spike, honey'" was the inflamed rhetoric from California attorney general Bill Lockyer.

About a month later in San Francisco, Skilling got hit in the ear by a protester's cream pie. "People in California are angry," said Skilling, wiping the tasty filling off his head. "And they should be."

When Liz and I met with Enron public relations before the California trip, we already knew the California-Enron relationship

was overheated. We were looking forward to getting some suggestions for how to deal with any "encounters."

"Don't worry about pies," PR explained. "They save those pies
for extremely high-profile targets. That same group that hit Skilling
also hit Bill Gates."

Okay. I crossed "pie anxiety" off my list.

"If anyone starts going off on you about Enron's role in the California energy crisis, just refer them to our department."

Okay. I made sure I had the right name and number.

"Just out of curiosity, what *is* Enron's role in the California
problem?" I was looking for the official spin.

"Well, first of all it's not the consumers' fault, it's the regulators' fault. They tried to revamp the state's energy system, but they
failed. Enron has done nothing wrong to manipulate power prices;
there's just no evidence of it." PR was telling us this like they had
explained it at least a thousand times already. "Their deregulation
plan put them at the mercy of price spikes. California would be
fine if they had done deregulation the right way, instead of the
stupid way."

Back in San Francisco, in the speech following the pie toss,
Skilling said: "California needs to get deregulation right, and the
rest of the country needs to get deregulation right. . . . Markets are
powerful, and they work."

The way I saw it, California was placing the blame on Enron,
when Enron was simply participating in the supply side of the
market. Enron was not a monopoly; consumers were not *forced* to
buy power from Enron. And the whole mess was oddly turning into
a California versus Texas thing—when in reality, Texas-based companies only supplied 13 percent of California's power. Californians
were angry that Enron was making tons of money while they suffered from high utility bills, but the reality was that Enron was also

getting *killed* by the California crisis, which had contributed to the 50 percent drop in ENE stock.

The deregulation Enron believed in was vastly different from the California version. The California Public Utilities Commission (CPUC) had created a set of requirements that prohibited long-term smoothing or hedging of prices; this equated to laying California consumers facedown on a price spike.

Price spikes are natural in any power market; after all, we were dealing in a commodity—electricity—that can't be stored. Storage is the way to smooth out supply and meet volatile demand; it's not an option with electricity.

In Ohio during 1998 and 1999, the day-to-day market ran into the same type of supply-demand imbalance that later hit California. Power prices, which usually ranged from $15 to $20 per megawatt, suddenly shot up to more than $7,000. Why didn't these price spikes crush Ohio the way they crushed California? Because in Ohio, the system had left only 2 percent of purchasers at the mercy of the day-to-day market. In California, on the other hand, regulators had left the *entire market* at the mercy of the day-to-day prices and potential spikes.

Enron *never wanted* California in that position. In fact, Enron had argued against it. In 1996, Skilling said that the plan California was putting into place was "ludicrous."

Everyone at Enron knew that our company would be much better off if California was successfully deregulated. Deregulation was the key to Enron's future across the United States. To have California's effort backfire, while masquerading as deregulation, was actually a massive blow to Enron's national potential.

The free-market theory, the supply-and-demand issues, the benefits of deregulation—all made sense to us. But Liz and I would be facing people who hated Enron. We had to realize that any opinion we offered someone from California would be viewed as "that's easy for you to say." The thought of such a confrontation made us nervous about the trip.

The subject of our meeting with PR quickly changed, after spending just a few minutes on California. The new subject was Enron's third-quarter earnings, which were being reported in three weeks.

"If anyone asks about the stock price, earnings, or the financial statements—tell them that *this* quarter Enron will be opening up the books. We have nothing to hide, and we really want to build trust by coming out with a much higher level of disclosure."

What PR was saying sounded like an answer to Bickers's warning. It sounded like someone inside Enron *was* listening and that it was time to turn over a new leaf. Ken Lay was in charge again, and he knew the value of relationships—especially Wall Street relationships that are based on trust.

One of the new twists after Lay was put back in charge was an employee survey. The Web-based questionnaire was called Lay-It-On-The-Line and was designed to measure the collective mental state of Enron employees. The results of the survey were centered on two things: Enron had strayed from its core values (RICE), and the PRC process needed to be repaired.

The results of the Lay-It-On-The-Line survey, the PR message about Enron's new level of financial disclosure, and the fact that Ken Lay was preaching positively about Enron all added up to a message that Enron was being *fixed*. It was a strange message for me to be getting, as I was still trying to comprehend the idea that Enron had even been broken.

I was sitting on a barbed-wire fence. I had Skilling, Bickers, Middleton, and Weston showing me a turn for the worse. I had Lay, Enron PR, and twenty thousand of the "best and the brightest" employees showing me a turn for the better.

The great equalizer—as always—was the stock market. As I waited in the Houston airport for the flight to California, I caught a stock ticker streaming across a television screen. ENE stock had climbed from $25 back to $33.

It was a turn for the better.

How to Conquer Corporate America, Rule #4: Never fly first class, because eventually you'll have to fly coach again.

I hated flying. I could never accept the physics of it. I *understood* the physics, but I had a hard time sitting calmly inside a thin, wobbly tube traveling at more than 500 mph, about thirty-five thousand feet above the ground, while burning twenty thousand liters of jet fuel at thirty-four hundred degrees (when steel melts at fourteen hundred degrees).

Through sailing I knew the mechanics of wings and lift; but if the laws of physics fail on a sailboat, there's no harm in just floating around.

The amount of sweat on my palms was directly related to the turbulence of a flight, and my sanity was thinly based on the status of the seat-belt light.

Maybe it was the two emergency landings I had experienced on past flights. Maybe it was having my six-foot-one-inch frame crammed into a coach seat. Maybe it was the pilots—who always seemed more like game-show hosts than professional aviators. In any case, I wished Enron would fly me first class; but Sharon Lay's travel agency didn't even bring it up as an option.

I was flying just a few short weeks after September 11. The airports were nearly empty, and security was extreme.

A guy with spiked hair and a homemade jacket that read EVE OF DESTRUCTION walked right through security, his clothing covered in trinkets and chains, his face pierced to look like a fishing lure. No hassle for him.

I was next: dressed in business casual, carrying an Enron bag, and transporting a suspicious-looking electronic device known to its users as a "laptop."

Bring on the body cavity search.

The conference was a success. The presentation went well, we made lots of contacts, and we even made a trip across the border to Nevada for some blackjack. During the entire visit, we only had two "encounters" with disgruntled Californians.

First, as we sat down at a large table for lunch, a man saw our Enron name tags and said to the group, "Ahh . . . the enemy is among us." The comment was greeted with silence from the entire table, including me. I decided to pretend the little bugger didn't exist, and ate my lunch.

Then I got a visit from an Unidentified Flying Opinion, who tried mercilessly to suck me up into his spacecraft for an anal probe. He was dumping evidence on me, as if he had just caught me red-handed:

"You guys were jamming the lines. Your traders were screwing us with phantom congestion," he declared. "You've been doing it ever since you entered this market. It's unfair. It's out-and-out greed."

"Sir, I don't trade power in California. If someone at Enron is doing something illegal, you're wasting your time telling me about it." I offered him the contact information that Enron PR had given me; he wasn't interested.

I was caught off-guard by an issue that our PR colleagues hadn't warned us about. It sounded unethical, possibly illegal, but what did he want me to do about it? I guess I could have called the power-trading people back in Houston and given them the order: "Stop making money! Forget the profits! Sell it for less than the market will pay!"

One of the first things I did for Enron upon returning to Houston was buy an Internet domain name for our group. The dot-com name was to be used for a new bankruptcy risk management product we were launching. We had selected the product name based on a zillion hours of brainstorming, and Enron's legal department had given it trademark clearance.

The only problem for us was that the domain name was already owned by someone . . . in California. He was "cyber-squatting." Nothing was more irritating than someone who tried to make a living buying domain names they never planned to use, except for resale. I could picture the guy brainstorming about which companies, products, or ideas he could beat to the Web. He would buy hundreds of www.names.com at $35 a piece, and then sit around waiting for deeper pockets to come along.

It took a few days to work the transaction, but I ultimately bought the domain name from this schmuck for a few hundred dollars. To hide my Enron identity, I used my mobile phone, a Yahoo! e-mail address, and a personal credit card. Enron later reimbursed me.

He never did learn I was with Enron. He never knew I had approval to spend *thousands* of dollars. He never knew he was dealing with the Fortune #7 company.

His game of cyber-squatting so irritated me that, once the

transaction was complete, I almost called him up to say, "Enron thanks you."

But then I thought about Enron's return to a better reputation. I thought about Lay-It-On-The-Line and the PR message. I thought about the core values. With the October 16 earnings report right around the corner, it was time to start showing the world a new and improved Enron.

5

Ken's House of Cards

"The price of leadership is responsibility."
——*Sir Winston Churchill*

Tuesday—October 16, 2001
ENE opening price: $34.30
ENE closing price: $33.84
ENE trading volume: 8,324,400

The third-quarter conference call sounded different without Jeff Skilling's attitude. The trading floor had tuned in at the usual 9:00 a.m. with a great sense of optimism. Expectations were high that Enron would deliver on its promise of greater "transparency" and "disclosure." There was also no chance of Ken Lay calling anyone crude names during the call, at least not with the microphone on.

As Enron's fearless leader began telling us the results from the previous three months, the newswires began delivering the headlines from the press release:

"*Enron Corp. announced today recurring earnings per diluted share of $0.43 for the third quarter.*"

"*Total recurring net income increased to $393 million, versus $292 million a year ago.*"

As usual, it was information overload. The numbers were spilling across my computer screen, echoing across the trading floor, and popping up on CNBC. It was all positive. Smiling, confident faces were all around me; and the voice of Ken Lay ricocheted calmly throughout the building:

"Our twenty-six percent increase in recurring earnings per diluted share shows the very strong results of our core wholesale and retail energy businesses and our natural gas pipelines."

The focus was on third quarter 2001 as it compared to third quarter of 2000, and the results were typical of an Enron earnings report. Growth of 26 percent was spectacular. These were *record* earnings.

Then, like a pile of bricks, he dropped it on us.

More than a billion bricks, to be precise. "Non-recurring charges totaling $1.01 billion . . . were recognized for the third quarter of 2001," read the press release.

Earnings Summary
(Millions)

	3Q00	3Q01
IBIT:		
Transportation & Distribution	$ 176	$ 87
Natural Gas Pipelines	*83*	*85*
Portland General	*74*	*(17)*
Global Assets	*19*	*19*
Wholesale Services	589	754
Americas	*536*	*701*
Europe and Other Commodity Markets	*53*	*53*
Retail Services	27	71
Broadband Services	(20)	(80)
Corp. & Other	(106)	(59)
Total IBIT	$ 666	$ 773
Interest & Other	302	255
Taxes	72	125
Net Income – Recurring	$ 292	$393
Non-Recurring Items	-0-	($1,011)
Reported Net Income	$ 292	($618)

09_01_3rd Quarter-3

Slide from Enron's October 17, 2001, analyst presentation, summarizing the income statement for the third quarter of 2001.

Ken Lay added, "After a thorough review of our businesses, we have decided to take these charges to clear away issues that have clouded the performance and earnings potential of our core energy business."

With the flip of a switch, the mood on the trading floor went sour. The total reported earnings came out to a loss of over $600 million. Never mind the crap about recurring and nonrecurring—that was just accounting language for "we'll try not to let it happen again."

My phone started ringing in the middle of the call. I only needed one guess.

"So you guys *are* disclosing more! You're disclosing a billion-dollar hit!" Bickers was simply freaking out, in a way that made me almost smile. The poor guy still had his highest rating on ENE stock, and he had a world full of clients he would need to explain this to.

"Chill, Bickers. It's a one-time charge for Azurix and Broadband and whatever other junk Enron invested in." I went on the defensive. The way I said it, he must have thought the losses were common knowledge to all Enron employees. I guess we all knew there were losses somewhere, but they had never really been quantified.

"Dude . . . this is NOT good. What a fucking mess!" He hung up to turn his focus back on the conference call.

The press release offered more details on what the *nonrecurring* charges were. The $1.01 billion loss was grouped into three parts:

- $287 million related to assets of Azurix Corp.
- $180 million related to restructuring of Broadband Services
- "$544 million related to losses associated with certain investments, principally Enron's interest in The New Power Company [an EES spin-off started by Lou Pai], broadband and technology investments, and *early termination during the third quarter of certain structured finance arrangements with a previously disclosed entity.*"

• • •

The phone rang again. It was Bickers.

"What the shit is this 'previously disclosed entity' . . . can't you hairy-backed idiots just tell us what the *entity is*?" He was livid.

I knew he was venting, so I didn't take it personally. Plus I agreed with him. I couldn't understand why Enron was still speaking in code. Did this "previously disclosed entity" have something to do with a "related party" whose managing partner was "a senior officer" of Enron? This was a billion dollars we were booking as a loss, and over half of it was accounted for as part of list of "certain investments."

Ken Lay's voice continued to echo across the trading floor. For the most part, it sounded like he was just mimicking the press release.

Then we heard something extra at the end of the loss description:

> . . . *early termination during the third quarter of certain structured finance arrangements with a previously disclosed entity.* **In connection with the early termination, shareholders' equity will be reduced by approximately $1.2 billion . . .**

Huh?

The phone rang again.

"Dude . . . what did he just say?" Bickers was no longer pissed. Now he just sounded confused.

"Something about shareholders' equity." I was confused, too.

I could hear other people at Bickers's firm arguing in the background. Bickers suddenly said, "Later," and hung up.

The day was filled with news headlines, analyst interviews, and angry phone calls from Bernie Bickers. The stock closed at $33.84 with NYSE volume around 8 million. Investors, brokers, employees, and analysts were all confused; and everyone was desperately looking for answers. The eyes of the Enron watchers were blurred by the double vision—created by "record earnings" crossed up with "billion-dollar charge."

We knew this much: The dust wasn't going to settle on the third quarter for a few days. Enron had delivered on its promise of transparency, but no one understood what they were looking at.

> Wednesday—October 17, 2001
> *ENE opening price: $34.00*
> *ENE closing price: $32.20*
> *ENE trading volume: 5,086,200*

One of the first things we were taught in business school was that if you don't read the *Wall Street Journal,* you *shouldn't be* in business school.

I subscribed to the online version; many others on the trading floor preferred the rain forest–destroying version.

So many people on the Enron trading floors read the *WSJ* that the papers were stacked in massive columns in the hallway. I could gauge my arrival time by the shrinking piles—if most copies were gone, then I was extremely late that day.

On October 17, I was practically the first person to arrive at Enron. The *Journal*s were still being stacked when I arrived. I knew Liz Perry was still on the conference circuit in Chicago, so I dug around and grabbed her copy. I was anxious to see what the *Journal* had to say about the previous day's antics.

"Enron Posts Surprise 3rd-Quarter Loss After Investment, Asset Write-Downs" was the headline. I read into the article as I walked to my desk. By the second paragraph, I knew the *Journal* had something much juicier.

" . . . a particular slice raises anew vexing conflict-of-interest questions." The second paragraph and dozens of other paragraphs were about Enron's chief financial officer and his connection to a pair of limited partnerships.

Say hello to Andrew S. Fastow, Enron Corp.'s CFO.

I remembered Liz Perry telling me months earlier that the *Journal* had some serious dirt on Enron—but I forgot about it, because that dirt never showed up.

Until now.

Regardless of the timing, the *WSJ* news was flowing in October like a muddy river. Andy Fastow had set up and run two partnerships, LJM Cayman LP and LJM Co-Investment LP, which were put in place to transact with Enron. The initials LJM were those of Fastow's wife and kids.

The *Journal* article went into details about the arrangements of the two partnerships, which were supposedly responsible for just $35 million of the billion-dollar charge; but the amount wasn't the point. The *Journal* explained that Fastow was making money off his role in the deals. More specifically, Fastow was "eligible for profit participation that could produce millions of dollars" engaging in transactions with Enron.

I sat at my desk and read through the article two more times. I stopped seeing the numbers and the partnerships and the Enron spin. I started to see a huge red stamp across the pages of the most respected business publication on earth. It read, "This company cannot be trusted."

Later that morning I got a call from Bernie Bickers. He sounded completely exhausted, and explained how his life was suddenly being taken over by Enron. He filled me in on how hectic his day was becoming.

Bickers awoke just before the crack of dawn. He sat up in bed after another one of his pigeon nightmares. Bickers hated pigeons, and sure enough a small crew of those stinky flying rats was lined up outside his window. They had ruined his slumber with their penetrating stares and gargled conversation.

Bickers normally would have stayed at his girlfriend's place on the Upper East Side, but he simply didn't have the strength to get there the night before. He crashed at his own place near the office, because the night before he had been hit by the Enron bus. He felt hung-over, like he had gotten high on red ink.

Bickers told me that as he got ready for work, he couldn't stop thinking about the mysterious shareholder equity comment. He didn't understand why it was barely a mention in the call, and not part of the press release. The J. P. Morgan guy had asked Enron execs about it during Q&A, but it was breezed over.

Ken Lay and the rest of the Enron leadership would be meeting with Bickers, and an army of other analysts, later that day. The meeting would be at the standard location, the Four Seasons Hotel on East 57th Street—but he suspected the meeting itself would be anything but standard.

Bickers picked up his *Wall Street Journal* just outside his apartment building. He was floored by the Fastow story, but also confused by the fact that the *Journal* didn't mention the share-holder-equity issue.

He explained that everyone else in his office was shocked, too. "They missed it, Bickers!" was the repeated cry heard over his shoulder. The *WSJ* had delivered Andy Fastow, but hadn't mentioned the $1.2 billion hit to equity.

Bickers told me his voice mail and e-mail were flooded with messages from brokers, fund managers, and irate investors. They were calling him to see what was going on with ENE, yet Bickers himself had no clue. They would ask him to "set the floor" on the stock price, when his ENE financial model was at a standstill due to a lack of information. Enron, among all the other surprises of the third-quarter report, had rearranged the product lines. This made it impossible for Bickers to do any calculations. As a result of the mess, there would be *no time* for price targets—they would only be able to deal with ENE in triage mode.

As we talked, Bickers paused to let out a huge sigh. Dynegy and Enron had both reported on the previous two days; two other energy companies, El Paso and Williams, would report the following week. He was already running on fumes, and the games were just beginning.

He then flashed back to the analyst meeting in Houston. Ken Lay, on the heels of Skilling's resignation, said there was "no other shoe to drop."

We wondered what other bullshit Ken Lay would feed analysts later that day at the meeting.

Thursday—October 18, 2001
ENE opening price: $31.95
ENE closing price: $29.00
ENE trading volume: 9,300,500

On Wednesday the Fastow story had delivered a huge blow to Enron's credibility. On Thursday the *WSJ* hit the street with a new headline:

"Enron Says Its Links to a Partnership Led to a $1.2 Billion Equity Reduction."

Finally the *Journal* was on it, and now investors and other analysts knew what had been giving Bickers a headache.

UBS Warburg analyst Ron Barone said, "We found it disconcerting that the company waited to disclose the additional $1.2 billion charge to equity in a fleeting comment in the middle of a conference call."

The *Journal* also reported that Enron spokesman Mark Palmer, when asked why the equity reduction was not in the press release, explained it as "just a balance sheet issue" that was not "material" for disclosure purposes.

Again, the issue was trust. That "balance sheet issue" increased Enron's debt-equity ratio, and Moody's Investors Service put Enron debt on review for a possible downgrade.

Shares of ENE traded down to $29. Bickers was stuck in irons. He struggled to gather information and sort through it, while at the same time fielding hundreds of calls to the tune of "What is happening?" and "What are you doing about it?"

The analyst meeting at the Four Seasons had left him spinning with mixed messages. The Enron leadership had delivered a presentation about growth, with hardly a whimper about partnerships and losses.

He decided to stop taking calls from brokers; he could only handle so much. He was starting to lose it. He had a nonstop buzz from inhaling Enron flatulence, and with no end in sight.

Friday—October 19, 2001
ENE opening price: $28.01
ENE closing price: $26.05
ENE trading volume: 15,702, 300

Yet another *WSJ* headline, and for the third day in a row, it was a whopper:

"Enron CFO's Tie to a Partnership Resulted in Big Profits for the Firm."

The story detailed some of the millions that Fastow was making off the LJM2 deals. In addition to those dirty details, the *Journal* story included statements like "Enron officials didn't have any comment" and "Mr. Fastow declined several requests for an interview."

I spun around to McLainey and Duffy. "Why aren't they talking? Every time they decline to comment they lose more trust. Did they forget we're a public company? It's not like they're being asked to open their underwear drawer."

Duffy and McLainey turned to each other to see what the answer was.

McLainey finally jumped in. "It would be nice if they had disclosed all this stuff months ago, but obviously they were hoping to disclose it . . . never."

"Okay, so they screwed up. Now is a good time to come clean, right?" I looked at Duffy like it was his turn to respond.

"I don't think they know *how* to give bad news. . . . They've just never had to do it before."

McLainey, Duffy, Waterston, and the rest of our group worked hard to keep things normal as the cascade of news was coming down. In fact, McLainey started to push me. I guess he thought it was time to dig in and work harder, that it was time to work for our survival.

But the truth is that during this week in mid-October, the phones on the Enron trading floor stopped ringing. Lazarri was relatively quiet, and the entire floor was no longer a profit party. The Friday afternoon footballs started flying as usual, but it wasn't accompanied by the usual laughter and joking. This time it was more like an exercise in self-distraction and tension release.

The week of October 15 finally came to an end. I pulled up a stock chart on ENE for the week. It opened Monday at $35 and closed Friday at $26, a drop of more than 25 percent in five days.

On my way home I called Bickers, who I knew would be working late into a Friday night.

"Dude . . . Thank God you're not a pissed-off broker," he answered.

"So when's it going to hit bottom?" I was asking him to set the floor on ENE stock.

Then he hung up on me.

• • •

A few hours later Bickers called me back from his wireless phone.

"I can't set a floor, because ENE blew through my floor days ago. I don't have a clue what to tell people." He sounded exhausted.

"So if it blew through the floor, we're going to bounce back up?"

"Yeah . . . I mean, I just can't see Enron going out of business. I can't see you losing your investment grade, and I can't see the government letting you fail." He paused to catch his breath. "As for the Fastow scams, I think you guys bent the rules like a pretzel . . . but you didn't break 'em."

"Well it's nice to hear that somebody still trusts Enron." I said it even though I was having a hard time believing it myself.

He caught his breath again. "Call it *intellectual inertia*."

And just like that, Bickers created a new buzzword for the modern investor. He believed in the Enron story—the fantastic future and the global growth, the bullish outlook for trading *everything*—and he was therefore unable to move his mind in the direction the news was heading.

Intellectual inertia. That said it all.

Monday—October 22, 2001
ENE opening price: $23.50
ENE closing price: $20.65
ENE trading volume: 36,425,600

Liz Perry returned to the Enron trading floor seventeen days after she left. She had spent the previous two weeks on the conference tour in Northern California and Chicago.

I approached Liz to ask how things went. "How was the rest of the trip?" She looked like a train wreck.

Things had gone well for us in California before I had come back to Houston, but that was before earnings came out.

"Ugh. Let's see." She was ready to vent. "Our plane almost piggy-backed another one when landing in Chicago, the conference bus had to make a surprise detour because of a bomb threat, and then all this weirdness about anthrax," she paused for the big one, "and oh yeah, my stock options are worth zero dollars. What are we at now?" She looked at Lazarri's Bloomberg screen, "Great! $23 is just great." She put her head in her hands, her elbows on the edge of her desk, and stared at the floor.

"So . . . glad to be back, I guess?" It sounded like a horrible trip. I was glad I came back to Houston instead of heading to Chicago.

"All people wanted to talk about," she popped back up, "was Andy Fastow. Until that *Journal* story, none of us had ever even heard of him."

I could picture the scene. It was the Association for Financial Professionals (AFP) Annual Conference, featuring keynote speaker Madeleine Albright. The AFP conference was a gathering of thousands of financial wizards from around the business globe. Our booth was hosted by Liz and a few other members of the marketing team—and as the earnings mess unfolded, they were suddenly faced with a curious mob of financial professionals.

"People started coming up to us and asking about him. I had to look Fastow up on the Internet before I realized he was our CFO."

Anatomy of an Enron Partnership—Part 1

Andy Fastow has been described as the quiet, low-profile type. While everyone in business knew of Ken Lay and Jeff Skilling, even people at Enron rarely heard the name Andy Fastow. He didn't send out company-wide e-mails, and he didn't appear in the public spotlight; he sat behind the curtain, performing his magic.

Born in Washington, D.C., and raised in Virginia and New Jersey, Fastow was always a finance geek. At Tufts University, he was an economics major. He and his wife, Lea (The "L" in "LJM"), got their M.B.A.'s from Northwestern University in 1986. He was learning the art and science of money, but he had also married into it. Lea came from a family that owned a chain of eighty-seven grocery stores.

He joined Enron in 1990 and in eight years climbed to rank of CFO. Aside from a passion for art and a few real-estate properties, Fastow didn't wear his net worth on his sleeve. His rabbi said it best: "You'd never even know what he did for a living."

What he *did* do for a living was keep Enron's debt off the balance sheets. In 1999 he bragged about it to *CFO* magazine, the year they honored him with their Excellence Award for Capital Structure Management.

In October 1999, it was worthy of an award. In October 2001, it was bringing Enron to the edge of a cliff.

Back in my business-school days, off–balance sheet partnerships were just part of the lesson plan. It wasn't a subject we spent a lot of time on, but it was a basic part of finance and accounting classes.

The concept was simple: If a firm could structure a special borrowing arrangement—one in which the obligation to repay isn't recognized on its consolidated statements—then the firm could reduce the amount of liabilities shown on the balance sheet. Off–balance sheet financing could take many forms, and most had been given a specific reporting standard by the Financial Accounting Standards Board (FASB). However, some situations lacked a specific set of accounting rules—in which case it was up to the analyst to apply *general* standards to the transaction.

For Enron, the use of partnership companies and special transactions was the common method of off–balance sheet financing. The partnerships would be set up to lend Enron money in a way that didn't need to be disclosed. Enron would promise the partners a delightful return and would back that promise with Enron stock. The public wouldn't see the transaction—all they would see is more profit and less debt.

The typical partnership transaction would involve the creation of a special-purpose vehicle or entity (SPV or SPE). The SPV is technically its own company, which is really nothing more than cash being put up by lenders and outside investors.

Enron uses the SPV to sell an asset, which doesn't have to be a power plant or a pipeline—it can be anything from shares of non-Enron stock to a Ferrari to a broadband deal. The SPV pays cash, which Enron can use to expand the business, pay dividends, and increase profits. The money Enron receives is recognized as debt to the SPV, not to Enron. For Enron, it just shows as income.

The whole point of the partnership is to raise cash for Enron and keep debt off the balance sheet—debt that would scare investors, lower Enron's credit rating, and be a hindrance to Enron's trading operations. For thousands of other companies to continue trading with Enron, they had to trust that Enron was in good financial health. The trick was to account for these transactions legally and according to FASB rules.

One issue that had to be addressed was maintaining the status of these entities as partnerships. The FASB rule allows for partnership status if at least 3 percent of the deal's capital comes from outside investors. If the amount of non-Enron investment drops below 3 percent, then the operation is considered a subsidiary and must be shown on Enron's consolidated financial statements.

It's all very complicated and worthy of masking tape on plastic-rimmed glasses, maybe even a pocket protector. But in October 2001, it was the gravity of these accounting games that brought Enron crashing down to earth.

With Fastow running two of these partnerships (the LJMs), and Michael Kopper another (Chewco), breaking news about them led the world to question how Enron could get away with sitting on both sides of the transaction table. Those questions escalated in October when it was revealed that Fastow personally made $30 million from the deals.

Suddenly the complex network of partnerships—which on the surface seemed perfectly legal and acceptable—was at the center of a scandal relating to conflict of interest and self-enrichment.

Even without these problems, the house of cards was already starting to wobble. When ENE stock was flying high, the structure of these deals was manageable. When Enron stock fell by more than half, as it did in 2001, the deals that were supported by Enron stock became problematic for everyone.

All of this financial engineering was deep inside the core of Enron's business—it was a black box wrapped inside the balance sheet and the income statement. This network of deals grew to become Enron's unseen shaky foundation.

Next time you build a house of cards, see what happens when you wreck the bottom layer.

An Enron press release hit the wire that same day:

FOR IMMEDIATE RELEASE: Monday, October 22, 2001

HOUSTON——*Enron Corp. (NYSE: ENE) announced today that the*

Securities and Exchange Commission (SEC) has requested that Enron voluntarily provide information regarding certain related party transactions.

"We welcome this request," said Kenneth L. Lay, Enron chairman and CEO. "We will cooperate fully with the SEC and look forward to the opportunity to put any concern about these transactions to rest. In the meantime, we will continue to focus on our core businesses and on serving our customers around the world."

Enron noted that its internal and external auditors and attorneys reviewed the related party arrangements, the Board was fully informed of and approved these arrangements, and they were disclosed in the company's SEC filings. "We believe everything that needed to be considered and done in connection with these transactions was considered and done," Lay said.

The law firm of Milberg Weiss Bershad Hynes & Lerach LLP filed a class-action lawsuit against Enron on October 22. The lawsuit pointed to Enron officers and directors, as well as auditors, with accusations of "massive insider trading while making false and misleading statements about Enron's financial performance."

As an ENE shareholder (in addition to being an employee), I would soon get a lawsuit invitation sent to my house from Milberg Weiss:

This letter and the accompanying materials are sent to you as a purchaser of the common stock of Enron Corp. (NYSE: ENE) between January 18, 2000 and October 17, 2001 (the "Class Period").

If you wish for us to act as your counsel in this litigation, please read the enclosed complaint, retainer agreement and certification, and sign. . . .

This firm has thoroughly and extensively investigated this matter, and believes that there is a valid legal and factual basis to prosecute this action against the defendants."

The focus from day one of the lawsuit was on Enron leadership, specifically the twenty-nine officers who sold huge amounts of stock during the class period. The list of defendants would later grow to include more Enron insiders, as well as Enron's auditors, lawyers, and banks. The class period would also later be expanded, eventually covering the time from October 1998 to November 2001.

For those of us sitting on the trading floor, as we were starting to worry about our jobs, the list of insider sales was sickening. Here are the more notable Enron executives named in the suit, and their proceeds from the sale of ENE stock during the Milberg Weiss class period:

J. Clifford Baxter	$34,734,854
Robert A. Belfer	$111,941,200
Norman P. Blake Jr.	$1,705,328
Richard B. Buy	$10,656,595
Richard A. Causey	$13,386,896
James V. Derrick Jr.	$12,563,928
John H. Duncan	$2,009,700
Andrew S. Fastow	$33,675,004
Mark A. Frevert	$54,831,220
Wendy L. Gramm	$278,892
Kevin P. Hannon	"Unknown but substantial"
Ken L. Harrison	$75,416,636
Joseph M. Hirko	$35,168,721
Stanley C. Horton	$47,371,361
Robert K. Jaedicke	$841,438

Steven J. Kean	$5,166,414
Mark E. Koenig	$9,110,466
Kenneth L. Lay	$184,494,426
Rebecca P. Mark	$82,536,737
Michael S. McConnell	$2,506,311
Jeffrey McMahon	$2,739,226
Cindy K. Olson	$6,505,870
Lou L. Pai	$270,276,065
Kenneth D. Rice	$76,825,145
Jeffrey K. Skilling	$70,687,199
Joseph W. Sutton	$42,231,283
Lawrence Greg Whalley	"Unknown but substantial"

I was amazed at how quickly Milberg Weiss filed the lawsuit. I asked Waterston about it.

"Shareholder class-action suits are big business," he explained. "As soon as something looks fishy about a stock drop, these law firms line up at the courthouse."

Big business, indeed. And Milberg Weiss was a monster force in the shareholder lawsuit "industry." The master is the firm's partner William Lerach, who turned corporate class-action into a billion-dollar dance, one that every corporation feared an invitation to.

Milberg Weiss was on the Enron case. Dozens of other firms would soon join them, all hoping to grab the lead-counsel role in a war between Enron and its shareholders.

• • •

Tuesday—October 23, 2001
ENE opening price: $21.40
ENE closing price: $19.79
ENE trading volume: 27,844,400

In a show of organized desperation, Enron announced it would hold a special conference call with investors—just a week after the earnings conference call—to address new concerns.

The trading floor listened again, this time in stunned silence.

Much of the call centered on two Enron trusts called Marlin II and Whitewing. Enron had established the two trusts to borrow more than $3 billion, using water-related assets.

We all had a wicked flashback as "guess who" showed up on the call—it was Richard Grubman, the same guy that Skilling called an asshole six months earlier.

We were shocked, as we had thought Grubman was banned from all future interaction with Enron. Grubman began grilling Lay on the subject of Marlin II. Grubman came up with $100 million for the value of the water assets, which would make it tough to use the assets for $1 billion in debt payments.

Lay didn't call him any names, but *did* accuse Grubman of trying to push ENE stock down. Lay then asked the operator to hang up on him.

Later that same day, Enron leadership held an all-employee meeting at the downtown Hyatt. It was not what you'd expect from the all-employee meeting for "The World's Leading Company": a crowded hotel ballroom with *Brady Bunch* decor, a crackling sound system, and a small podium possibly borrowed from a nearby high school. It was standing room only, and the sixteen hundred Enron faithful were squeezing together in the doorways and the halls just to hear Ken's voice—the man who would save our company. Another five thousand employees were watching on their computer screens.

Finally the moment came when Chairman and CEO Kenneth L. Lay stepped up to face the crowd. For many of the newer employees, it was their first time actually seeing the man in person. They would be shocked, as I was the first time I saw him, at his surprisingly small stature. A man next to me said he looked like Elmer Fudd dressed in late '80s business attire.

When Lay enters a room or steps up to a podium, it's never about dogs and ponies. It's about words; and no one in corporate America could spin words more skillfully than Ken Lay. Forget special effects and high-tech gadgetry. This guy's specialty, like any good politician, was the art and science of *making you like him*. He had done it his entire career. He was a master at it.

He had a rugged, serious expression on his face—as if he knew this was going to be a tough one. It could also have meant he wasn't sleeping much.

As usual, the Enron all-employee meetings consisted of a few words from company leaders followed by a question-and-answer session. Questions were either asked directly from the audience or via a small card passed up to the front.

After a one-sided regurgitation of press-release propaganda, I watched as Lay stepped to the podium with a handful of question cards submitted by the impatient Enronians.

"I would like to know," Lay began reading, "if you are on crack. If so, that would explain a lot. If not, you may want to start because it's going to be a long time before we trust you again."

A sharp silence; then a few barely audible laughs—the nervous kind—came from the crowd. You could hear the thud of a thousand jaws dropping to the floor. Someone had just asked the chairman and CEO of a $100 billion corporation if he was on crack! Surely someone was supposed to screen the cards. Certainly Ken Lay himself could have skipped over *that* card.

Mr. Lay looked up at the sea of wide-eyed employees and responded, "I think that's probably not a very happy employee, and that's understandable."

Ken Lay was heartbroken, and he told us so. He pointed out that it wasn't just the past few days, but the past few months that were heartbreaking. Enron was his life, and Enronians were his people. Everything was falling apart; the stock was down 75 percent for the year.

"Many of you . . . are now concerned about college education for your kids, maybe the mortgage on your house, maybe your retirement—and for that I am incredibly sorry."

He paused. "But we're going to get it back."

Aside from the crack question and the apologies, the meeting was very similar to the morning conference call. Lay also expressed his support for Andy Fastow, who was sitting in the front row: Lay indicated that Andy would remain as Enron's CFO.

Lay then produced a cheer from the crowd when he announced bonuses would be paid in full for 2001, *if* Enron met its targets. It was a questionable statement, but seemed cheer-worthy to most Enronians anyway.

Lay's words always had a calming effect, and the all-employee meeting of October 23 was no exception. In this moment of lost trust, it appeared Ken Lay was being honest. Perhaps it was because he truly believed what he was saying; maybe he didn't really know the whole truth, and his mind was simply defaulting to the most optimistic answer. I didn't know. I just couldn't tell.

After all, Ken Lay's career paralleled Enron. Ken Lay *was*

Enron. Everything to date had been a skyrocketing success: more than a decade of mammoth deals, seven-figure bonuses, management awards, and global recognition.

And now an irate employee was asking him about a possible crack habit?

I was dumbfounded.

I arrived at my second visit to Dr. Muckenberger's office five minutes late. Once again, the waiting room was empty, which I decided must be quite normal for the 7:30 P.M. appointments. I waited for another half hour before he appeared. I had grown impatient.

"Mr. Cru-vay . . . right this way." His spiky gray hair and goatee had grown significantly since my last visit.

I took my usual position and stared at the Monet print. I wasn't really there. I couldn't imagine there was anything to say.

"So," he began slowly while reading frantically through a pad of notes, "everything still going well at Enron?"

I answered without hesitation, "Yeah. It's going great." I suddenly found myself in Ken Lay's shoes.

"Good . . . good . . . good." He kept looking at the notes.

"How are you feeling?"

I stared deeper into the Monet; if I zoomed in on one area, it turned into a painting of splotches. Maybe twenty-nine years old *was* a little young to be on blood pressure medication and banned from caffeine. Maybe my wife was right—Enron was turning me into an absolute wreck.

"I'm fine—feeling better than ever," I answered, even as I felt my pulse pounding through my head.

"Good . . . good to hear." He was speaking in a tone that left me thinking his mind was on something other than me. "Oh yes! And you're married now! How's that going?"

The Monet seemed oddly colorful for such a simple scene. It was generally blue, but looking close I could see the entire spectrum.

Marriage was pretty good, considering I had spent the first few months of it sitting on the Enron trading floor. Now I was probably about to lose my job, and the new house would suddenly become unaffordable. I thought we might have to sell the dog.

"Marriage is great," I said as I lost patience with him. I couldn't believe this guy. I felt like ripping the notepad out of his hands and asking him to guess my name.

"Great . . . that's just great." He was checking things off as if he had completed them. "Maybe we can explore . . . "

"Is there a point to this?" I cut him off; I was losing patience.

"The point, Mr. Cru-vay, is to evaluate your progress . . . "

"Progress! Progress?" I could feel myself starting to snap. "Progress from what to where? You don't know anything about me! You sit there with your stupid notepad, probably sketching daisies or something, and you ask me this mind-numbing garbage like you're reading from a grocery list. Progress would be if I was promoted to director with a truckload of stock options and a fat fucking bonus at the end of the year! Progress would be a stock that was headed up to $120 where Goldman Sachs said it would be. Progress would be if you learned how to pronounce my last name."

I sank back into the seat and refocused on Monet's blurry boats.

With a look of sheer boredom, Dr. Muckenberger paused to make certain I had finished. "Very well done. How did that feel?"

"Good." I was glazed.

"Great . . . let me write you a prescription."

• • •

Wednesday—October 24, 2001
ENE opening price: $19.00
ENE closing price: $16.41
ENE trading volume: 75,797,104

Just a week after the *Wall Street Journal* had thrust Andy Fastow into the spotlight, Enron decided to send him packing. Just one day after Ken Lay said Fastow was staying, our CFO was given a "leave of absence."

The press release explained that Lay had come to realize the move was needed to restore investor trust.

And that new trust came in the form of Jeff McMahon. He had been Enron's treasurer from 1998 to 2000, and then head of Enron's Industrial Markets group—a position that had put his glass office directly in front of us on the trading floor. When the announcement was made, McLainey, Duffy, and I looked up to see if McMahon was in his office dancing around. He wasn't dancing.

I asked Waterston about McMahon.

"It's an interesting choice," he explained. Waterston looked surprisingly content considering the state of Enron affairs, perhaps because he was without the daily stress of running an active group. Our credit-risk business had suddenly gone silent, and Waterston's sleeves were not rolled up. "There has always been a lot of tension between McMahon and Skilling."

"How so?"

"Well, there's a reason McMahon is sitting in that office over there. He had an issue with these Fastow deals, so Skilling sent him down here." I noticed Waterston had lowered his voice.

In any case, the forty-year-old blond-haired accountant was now in charge of Enron's finances and, more important, rebuilding the company's reputation.

• • •

Instant message software was becoming more common in business; it wasn't just for teenagers anymore. At Enron we were all linked to an IM system that allowed us to see when others were at their desks, send instant questions or comments around the world, and have virtual conversations without making any noise. I had also linked non-Enron people to my list of IM contacts. It was much more interactive than old-fashioned e-mail.

I was listening to ESPN on my phone when suddenly an IM message popped up. It was a friend of mine from Arthur Andersen:

carriemills: hey you! how are things going?

briancruver: how are things going! how do you think?

carriemills: it'll turn around. but it IS kinda nuts. there's a lot going on around here too.

briancruver: funny you should mention that. the shredder across from my desk is about to burn up from overuse!

carriemills: for us it's just policy . . . to minimize paper—we'd never be able to store it all ;-)

briancruver: anyway . . . the whole thing's pretty sad. people here are losing their life savings, and it's going to be tough to recover.

carriemills: that sucks. how are you doing?

briancruver: fine. i just can't believe it's happening to enron. this was always the place to be, you know?

carriemills: sorry. hope you're okay. i've gotta run but lets have lunch when things get back to normal. bye! ;-)

briancruver: thanks. sounds good. bye.

Carrie was funny in a hyperactive sort of way. She had gone to Texas A&M for her accounting degree, a fact that I tried desperately not to hold against her. She had a ton of spastic energy, which I guess was needed to spend a lifetime as an accountant.

I remembered an e-mail I had been sent back when I first joined Enron. The writer had discovered some analysis on Enron's accounting procedures. According to the e-mail, if Enron had recorded trading profits as revenue (like brokerage firms do), instead of recording the entire transaction amount, then Enron would have only $6.3 billion on the revenue line in 2000.

That amount of revenue was slightly less than the $100 billion that put Enron in its current #7 spot in the Fortune 500— between Citigroup and IBM. Instead, the revised revenue number would put Enron at #287, right next to Campbell's Soup.

"If you liked it at $40, you *love* it under $20," yelled Lazarri across the trading floor. We all shook our heads. With the trading floor coming to a screeching halt, I should have been left with little to do. Except that McLainey kept dumping work on me—I thought it must be his way of being in denial.

But I did my work, even as Waterston walked around to make sure I was also job searching. In between McLainey assignments, I worked on my résumé and a handful of other people's résumés. I listened to ESPN on the phone just to take my mind off of the constant barrage of Enron mudslinging. I would spend all day talking to friends via e-mails and IMs.

I stared across the once lively trading floor. Enron was on all the news channels. News trucks had arrived outside the building. It was becoming a circus.

Forget the fact that our CEO had left us, that was months ago. In just over a week:

- Enron had reported its first quarterly loss (of more than $600 million) in over four years.

- The CFO had been canned after the *WSJ* brought out conflict-of-interest issues and a $1.2 billion hit to shareholder equity.
- The SEC was beginning an Enron inquiry.
- The Street lost nearly all of its trust and confidence in Enron. ENE was down to its lowest levels in more than five years.

And our business, the business I was trying to help start up, had suddenly shut down. There would be no more deals, and we would simply burn up cash as a hopeless new idea. Part of Enron's desperate cry to stabilize the failing business was to focus on Enron's core operations. In other words, it was time to go back to basics—and our new group, along with dozens of other new groups, was far from basic. The writing was on the wall, on the floor, and on the ceiling. There was no escaping it. Our group was finished in mid-October.

All we could hope for was a good deal on our way out the door, and Enron's standard severance package was spectacular. We knew the severance package was at risk if Enron ran out of money, and we were starting to get nervous.

I spun around to McLainey. "Hey, Greg. You got a second."

He spun around to me. "Sure. What's up?" He looked beaten up. I guess we *all* looked beaten up.

"I don't know how to ask this. In fact, I'm not sure how this works." I paused to make extra sure I said it right. "Is it possible you can get me laid off . . . like, soon?" I couldn't believe I was asking my own boss to get rid of me.

To my surprise, he laughed. "I wish I could. In fact, I wish we could all get laid off—I've been bugging Waterston about that for days." He saw that I needed more of an explanation. "It's just not up to us; Enron basically has a hold on all personnel changes until things settle down."

Later, I spoke to Liz and found out she had asked her manager for the same favor.

I also asked her what was happening in PR land.

"They don't have a clue how to handle this mess," she said.

"Why not? Aren't these the best PR people *in the world?*" I said as sarcastically as possible.

She laughed, "The truth is, they've been dealing with Enron's good news for the past fifteen years. This is the first time they have ever encountered bad news."

I wondered if it was really that simple. "Isn't this more a question of damage control, like, how to rebuild a reputation?"

She responded sharply, "*But they aren't doing that!* They're trying to spin things, while acting like nothing is really wrong. They should just admit what went wrong and then share the plan for fixing it. But right now, they can't even handle the basics!"

"The basics?" I asked.

"You know," she rolled her eyes, "like putting the equity thing in the earnings press release, or screening the index cards for questions about Lay's crack habit."

Friday—October 26, 2001
ENE opening price: $16.00
ENE closing price: $15.40
ENE trading volume: 28,328,500

How to Conquer Corporate America, Rule #5: Don't put anything in writing, unless you are willing to let the whole world read it.

The shredder for the trading floor was about ten feet from me, just on the other side of my desk. It was hard not to notice a steady stream of people using it, each with stacks of unstapled and un-paper-clipped documents. There was no one I recognized; it seemed more like assistants doing the shredding for other people.

I could almost imagine the shredding machine, which I had nick-named Sherman, shouting across the trading floor, asking for food. He was constantly growling, demanding more and more. Once Sherman got hooked on the pulp, there was no stopping him. I thought if we stopped supplying it, he might just sprout legs and race madly across the trading floor, sucking down every scrap of paper in his path.

I think I read every single column inch of the *Wall Street Journal* that day. It was easy to steal one of the printed versions from the hall, since hardly anyone wanted to read them anymore. It was too much bad news too many days in a row.

The headline was "Despite Losses, Complex Deals Analysts Remain High on Enron." The story pointed to a sort of "blind enthusiasm" surrounding ENE, in the sense that analysts would rec-ommend Enron without really understanding it.

The article focused on David Fleischer of Goldman Sachs, the analyst who spoke to me during my first week at Enron. He was a little off from the $120 price target he had predicted back in April. I felt they were picking on him, probably because he was always the most bullish on Enron. Then I wondered: could he still be bullish?

At $15 down from $90, it was time for Enron to be removed from Goldman's elite U.S. Select List—but ENE did remain on its distinguished Recommended List, which holds about two hundred stocks above the rest.

From the *Journal* story:

"Just because I can't be specific in being able to create a simple model . . . doesn't mean that you write off that industry and say 'I

can't analyze it' or 'I can't figure it out,'" says Mr. Fleischer, who
owns an undisclosed number of Enron shares. "If that were the case,
there would be an awful lot of industries we couldn't follow."

The *Journal* story continued to quote Fleischer in describing his personal Enron investment as "meaningful" and "not small." The story also mentioned that Enron had been an investment banking client of Goldman. Fleischer disputed the idea that his objectivity was compromised by his own interest in the ENE share price, claiming that his clients were happy that he was putting his money where his mouth kept going.

The *Journal* story made me think about the predicament that Bickers must be in.

Monday—October 29, 2001
ENE opening price: $15.15
ENE closing price: $13.81
ENE trading volume: 36,423,500

Enron had already been stabbed in the chest, but the twisting of the knife came on October 29.

Moody's Investors Service, which is a global leader in publishing credit ratings, downgraded Enron Corp.'s long-term debt. The downgrade came about two weeks after Moody's announced Enron had been put on "review." We all knew it was coming; in fact, we wondered why it hadn't happened sooner.

The impact of a lower credit rating on Enron was increased financing costs and, more important, demands by lenders for debt repayment. Enron's trading business accounted for 90 percent of the company's operating earnings, and a credit downgrade was a huge hit to the trust of Enron's trading partners. The downgrade was to a level still two notches above junk status. However, Moody's also announced it would keep Enron Corp. on review for further downgrade actions. It was absolutely mission-critical that Enron stay above investment grade, or else Enron would default on billions of dollars in debt and be forced to issue millions of new shares of ENE.

Meanwhile, in the world of bond trading, Enron was priced at noninvestment-grade levels.

Somewhere inside Enron, the focus was on getting cash to keep the business running. Enron was madly trying to negotiate new credit lines of between $1 billion and $2 billion. Suddenly there was a run on the bank for the world's largest energy trader. Enron insisted things were still running smoothly and trading operations were strong. With some liquidity support, a breather from bad news, and maybe a favorable word from the SEC, then perhaps Enron could pull out of the dive. But without all of that, it would be game over.

I looked around and didn't see *any* trading operations; I wondered where inside the Death Star things were still "running smoothly."

On October 11, 1999, the board of directors of Enron Corp. met in the Whitney Room of the Four Seasons Hotel in Houston. This "executive session" began at 7:20 P.M. CDT and was to be followed the next day by an "open session."

Almost all of the directors were there, including Ken Lay, Jeff Skilling, Rebecca Mark, and "Pug" Winokur (only Director Ronnie Chan was absent). Other executives were there as well, including Andy Fastow, Jeff McMahon, and Joe Sutton; and Secretary Rebecca Carter took down the minutes of the meeting.

The meeting was fairly standard. The board discussed new candidates for election to the board, company earnings, the stock plans, and dividends. Rick Causey talked about Enron's Y2K preparations. Joe Sutton talked about a proposed Human Rights Policy. And, according to the minutes . . .

> *Mr. Winokur then discussed information concerning an unaffiliated investment partnership, LJM2, and stated that the partnership could possibly provide the Company with an alternative, optional source of private equity to manage its investment portfolio risk, funds flow, and financial flexibility. He noted that Mr. Andrew S. Fastow would be acting as the managing partner of LJM2 and discussed Mr. Fastow's role in the LJM2 partnership. He commented on the controls that would be put in place to manage any transactions between the Company and LJM2 and noted that the Company and LJM2 were not obligated to one another in any way. He noted that the controls include review and approval of all transactions by the Chief Accounting Officer [Rick Causey] and the Chief Risk Officer [Rick Buy]. . . . He stated that the Company's Conduct of Business Affairs Policies would prohibit Mr. Fastow from participating in LJM2 as managing partner due to his position as Executive Vice President and Chief Financial Officer . . . absent appropriate reviews and waivers from the Board and a finding that such participation does not adversely affect the best interest of the Company.*

Winokur then recommended that the board endorse Fastow's role in LJM2, his motion was seconded, and the board approved it. Among the resolutions: that LJM2, "as a potential ready purchaser of the Company's businesses and assets or as a potential contract counterparty, could provide liquidity, risk management, and other financial benefits to the Company."

The executive session of the Enron board meeting ended at 9:02 P.M. CDT.

At the time of the October 1999 board meeting, ENE stock was around $39. Over the following eleven months, the stock price increased 125 percent.

LJM2 was working just fine.

Wednesday—October 31, 2001
ENE opening price: $11.80
ENE closing price: $13.90
ENE trading volume: 43,726,500

For Halloween I decided to dress up as an Enron employee. Imagine my disappointment when I saw that everyone else on the trading floor had on the same costume.

There was no work for our group; there hadn't been for weeks. Ken Lay was comparing the "attack" on Enron to that of terrorists; I failed to see the connection but could appreciate the way he must have felt.

All across the trading floor were computer screens showing résumés. It was an odd site to see in broad daylight. People were walking around the trading floor with draft copies to get second and third opinions. I reviewed a few résumés myself; Liz Perry and I exchanged résumés and agreed to pass them around for each other.

By the end of October, I had a copy of just about everyone's résumé in the group, except for Waterston. He didn't seem too concerned about his own future, perhaps because he was so focused on all of ours. Waterston made sure we were all working toward new jobs. He offered help as he walked around the trading floor. I asked if he didn't mind me using him as a reference, and he agreed. For some reason he must have felt responsible for our circumstances. He felt the need to apologize. I hated when he apologized, when he was the last person fingers should be pointed at.

To my right I could hear a phone interview. To my left I could hear a discussion about the best résumé fonts. In my own head I was angry and frustrated. I couldn't believe I was in such a place: looking for a new job, talking to headhunters, and wishing McLainey would spin around and say, "You've been laid off. Here's your severance package."

Halloween was an eventful day, full of many tricks and very few treats. The stock was bouncing around $12. The SEC announced they had changed the "inquiry" to a full-scale investigation. Enron elected William Powers Jr. to the board of directors. The dean of the University of Texas law school was asked to lead a committee in an internal investigation into Enron's transaction history.

I left Enron that evening in a wicked daze. No matter how Ken Lay sliced it, the Empire was falling apart. I reached my car parked on the seventh floor of the garage and began to spiral down, down the drain, down into the depths of Enron Hell.

It was a hypnotic right-hand turn that seemed truly infinite. The messages on the garage walls were intended to remind me of who I was; they were meant to instill in me the meaning of Enron. Instead, the walls reminded me how phony those messages were.

As I circled the garage, the huge words on the walls began to look different.

Level 7—"COCKINESS . . . because we'll always be better than you, even after we lose our jobs."
Level 6—"BULLSHIT . . . because the truth is just too damn risky."

Level 5—"FIRE . . . me now, please! Before you run out of money and can't pay me my severance package."

Level 4—"LAY . . . because true to his name, who else could screw so many people."

Level 3—"MISLEAD . . . because we never realized that 'CFO' stood for Chief Felony Orchestrator."

Level 2—[this one was still there] "INNOVATION . . . because even the accounting department has mastered creativity."

Level 1—"DANGER . . . because at Enron, every day makes you feel like a toad in a tornado."

I reached the safety of Smith Street traffic and looked up at the mirrored towers. I was bent and I was bitter, but I would keep coming back.

Enron wasn't dead yet.

6

Buy High, Sell Low

> "Everyone has the brainpower to follow the stock market. If you made it
> through fifth grade math, you can do it."
> —*Peter Lynch, legendary manager of the Fidelity Magellan Fund*
> *(best-performing fund, 1977–1990)*

T he phone call I got from Mr. Blue in early November was
unexpected; but what he called to tell me wasn't a surprise.
He had left Enron.

A month before I would have been shocked, but as Enron
began to quickly unravel, I started to get the picture. The
Enron executives had been evacuating at a steady pace for months.
I was disappointed to hear that Mr. Blue, my best Enron contact,
was gone—but that would hardly matter if Enron ceased to exist.

In any case, it was good to have a real conversation with him. I
quickly discovered that without Enron, he suddenly had all the
time in the world to talk my ears off.

He told me the story of his decision to resign.

The driver pulled up to the Enron hangar at Houston Intercontinental Airport. Mr. Blue set his cocktail down, took a deep breath,
and stepped out of the car. He stretched his shoulders back and put
on his sunglasses.

He scanned the aircraft and saw that the Gulfstream V was
there. That was Ken Lay's new one—bought by Enron in 2001 for
a measly $40 million. Mr. Blue thought about the one and only

time he was on the G-Five. He fell in love with it: the smooth and
seamless BMW Rolls-Royce engines whipping him around the
globe at four-fifths the speed of sound; the smell of new leather
meeting the sparkle of a fully stocked bar. He remembered they
had thrown *A Few Good Men* into the video player. He remembered
that the Gulfstream people had brought the seats in for the Lay
family to try out.

But that seemed like a long time ago. This day, Mr. Blue was
met by the two Enron pilots, who would be taking him up on a
Falcon 900, the plane he had probably flown in the most. It wasn't
the G-Five, but it was still a magnificent aircraft. The performance
specs were not as good, but the comfort level was just as high.

He stepped up into the plane, which sported Enron's colors.
There was no logo on the outside of the aircraft, but plenty of
Enron cups and napkins inside to remind passengers whose plane
it was. Mr. Blue's lunch was waiting for him. So was a bottle of
Blue Label. The pilots were friendly as usual—as if they had no idea
what Enron was going through.

Mr. Blue sat in his favorite leather chair on the Falcon. It was
strange to be on the plane alone, but for that he was relieved. He
needed the time to think.

He squirmed deep into the chair, closed his eyes, and his mind
drifted back to the glory days of Enron.

It was a hot, musty morning in the Philippine jungle. Mr. Blue and
his team climbed aboard a Cessna that looked like it had crash-
landed a dozen times. They were on the last leg of a journey to
what was once the Subic Bay Naval Station. The base had been a
U.S. military installation for almost a hundred years, except for a few
years of Japanese occupation during World War II. It was a major

staging area during the Vietnam War. After the base was abandoned in 1992, Enron had decided to move in.

The Philippines was suffering from six hours of blackouts each day. The classic joke in the Philippines was: "What did Filipinos use before candlelight? . . . Electricity!" They needed power, and Enron saw an opportunity to get 116 megawatts up and running quickly. Mr. Blue and his team were there to evaluate the situation, and Enron International exec Joe Sutton would soon be joining them.

The Cessna pilot was a Filipino boy who must have been about fifteen years old. There were holes in the cockpit instrument panel where gauges used to be. As the plane lifted off and turned low over the trees, Mr. Blue leaned in toward the pilot.

"You know where we're going, right?"

"Yeah . . . Subic Bay . . . no problem," he answered with surprisingly clear English.

The plane teetered side to side. Mr. Blue had no idea where they were, only that the capital, Manila, was to the south, and that the South China Sea was to the west. He thought about Enron International's objectives for the region. He thought the CIA would be helpful in gauging the risks and the competition for the project. Enron was eyeing a number of power deals in the Philippines; Enron's Subic Bay plant would sell power to the state.

He scanned the horizon. It was a country with more than seven thousand islands and way too many volcanoes. Mr. Blue thought for a second about how far he was from Houston. There wasn't much volcanic activity in Texas.

Mr. Blue saw plumes of smoke on the horizon, about sixty degrees off the plane's course.

"Excuse me!" He leaned in again, so the young pilot could hear him. "Is that Subic Bay over there?" He pointed.

"No, no. Subic Bay this way."

Mr. Blue wasn't satisfied with the answer. He wasn't exactly looking forward to getting there—the Philippine military presence, the civilian protesters—but he knew Sutton would be all over his ass if he was late. The plane was heading farther out of the way, so he needed to change the pilot's direction.

"I'll tell you what." He pulled a few hundred pesos out and stuck them in the pilot's shirt pocket. "We've decided to check out that smoke over there, instead of going to Subic Bay."

As the plane finally banked toward Subic Bay, the pilot responded, "*Hindi ko alam kung papaano ko po kayo mapapasalamatan sa inyong kabutihan*" [thank you very much].

Mr. Blue looked at his Enron colleagues. They all shrugged their shoulders. It didn't matter; at least they were headed in the right direction.

He turned his head to look out the side of the plane. He noticed a wing strut was separated from the wing. Despite the danger, it somehow made him laugh.

Mr. Blue was still laughing when he woke up. He wasn't on the forty-year-old Cessna anymore; he was on the Falcon 900. He wasn't in the Philippines; he was cruising several miles above East Texas.

The video monitor showed the aircraft's speed and altitude, as well as the outside temperature. One of the pilots had cleared away his uneaten lunch.

He laughed again as he thought about the Subic Bay project; he had come a long way in his Enron career since then. All the countries and projects and plane flights flashed through his mind.

He looked around at the plush interior. He got up from his seat and headed to the back of the plane, where he stretched out on the sofa. It was a luxury he had earned after a long career at Enron: *a sofa on an airplane.*

But that long career was reaching its end. The glory days of Enron were gone, and the game just wasn't fun anymore. He thought about his Enron stock and the future of the company.

There was no future. It was time to cash in his chips and walk swiftly out of the casino. If he didn't do it soon, he might get stuck as part of the cleanup crew.

After my conversation with Mr. Blue, I searched through the Internet to see just how noticeable the Enron executive "evacuation" was.

Wow! In just over twelve months, many of Enron's key leaders had permanently evacuated the building:

Rebecca Mark—She was Enron's vice chairman (a.k.a. the Ejection Seat), head of Azurix, and former chairman and chief executive officer of Enron International. She left Enron in August 2000.

Joe Sutton—Sutton took Mark's place in the Ejection Seat (Enron vice chairman) in 1999. Prior to that, he was president and chief executive officer of Enron International. He left Enron in November 2000.

Cliff Baxter—He was chairman and chief executive officer of Enron North America, before being promoted to the Ejection Seat after Sutton left. Baxter then resigned in May 2001.

Lou Pai—Pai was chairman and chief executive officer of Enron Accelerator for three months, and before that he was in charge of money-losing deals for Enron Energy Services. He cashed out and left in May 2001.

Tom White—The West Point grad left Enron to become secretary of the army in May 2001. White was head of Enron Engineering and Construction, but most recently was working with Pai on the money-losing Enron Energy Services deals.

Jeff Skilling—After an eleven-year career building Enron, the director and chief executive officer unexpectedly quit in August 2001, just eight months after being promoted from president and chief operating officer.

Kevin Hannon—Hannon left his position as operating officer of Enron Broadband Services in August 2001. According to the securities class-action lawsuit, he had previously requested nonofficer status so that he wouldn't have to report his stock sales. Also, months prior to leaving Enron, Hannon made an options bet on ENE that the price would go *down* below $70. He was right, and made money on the options.

Ken Rice—The chairman and chief executive officer of Enron Broadband Services—the biggest money-losing flop of all Enron's new ventures—bailed in August 2001, perhaps to focus on his Ferrari collection.

Andy Fastow—After about four years as Enron's chief financial officer (and a prior stint as senior vice president of finance), Fastow was asked to leave in October 2001 due to his involvement in scandalous partnership deals.

All of these critical departures added up to one thing: It was time to start buying a boatload of ENE stock. Yes, I *was* losing my mind.

I didn't have any special information; it just seemed like a worthwhile bet. In the low teens, Enron was clearly oversold. With the SEC investigation, the credit downgrade, and a steady stream of negative news, it seemed like an opportunity to buy. Bickers and I still believed that if Enron could catch a break and buy some time, some parts of the Enron business could maintain value going forward.

Plus, the stars were aligned for a possible acquisition of Enron, which could have drawn at least a slight premium over the current share price.

Merger rumors were flying at the beginning of November:

Royal Dutch Shell seemed to be the front-runner. In fact, a Shell buyout of Enron had been rumored for several years—especially when I was at the Shell trading firm, where we would joke that buying Enron was the only way to compete with Enron. Analysts pointed to the potential marriage between Enron's wholesale trading and Shell Energy Services, but people who knew the two companies realized they were completely *opposite* in terms of culture and organization. It was simply impossible to imagine.

Warren Buffet's Berkshire Hathaway was hot on the rumor block as well. Buffet had taken over Mid-American Energy and some analysts saw that as just the beginning of his energy deregulation play. The only problem was that Buffet liked companies that were "well managed, selling tangible products." Uhh . . . that wasn't Enron.

The hottest rumor spinning in our circles on the trading floor was a GE Capital merger. This rumor didn't have the same degree of synergy attached to it, but the word *synergy* was just an overused '90s term anyway. Enron would simply be a lucrative energy investment for GE, one that was primed by Enron's sagging stock price, massive revenue streams, and dominant position in the trading space.

There I was, watching ENE tick north and south (mostly south) over Lazarri's shoulder, waiting for the right moments to jump in and out. I *was* more than a little intrigued by the small flocks of suits walking through the trading floor on guided tours. These overdressed packs of wide-eyed businessmen ranged from the local Houston look to the yellow-tied investment-banker look. One group was entirely Japanese with a translator. I could only guess who these groups were, and I was probably guessing wrong. They could have been buyers for

Enron, or maybe buyers for the building. Maybe they weren't buyers at all, and Enron had decided to give guided tours for extra revenue.

Even if Enron wasn't bought out, the liquidation value of the hundreds of giant flat-screen televisions had to be worth $12 per share. Okay, so maybe I was reaching a bit.

In addition to the rumors, news, and endless speculation came a wave of Wall Street downgrades. Analysts were backing out of their support for the stock; on November 1 it was Merrill Lynch. In the ten days before that, it was Salomon, Bank of America, J. P. Morgan, and two downgrades by Prudential. The downgrades brought back memories of the "dot com" bubble-bursting action just a year and a half before. When those stocks were peaking—and everyone was jumping on the high-tech bandwagon—all we heard about was initiated coverage or upgrades or price targets by analysts that screamed, "Buy! Buy! Buy!" When those same high-flying stocks were worth just a tiny fraction of that "buy" price, analysts reversed their outlooks and screamed, "Sell! Sell! Sell!" If an investor reacted to that ratings action, and in many cases I did, then an investor would consistently be buying high and selling low. That's just not the way to play the game.

During a period of several consecutive down-ticks, I got nervous and gave Bickers a call.

"Hey Bickers. How low can this thing go?" It was a straightforward question.

"Dude . . . I know! This is nuts—just fucking nuts!" He was exasperated, and he was probably dealing with ticker hypnosis like I was.

"No, really. I want you to give me a real answer. How low can this thing go?"

He thought for about two seconds, and then gave me a logical answer: "Uhhh . . . about zero dollars."

Ouch.

It was hard to think that Enron could really just disappear. I couldn't help but think this was a different situation from that dot-com hype-driven drool. We had two enormous towers standing at the leading end of the world's energy corridor. I saw thousands of employees, futuristic technology, and a history of dominance in the gas and power markets. This wasn't a garage full of Web designers, trying to resuscitate roadkill on the information superhighway. It wasn't a virtual pet store, or some new software designed to manage software-management software. This was Enron Corp.! I had to believe that something—anything—was going to happen and turn things around.

So when the wave of analyst downgrades hit ENE, we barked at the reverse logic and felt like giving those analysts the middle finger. Bickers and many other firms didn't downgrade, even though they stopped pumping up the stock. As mentioned before, it wasn't saving any face to tell the world to "sell" at 80 percent below the level they had said to "buy."

Don't get me wrong—my perspective on buying ENE stock was unrelated to the fact that our start-up group was history. Waterston, McLainey, Duffy, Perry, Lazarri—we all knew that regardless of the direction the Enron mess was swept in, we would all be sent packing. In early November, it wasn't a question of "if," but "when" and "how." The business of selling bankruptcy protection was about as far as any-thing from being a core business at Enron. The funny thing was, the same customers who wouldn't listen to me when I talked about credit risk were now shitting bricks because they had huge exposures to Enron. In a truly bizarre and worthless way, the collapse of Enron was finally giving our business idea the attention it had merited all along.

What else could I do at that point but load up on ENE stock? I wasn't the only one.

A young analyst to my right dumped her life savings in. Calls came in from other trade floors within Enron to let us know that everyone was buying. It was like we had our own ENE transaction board being passed around the company. We all talked about the trades we were doing, mostly in terms of where we thought the price would be just a few hours later. Most people had their Web-based trading accounts open at all times. Even Lazarri took a break from his beef jerky futures and did some quick in-and-outs on ENE.

It was an exciting way to kill time during those weeks when we had little work. It was a desperate attempt to get back the money we had lost in our stock options. It was madness. It was denial.

And it was an efficient way to lose a lot of money.

The news was constant, as Enron was finding itself at the center of the business world. It became a daily downpour of wire-service stories, *WSJ* headlines, magazine articles, CNBC commentary, and Enron press releases. If a story was new and just hitting the wire, Lazarri would announce it to the floor. I couldn't decide if he did it to keep us informed, or just to let us know he was still ahead of everyone.

One story that turned thousands of heads was an article in *Texas Monthly* magazine. The article was written by Mimi Swartz and covered the history of Enron through the eyes of Jeff Skilling. Needless to say, everyone on the trade floor was furious. Even in November, and even with Fastow looking down the barrel of everyone's finger, the consensus was that Jeff Skilling had betrayed us all.

When Swartz's article came out, Enronians were floored by the pure and positive light shed on Skilling. No one cared about the article's portrayal of Enron's scandalous history and culture; that was acceptable. But everyone did care that she made Skilling look like Enron's lonesome hero. Swartz breezed over the financing mess with just a one-sentence blurb in parentheses: "(It was essentially risk management against Enron's possible failures.)"The article also read, "Skilling's supposedly brilliant colleagues were as shocked at the news of his departure . . . may be a testament to their lack of emotional intelligence." She had bought his spin about why he left; she had bought his flashing eyes; she had bought his prophecy for the future. In this article called "How Enron Blew It," her story had utterly failed to explain what everyone at Enron believed: that Skilling was the reason Enron blew it.

Which may explain why I walked by one of the columns on the trade floor and saw the magazine's page taped to it. A marker had been used to change the title to, "How Mimi Blew It."

Frustration with the media was not limited to just those who were off-target. Some of the frustration was directed to those who just seemed overly vindictive.

In addition to Bloomberg news, most people on the trading floor had Yahoo! Finance open on one of their computer screens. Yahoo! was a reliable way to track the top ENE headlines, while also having a very active message board. One of the news sources that Yahoo! pulled stories from was TheStreet.com. The writer covering Enron was named Peter Eavis.

In October and November 2001, Eavis managed to become the most hated man on the Enron trading floor. He was relentless with his production of Enron-bashing stories, which appeared frequently among more neutral Enron news. Just when we thought Enron was going to have a positive day, there was Eavis to shed a negative light on things.

Even as far back as July, Eavis got our attention with the article "With Growth Slowing, Enron's Fall Is Far From Over." So in October and November, you could imagine what a field day he was having:

"Lessons From Enron's Meltdown"—October 1
"Still No Clarity at Enron"—October 16

"Trusts Keeping Enron Off Balance"—October 22

"Enron Fails to Smooth Things Over"—October 23

"Shell-Shocked Enron Parts With CFO"—October 24

"Enron's Problems Go Way Beyond Its CFO"—October 26

"Enron Troubles Only Tip of the Iceberg"—October 26

. . . and many, many more. On any given day someone would say, "Oh shit, another Eavis."

As the anti-Enron bandwagon became more and more crowded with other journalists, the term "Eavissed" was used to describe other rancorous reporters, as in, "Did you see the *Times* again today . . . looks like we're getting Eavissed."

Of course, we couldn't get *that* pissed off at Eavis. He was absolutely right about absolutely everything.

The only positive spin coming from anywhere was from Enron itself, and there wasn't much of it. In early November, press releases declaring new financing help and the sale of Azurix North America were put out; executives were also hitting the street talking to Wall Street analysts and reporters: "The business will survive" and "Enron will refocus on its core business" and "Enron continues to run smoothly" were the three cheers for the day.

The financing deal on November 1 was part of the continued effort to manage cash in the short term. Liquidity was an issue, as well as other debts that needed to be paid. Enron had drawn down on almost $3 billion of its total credit lines a week earlier, so this deal would secure another $1 billion from J. P. Morgan Chase and Citigroup.

Jeff McMahon, the new CFO who replaced Fastow, had moved out of his nearby office from right under our noses. We decided he must have been busy trying to gobble up a billion here and a billion there. I decided not to move into his empty office—again, the goal was to get laid off, not fired.

Thursday—November 8, 2001
ENE opening price: $8.50
ENE closing price: $8.41
ENE trading volume: 60,882,700

"If you liked it at $20, you love it under $10." It was Lazarri again. I rolled my eyes.

Enron dropped a pair of press-release bombs on Thursday, November 8. One was to confirm the merger rumors that had zeroed in on a possible deal with Dynegy, a small Enron competitor down the street.

The other was a restatement of Enron's earnings back to 1997.

As for the Dynegy news, it hardly left us dancing in the aisles. Dynegy had always been, for lack of a better word, Enron's "bitch" in the world of energy trading. I knew a few people there; in fact I had already sent some résumés over. We would have preferred GE Capital. We would have preferred to remain Enron.

First came a phone call from my baseball fanatic brother. He called to ask me if the name of Enron Field would change. As if I would know.

Then came an e-mail from Bickers:

Cruv—
The last one is my favorite . . .
Dynron
Dron

Enronegy
Geritol
DyEn (pronounced Dyin')
—Bickers

I wasn't amused.

In the earnings restatement, Enron officially reported to the SEC and to the world that it had "more information" (read "more of the truth") about the off–balance sheet transactions.

Enron and Arthur Andersen had determined, among other things, that many of the off–balance sheet entities should have been part of the publicly disclosed financial statements. More specifically, the financial impact of JEDI, Chewco, and LJM1 needed to be factored in.

The summary of the adjustments released by Enron was as follows:

Year	Reduced Income	Increased Debt
1997	$96 million	$711 million
1998	$113 million	$561 million
1999	$250 million	$685 million
2000	$132 million	$628 million

Then came another headline from Peter Eavis: "Enron's Restatements Don't Go Far Enough."

The earnings restatement would have pummeled ENE stock into the ground for good, but the Dynegy deal was a valuable distraction. The speculation over the per-share value of a Dynegy deal was enough to keep ENE in the $8 to $9 range. Most of us couldn't care less about either piece of news, except for one thing: A deal with Dynegy would mean a severance package.

• • •

That evening I found myself with another McLainey assignment. He was still working hard on plans B through E, since plan A (a future at Enron) was sinking like a brick. It was a little frustrating to be working late that night, considering I was going to lose my job at any minute.

Sherman the shredder was working late.

The Enron tour guide was working late.

And Bernie Bickers was working an hour later on the East Coast. He called around 8:00 P.M. my time. "Dude." He sounded delirious like me. "What are they going to do about the name for Enron Field?" I could have strangled him through the phone.

Also working late was Ron Middleton. I saw him in the elevator as we were both leaving. Once again, he looked like his eyes were bleeding.

"Wow. When was the last time you slept?"

Ron laughed. "Man, this is just crazy." The elevator door closed with just the two of us inside.

"How can RAC be crazy right now? What deals are we doing?" I didn't understand.

"I've been here since early Wednesday morning—and it's got nothing to do with RAC." He wiped his eyes as they continued to water.

Now I was curious. "Dynegy?"

He didn't answer me. Instead, he gave me a look as if it hurt not to talk about it.

I knew it was a short elevator ride, so I wasted no time in begging for an explanation. "Aw, c'mon. They're letting you go home, so it must be finished, whatever *it* is."

Again, he didn't respond. The silence was painful.

The elevator opened. I stepped aside to let him go ahead; after all, I had slept at home the night before.

He couldn't keep his silence. "Everything's worked out—we're gonna be fine."

Friday—November 9, 2001
ENE opening price: $8.00
ENE closing price: $8.63
ENE trading volume: 75,508,704
DYN (Dynegy) closing price: $38.76

The Enron press release:

"*Dynegy and Enron Announce Merger Agreement.*"

The deal was done, and an audible sigh echoed across the trading floor. The sigh was 20 percent for avoiding bankruptcy, 80 percent for the depressing realization that Enron was no more. It was a strange realization to have while sitting in the middle of the culture, the people, and the sea of E logos. It was strange to think that Enron was going away forever.

Under the terms of the merger agreement, the new company would be called "Dynegy." If only I had forwarded Bickers's e-mail to Dynegy CEO Chuck Watson, we could have *merged* under a more creative name.

More important than names, the deal set forth a stock transaction ratio of 0.2685—which meant that each share of ENE would be converted to that fraction of DYN shares (at the time of deal closing, which was expected in eleven months). For example, if DYN was up to $100 per share at closing time, then the holder of an ENE share would get $26.85 worth of DYN.

In theory, that ratio should stay constant between the two

stocks from the time of the agreement until the final close; ENE would therefore move parallel to DYN. If the actual ratio ever dropped to below 0.2685, the difference would represent shareholder skepticism over completion of the deal.

At the Friday close on November 9, the ratio between Dynegy and Enron stock was about 0.22, with Dynegy stock trading in the high $30s. The total value of the transaction was around $7 billion.

In addition to the stock transaction, Dynegy immediately invested $1.5 billion in Enron (which came indirectly from ChevronTexaco, a 26 percent owner in Dynegy). In exchange for the immediate cash infusion, Enron gave Dynegy an option to acquire 100 percent of Enron's Northern Natural Gas pipeline subsidiary.

Chuck Watson was named CEO of the merged company. The board of the new company would have a maximum of fifteen members; Enron was given the right to pick just three of them.

After soaking in the details and looking through the news, an e-mail arrived from my friend across the street at the Enron competitor (not Dynegy):

Cruver:
So what are they going to call Enron Field?
—J

I decided not to respond.

After an alarming failure in management-to-employee communications, Enron finally gave us some; only this time it was not an e-mail from Ken Lay. Instead, the "Dynegy Deal Q&A" was posted on our company intranet.

Among the more entertaining highlights:

Q: From a business standpoint, are Enron and Dynegy now one company?
A: Not until closing, which may not occur for a number of months . . .
We will act toward Dynegy the same way that we would act toward any
other competitor.

Q: Has Dynegy completed due diligence? Are they satisfied that the
potential exposure is manageable?
A: Dynegy has completed significant due diligence and there is no due
diligence out as such. Dynegy was fully aware of the matters reported
recently with respect to certain financial statement restatements and
related party transactions.

Q: What are the immediate business benefits of the transaction?
A: This deal confirms the value of Enron's core business and strengthens
the company's liquidity. This transaction enables the shareholders of
both companies to participate in the upside of the combined enterprise.

Q: What happens to Ken Lay?
A: Ken Lay will remain as Chairman and CEO of Enron until the transaction closes. He will not join the Dynegy Office of the Chairman.

Q: Will Enron complete its new building?
A: Yes.

Q: Is Enron's vision still to be the world's leading company?
A: Enron's vision will be revisited once the companies are merged.

Q: Will this affect Enron's innovation?
A: A key strength of Enron and Dynegy has been their employees' innovation and we expect this to continue.

Q: Will Enron Field be renamed?
A: The combined company will determine this.

Q: What does this merger mean for Houston?
A: We believe that it is positive for Houston because two premier energy
companies will join forces and remain in the city.

Q: If I am laid off, either prior to the merger completion (or as a result of it), what will my severance package be? Will the severance plan change?

A: If an Enron employee is let go prior to the merger, and is eligible for benefits under the Enron Corp. Severance Plan, then the terms of that plan will govern. Postmerger, employees will be eligible for benefits under whatever severance plan the merged company adopts. No changes to the severance plan have been made at this time.

Q: What happens to our bonuses this year?

A: The 2001 bonus process will continue as usual and will be consistent with previous practice based on company and individual performance.

Q: Will there be a year-end PRC?

A: We are still reviewing the year-end process.

Q: Will the Enron Body Shop [the health club] remain open?

A: The Body Shop will remain open and continue with normal hours. Once the merger is nearing completion the program will be evaluated.

After having a cow over the baseball field question, I went back and reread the question about being laid off. I must have read it a dozen times. McLainey, Duffy, and I all spun around to discuss it, and others joined us. Duffy printed out a copy of the question to add to his new folder of "claim evidence."

Needless to say, it was quite a relief. With eleven months until the deal closed, and a 100 percent chance of being laid off before then, we were set to receive Enron's standard severance package.

The Severance Pay Plan from the Enron benefits handbook:

*Enron **may** grant the following severance benefits if your employment is permanently terminated by Enron under one of the following reasons:*

Cause—If you are terminated for cause or misconduct, you will not receive a severance benefit.

• • •

This first one is what kept me from moving into McMahon's empty office, running naked across the trading floor, or trying anything else to get fired.

Failure to meet performance objectives or standards.

I thought perhaps, since none of us had any work, we might get canned for this second one—in which case we would get a week of pay for each year of service (up to a maximum of six weeks).

Reorganizations or similar business circumstances.

Bingo! That was our ticket. Under a merger situation, we would get a week of pay for each year of service, plus a week for each $10,000 of base salary. On top of that, we could *double* those weeks by signing a "waiver of all rights and claims relating to your termination of employment."

Perry and I were looking at five months' pay if we were laid off. McLainey, Duffy, and especially Waterston were eligible for much more. With the holidays coming up, with the nation heading into an economic recession, and with a pathetic Houston job market—we would need every penny. In our hearts we were all banking on the severance package, while in our heads we knew that there is no such thing as certainty—especially with respect to Enron in 2001.

So we marched forward with McLainey's plans for preserving our ideas for a bankruptcy risk management business.

The research and analytical work he had been dumping on me was fodder for a business plan, which we planned to use in a number of different ways. It could be sold to a surviving group within Enron;

it could be sold to the new Dynegy; it could be sold to a competitor, consulting firm, or group of independent investors.

It was hard to tell if the business plan was something we all believed in, or if it was simply a way to keep ourselves employed. We knew that with Enron's sudden collapse, our concept of bankruptcy risk would be much easier for the market to believe. As for me, I just wanted a paycheck from somewhere. Anywhere!

In any case, the plan included about ten key people from our group who understood different pieces of the bankruptcy risk puzzle. If anyone did buy our business plan, they would be bringing a small piece of Enron's failed future back to life. If no one bought in, our ideas would end up in a trash can.

Late that Friday, I got two phone calls from friends in Dallas and Los Angeles. One wanted to know about the name change for the baseball field. The other wanted to know about the name change for the baseball field. Enough already!

As I walked out of the Death Star that day, it just didn't feel like Enron. As I passed Enron logos in chrome and neon, I imagined the hideous Dynegy logo in their place. The building now had a quiet, somber atmosphere filled with an odd combination of bitterness and remembrance. Thankfully it was the weekend; I would need at least two days to produce enough motivation to show up on Monday.

On the drive home, several Houston radio stations were discussing the future name of Enron Field. I turned off the radio and threw in a Limp Bizkit CD.

Tuesday—November 13, 2001
ENE opening price: $9.50
ENE closing price: $9.98
ENE trading volume: 33,245,100
DYN closing price: $46.94

For the first time in forever, the stock seemed stable; it even had an up-tick to nearly $10. It was good timing, since November 13 was the end of the blackout period for the Enron 401(k) savings plan.

The Enron savings plan, just like any other 401(k) plan, was a way for employees to save their money—with tax advantages and contributions from Enron. Employees could set up automatic deductions of up to 15 percent of their salary. For amounts up to 4 percent of salary (it was 6 percent for newer employees), Enron would add funds to the account equal to 50 percent of that 4 percent amount.

For the amounts contributed by the employee, there were nineteen investment options besides ENE stock, though only the Enron contributions were locked up in the ENE stock fund.

In 2001, Enron had decided to change plan administrators—a process that caused the blackout period. The blackout lasted only ten trading days—from October 29 to November 12—a period during which the stock dropped $3.83 per share. Prior to October 29, during the eight months when the stock traveled from $90 down to $14, employees were free to transfer their savings to and from the nineteen non-ENE investment options (again, with the exception of the Enron-contributed amount).

A month before the blackout, Enron began sending letters and e-mails to employees warning of the ten-day period. Was this correspondence enough notice? If someone didn't read mail and they didn't follow ENE stock, was Enron also responsible for tapping them on the shoulder?

On November 13, after the blackout ended, I started to hear the grumbling of employees who were "locked out during the collapse" and who had "a life's savings trapped in ENE stock." I wondered how that could happen inside a company that always preached risk management and diversification to the business community. Was Enron preaching something different to its employees with respect to the 401(k)? At a minimum, the blackout period caused people to lose $3.83 per share, but only their Enron contributions were forced to take that hit. As for the employee portion of the 401(k) contributions—what was it doing in ENE stock on October 29 after an 80 percent decline? Who was advising these people? Was *Enron* telling these people what to do with their money?

I just didn't get it. Yes—we were all buying ENE in early November; but that was a risk we were taking on our own. If we lost that bet, we had no right to blame Enron for putting our money there. I didn't understand why plaintiffs' attorneys were making such a big stink about the blackout period.

On November 13, Ken Lay left me a voice-mail. It should have been something to the effect of, "Hey, Brian, sorry about this nasty little mess we created; don't forget that Jeff had a little something to do with it, too. I promise I won't hide anything else from you. From now on, I'll be honest and up front. Even if I don't have all the facts, I'll be honest in telling you I don't have all the facts. I'm working out the details of your severance plan this afternoon. Tell your wife hello. Let's have lunch soon. Bye."

No such luck.

Instead, the voice mail from Ken Lay was sent to all employees at Enron. It started out with, "Hello, this is Ken Lay." It sounded like it could have been a computer-generated version of Ken Lay rather than a real one.

Ken explained that his own employment contract with Enron arranged for him to receive a $60 million severance payment as a result of the Dynegy deal. Ken was leaving all Enron employees a voice mail to share his decision *not* to accept the $60 million.

As people picked up that voice mail across the trading floor, I heard hissing and laughing and a variety of vulgarities directed at Mr. Lay. Some people were so pissed, they slammed their phones down with a resounding "Fuck you!"

Once again, I was dumbfounded. The point of the voice-mail message was *what*? Did he think we'd be jumping for joy? Or perhaps we would all applaud his dedication to Enron.

Middleton called me and said, "Like we would have let him get away with that anyway." His statement caused me to picture an angry mob storming Lay's office.

Afterward, it occurred to me: "Ken, take the $60 million! Later you can distribute it fairly among the people who got screwed by Enron!"

John Walker began creating whiskies in Scotland in 1820, and soon he perfected them with the help of his son Alexander. Two centuries later, their work is epitomized by the ultimate blend of character and style: Johnnie Walker Blue Label. It's a masterful combination of sixteen rare whiskies, designed exclusively for the connoisseur. Because the whiskies in the blend are rare and production is limited, Blue Label costs thousands of dollars per case.

As I approached the back table where Mr. Blue sat, I noticed a double shot of his favorite drink poured over ice. At $50 per glass, it looked like he might have had more than a few.

How to Conquer Corporate America, Rule #6: If somebody important is drunk, listen to him or her *very* carefully.

The meeting with Mr. Blue was at the Lobby Lounge in the Four Seasons Hotel in downtown Houston, where he was staying as a guest. He stood awkwardly to shake my hand and we exchanged pleasantries:

"You look like shit," he said.

"Thanks." All I could do was laugh. "You look a bit out of sync yourself."

He smiled at the way I returned his noncompliment. "Well, I guess we've both been exposed to the Enron virus."

I had no idea why Mr. Blue was staying at the hotel. The Four Seasons was on the exact opposite side of downtown from the Death Star—I figured that much made sense. Was he hiding from something? Did he sell his house? Was some special meeting taking place at the hotel? I decided not to ask, and I never found out.

I didn't feel qualified to drink Blue Label, so I ordered a bottle of Shiner—a favorite Texas beer.

"It's amazing how many executives have left Enron," I said, hoping for some insider explanation.

"Yeah, well, Enron is finished. No one wants to hang around and be part of the cleanup crew or take the blame." He sipped his legendary drink.

I reciprocated by sipping my beer. "And you're not interested in Dynegy?"

He chuckled, "Oh, that . . . I left before that was announced." He saw me waiting for more information. "It's a joke. It's not going to happen."

At that moment I felt like changing the subject. The Dynegy deal was the key to saving our severance packages; I didn't want to hear that the Enron roller coaster still had more dangerous curves ahead. Unfortunately, he continued with his explanation.

"Dynegy has no clue what they are buying. They have almost

a year to open up can after can of Enron worms." He looked around the lounge; we were the only ones there. "We've got a lot of worms."

I thought that was a fair statement; after all, I had personally been learning about those worms for the past few months. Most of all, I was struck by Mr. Blue's use of "we" when describing his former employer. It must have been hard for him to let go.

He continued. "We've got huge cans . . . huge buckets of worms. Warehouses full of crates full of buckets of worms. Eventually, Dynegy will get the keys to those warehouses."

"I'm afraid you lost me on the warehouse thing."

He brought his eyes back to me and overlooked my last statement, as if he had forgotten I was there. "Are you looking for another job yet?"

"Yes, have been for weeks," I answered.

"Good . . . that's good." He returned to staring at his bronze-coated ice cubes. He started to spin them in the glass with his index finger, and then returned to the subject of the Enron worms—only he switched metaphors. "This storm that Enron is unleashing . . . it's been brewing for fifteen years."

I didn't dare try to lead the conversation at that point. I sat on my tongue and let him run back to Enron's past for a while.

The Enron Oil mess he was referring to was in 1987, when two rogue Enron traders—guilty of arranging a multimillion-dollar trading conspiracy—were kept on Lay's payroll.

"Enron's been a game of dirty tricks ever since. It's a game you learn to play, or you just don't last. You learn to do what management tells you to do, even if it violates the laws of nature."

"And that Code of Ethics thing?—it only exists on an 'as needed' basis."

Oh, what the hell—I decided to jump in headfirst. "You lasted a long time; you must have been pretty good at the game yourself."

Mr. Blue just stared at me for what seemed like days. I over-swallowed some beer, which left a lump in my throat and caused my eyes to water.

He leaned in. "There was an unwritten rule . . . a rule of 'no bad news.' If I came to them with bad news, it would only hurt my career."

"Bad news about what?"

"About Enron's deals—how little sense they made, how they would lose money, how they were run by unqualified egomaniacs." The waitress brought him another glass; I wondered if he got some sort of frequent-flyer discount on the good stuff. "These guys were ex-military, ex-Harvard, ex-whatever Ken Lay was looking for. They were brilliant people, and somewhere they fit the strategy—but on a project to build a billion-dollar power plant, you needed someone who knew how to build a billion-dollar power plant."

"You're talking about India?"

He sat back and looked up. "I'm talking about India, Guatemala, Puerto Rico, the Dominican Republic, Brazil, the Philippines . . . I'm talking about the globalization of stupidity. I'm talking about Enron executives jetting around the world, pissing off foreign governments, and destroying people's lives." He was starting to get angry. About $5's worth of Blue Label sloshed out of his glass. *"All in the name of someone's fucking bonus!"*

I sat quietly. He wiped his forehead. He adjusted his position in the chair to get more comfortable. He was just getting started.

"Subic Bay, the Philippines . . . The Philippine government gives Enron a list of potential partners, and we have the gall to pick someone not on the list. We barge into meetings, cut corners on the project, start the project without a contract, and on and on . . . Apparently Joe Sutton and Rebecca Mark piss off some people in the Philippine government, all in the name of hitting their bonus targets."

I nursed my beer as the conversation became even more entertaining.

"The Puerto Plata plant in the Dominican Republic . . . we build a ridiculous plant on a barge and float it into an area where garbage flows into it. The plant is at the bottom of a hill, with a hotel called the Bayside Inn at the top of the hill. As soon as we crank the thing up, all the poolside guests get covered in black flakes. The steam turbine is constantly filling with garbage, and we don't get paid for the power. The locals get pissed because the hotel has to be closed down and the local real-estate values collapse. Does Enron care? No, because even a dumbass idea like that somehow allows Enron execs to be paid their sacred bonus money."

I thought I was starting to get his point. "So in the ongoing struggle between Rebecca Mark and Jeff Skilling, you were on the side of Skilling and his 'virtual assets' strategy."

"No, no, no." He was gaining momentum and energy as he bore deeper into the subject. "Skilling and Mark *both* blew it, because the Enron system was designed for speed and altitude— not for direction and control. Skilling wanted to eliminate assets altogether—but sooner or later you need something of value as a fallback to your gambling problem. Mark wanted to buy and build the world's energy assets as fast as possible—which is why we ended up with the disasters I'm telling you about.

"The Dabhol plant in India . . . the local protests and police raids aren't because Indians don't want power; the police didn't drag a pregnant woman naked into the street and beat the shit out of her for business reasons. It's an issue of human rights and human disrespect. The Indians on Enron's side get bribes, while opponents get arrested. Land gets stolen, water resources are destroyed. . . .

Take Joe Sutton for example: As Indian officials are listening on the other end of a conference call, he says, 'I'm tired of getting screwed by these goddamned Indians!' I would say that's a problematic way of doing business."

The Sutton quote threw me, as I was still trying to understand the bigger picture. "Okay, that may be unprofessional—but aren't these foreign countries tough to deal with in the first place; aren't bribes and political maneuvers always needed to get these projects done?" I remembered an Enron attorney telling me that Enron was known for delivering cash kickbacks to political leaders around the globe. "And Enron is certainly not responsible for the actions of India's state police." I finally needed another beer, and got the waitress's attention.

"It may not be Enron in the streets wielding batons, but it is Enron arrogance and Enron greed that pushes a project to that dilapidated state." His glass was empty again, but this time he waved off a refill. "The San Juan Gas explosion in 1996 . . . I was involved in a report to management that showed the pipeline problems a year before it happened."

"Excuse me?"

It was approximately 8:30 A.M. in San Juan, Puerto Rico, on the morning of November 21, 1996. An air-conditioning system was turned on in the basement of the six-story Humberto Vidal Building. The air conditioner ignited a mixture of oxygen and propane, and the resulting explosion wiped out the building—killing thirty-three people and injuring eighty others.

The propane came from a cracked pipeline belonging to the San Juan Gas Company, an Enron subsidiary. In the seven days before the explosion, San Juan Gas had responded to complaints about a gas odor, but despite checks, no leak was found.

The National Transportation Safety Board (NTSB) investigated, and they spread the blame across multiple parties: the U.S. Department of Transportation, the Puerto Rico Public Service Commission, and Enron for their failure to oversee pipeline safety and operations. The NTSB urged Enron to require its subsidiary, San Juan Gas, to develop evacuation procedures so that when a leak is suspected, lives could be saved. The NTSB also asked Enron to beef up employee training. Enron disputed the NTSB report and would not admit responsibility. Enron chose to skip litigation (avoiding furthur discovery) that would have determined the precise responsibility for the accident. Enron was ready to move on, and agreed to go ahead and settle the size of damage claims.

I wanted some clarification from Mr. Blue. "So there was a report to Enron management about San Juan pipeline leaks . . . a year *before* the explosion?"

"Seven leaks per mile . . . a month's worth of gas was missing." He thought for a second. "The report was in 1995."

My beer arrived, and I took a quick gulp. I asked, "What was management's response?"

"They transferred me to another project on the other side of the world." He paused before summing things up. "Like I said before . . . the rule was always *no bad news*." Now he was ready for a refill and caught the waitress's eye. "I learned to follow that rule." His voice was becoming softer.

I suddenly realized that I was hunched over, with my chin resting on the lip of the beer bottle. I was lost in thought, dazed. I was having a hard time with all this international insanity. I asked the question, "Is it Enron, or just a small group of people?" I'm not sure what I meant by the question, but I wanted to believe it was a just a handful of unscrupulous executives.

"It *is* just a small group of people . . . but those people were created by the Enron system—a system that also creates hundreds of other sheep who are easily led by others." Another $50 double shot arrived for Mr. Blue. "It wasn't just bad luck that Lay brought in the people he did. It made the best strategic sense for him in terms of ruthless, high-stakes behavior. Military, Harvard, McKinsey, Andersen—he was looking for the cream of the elitist crop, and he got exactly that.

"The system was designed to make people rich without making real profits. The goal was to keep the stock price rising and the doubters muted—usually by sheer confusion. We would reorganize the company every six months just to keep the accounting books in limbo.

"All the financing games were basically an elaborate Ponzi scheme—old investors were paid with money from new investors."

The term *Ponzi scheme* derives from Charles Ponzi, who created such an investment scheme in 1920. With the promise of a 50 percent return in just forty-five days, Ponzi found over ten thousand willing investors to give him $9.5 million (which was a *ton* of money in the 1920s). By the time Ponzi's scheme ran out of steam, he was bankrupt (and in jail), leaving thousands of people in the streets holding worthless paper.

Mr. Blue continued, "Enron would even issue 'phantom stock' to executives—stock with value tied to capitalized expenses like hotels, limos, and booze. It's no different than the financing games we're all hearing about now: keep the public confused, keep reality off the books, and keep the auditors on your side."

I wanted to hear more about his last point: "Andersen?"

He welcomed the new subject. "See, everyone makes the mistake of thinking Andersen and Enron are separate companies. AA was just $52 million on the payroll. There are hundreds of ex-Andersen people inside Enron.

"And it made perfect sense for what Enron management wanted: replace the experienced Enron auditors—who have spent years combing through Enron's books—with a bunch of young kids just out of college. Give those new Andersen kids a downtown loft, a new Lexus, and show each one the golden path to becoming a partner. They learn to do things the Enron way, and they may never understand the liability of it—until it's too late."

As Mr. Blue continued on and on, I started to sense his relief in telling me all of this. It was therapeutic for him. He was clearing his conscience. But it dawned on me that this meeting wasn't really about that.

So I had to ask, "Look . . . this is all *very* fascinating . . . but I don't understand why you asked me here. Why are you unloading all of this on me?"

Mr. Blue looked down at his drink on the table, as if he was about to get philosophical. "Well, we never had a chance to talk when I was at Enron."

Was that it? That wasn't philosophical at all.

He continued. "The merger's going to fail, then Enron's going to declare bankruptcy . . . and eventually, everyone will move on to something else." He paused for a few seconds. "I'd like to think that people will learn from this, and take those lessons with them . . . but I'm afraid some people will just plant new Enron seeds wherever they go."

He wanted me to learn lessons from Enron? My head was spinning far too fast to process what those lessons could be. But I did appreciate his point, as well as his concern.

"So what about you?" I left the question open-ended, curious how he would interpret it.

"I'm an old man now. I'm not going anywhere." He sat back in his chair. "I had a very lucrative career." He paused as he looked out into a meaningless direction. "But it cost me my soul."

The Dynegy deal was indeed turning sour. The likelihood of the deal ever closing was measurable by the actual ratio between ENE and DYN, which had never quite fixed itself at the buyout ratio of 0.2685.

For each of the nineteen days the deal was alive, we followed the ups and downs of the Enron-Dynegy saga as they unfolded on CNBC.

In 1997, during my first year at the University of Texas business school, my M.B.A. classmates and I became hopelessly addicted to CNBC—the monetary moods shown in green and red, the hypnotic flow of infinite stock tickers, and the commentators' bullish outlook on life and the market.

CNBC has only been on the air since 1989. Rival Ted Turner once called CNBC a "piece of garbage," but in the year 2000, CNBC passed CNN in daytime viewership. The stock-talk lineup was a hit—with advertisers fighting to reach viewers that had a median net worth of over $1 million.

The biggest reason people tuned in was *Squawk Box,* CNBC's premarket funhouse. Every morning from 7:00 to 10:00, live from their New Jersey studios, the *Squawk Box* personalities would set the tone for the day. Maria "Money Honey" Bartiromo would dance around the floor of the NYSE as the market opened; Joe Kernen and David Faber would rally back and forth, ripping on ridiculous stocks and jabbing at irrational analysts.

On the Enron trading floor in November, it was Faber who took control of our minds. Nicknamed the Brain, Faber was CNBC's Wall Street correspondent most known for breaking big stories— especially merger and acquisition scoops.

Ahead of the Enron-Dynegy deal, Faber busted out with, "While such an outcome [a Dynegy purchase] is only one of a number of options being discussed, sources close to the talks tell me it's a possibility in the near term."

Sources close to the talks? We were sitting in the middle of Enron, and yet we felt worlds away from any "talks." At that moment, we realized Faber might be our best communication link to the future of our own company. If his face showed up on the big screens, we all hit the CNBC button on our phones and dropped what we were doing. The guy could move markets, and he moved Enron in November. Of course, the "sources" them- selves knew that Faber had this power—so it wasn't out of bounds to think he was continually being used by them. That was okay, since he seemed to be in touch with that possibility himself. It seemed he knew how to handle it.

Wednesday—November 21, 2001
ENE opening price: $7.00
ENE closing price: $5.01
ENE trading volume: 115,642,000
DYN closing price: $39.76

It was the day before Thanksgiving, and the day before my thir- tieth birthday.

Liz Perry dropped by my desk to ask, "So . . . what do you want for your birthday?"

"My severance package," I answered without hesitation.

I was *extremely* nervous that the collapse of the Dynegy deal was moments away. My conversation with Mr. Blue wasn't the only reason. The word on the street from Bickers and other analysts was that Enron wouldn't last a week without more cash, let alone ten months until closing. Faber and CNBC were down on the deal, and the market itself was trading ENE at a 50 percent discount to the Dynegy offer. The ratio between ENE and DYN was 0.1260, not 0.2685 as the deal promised.

The stock hit $5, causing a sea of dazed Enron employees to actually start cheering and laughing. A $5 share price, by many definitions, is the line between a real stock and a "penny" stock. At that moment, the feeling on the floor changed. We weren't Enron anymore; we weren't even part of Dynegy. We were history, and we were pathetic—and all we could do was try to have a sense of humor.

The day before Thanksgiving is typically a slow one for the stock market, but ENE volume hit 115 million shares that day. I decided to "puke" some of the stock I had bought earlier in the month—which I had been hanging on to like a symbol of hope.

Then Enron sent out a press release: "Enron Announces Progress In Efforts To Boost Liquidity; Reaffirms Commitment To Merger With Dynegy; Working With Major Lenders To Restructure Debt Obligations."

"Oh, no!" Duffy said as he spun around.

McLainey and I both spun around as well. "What?"

"Enron just said the Dynegy deal is going to go through," he said.

McLainey responded, "Aw, shit."

I just shook my head.

By November we had created a simple methodology for predicting Enron's future: Whatever Enron said would happen, expect the opposite to come true.

Then Peter Eavis showed up again, slapping us with the headline: "Plunge Says End Is Near At Enron."

"Thanks, Peter—shouldn't you be on vacation or something?"

> Wednesday—November 28, 2001
> *ENE opening price: $3.69*
> *ENE closing price: $0.61*
> *ENE trading volume: 345,367,808*
> *DYN closing price: $35.97*

On Wednesday, November 28, we were put out of our misery. The day was absolutely insane. After talks with Dynegy to cut the buyout price by 40 percent, and days of threats by ratings agencies to downgrade Enron to junk status, the end finally arrived.

Standard & Poor's did lower Enron's credit rating to junk, and any company that was somehow still doing business with Enron decided to stop.

EnronOnline was shut down.

Dynegy announced they were calling off the planned merger— the deal was officially pronounced dead. No one was surprised.

Enron then announced it would begin taking steps "to preserve the core franchise."

By midday, news vans had surrounded the Death Star, as the media frenzy reached a new peak.

But the biggest news on the Enron trade floor was *not* the failed merger or the credit downgrade. The big story was how things unfolded on Wall Street.

ENE stock, which started the day at $3.69, freefell more than

80 percent during a truly surreal and exasperating day. The stock price ended up at $0.61—*with ENE trading volume over 345 million shares.* This astounding number set a new record for a single NYSE stock on a single trading day.

That much volume is difficult to put in perspective, but I'll try: It was only a few years before, during the calendar year 1995, when the average daily volume for *all twenty-six hundred NYSE stocks was 346 million shares.*

Fortunately, Lazarri was in New York looking for a new job. If I had heard him say, "If you liked it at $10, then you love it at $0.61," I probably would have thrown my chair at his tanned head.

Meanwhile, people in my group—including McLainey, Duffy, and Perry—began stuffing personal belongings into their brief-cases. The common belief was that one day soon—most likely the next day—we would all show up for work and find ourselves locked out of the building.

7

Shredding and Scrambling

"I've seen the devil of violence, and the devil of greed, and the devil of desire; but, by all the stars! these were strong, lusty, red-eyed devils, that swayed and drove men—men I tell you."
—*Joseph Conrad,* Heart of Darkness

At the end of November, just 248 days after I joined the ranks of the best and the brightest, just eight months after my first day at Enron, it was all over.

During my short time at Enron, I had seen the stock fall from exactly $61 to just $0.61. That was a 99 percent drop in the value of my dream job, and it felt like a 99 percent drop in the value of my future.

On a realistic, short-term level, the question was more about paying the bills than the overall impact of Enron on my life. The promise of the millionaire factory had been broken, but that thought sat way in the back of my mind. In the front of my mind was survival. I was still getting a paycheck, and I was still technically an employee. I decided I would be happy about that, for however many more seconds it lasted.

The moment Enron got hit with a junk credit rating, the trading screens literally started going blank. The moment Dynegy called off the rescue attempt, the bankruptcy filing seemed just a matter of paperwork. Nearly twenty-one thousand Enron employees were on pins and needles awaiting their fate, with about seven thousand of those at the Death Star in Houston.

EnronOnline had been shut down, putting an instant halt to

$2.8 billion worth of transactions. A large section of EnronOnline employees were on our trading floor—I looked over at them to see dozens of empty chairs and a few people surfing the Internet.

The credit downgrade by S&P was followed by downgrades from both Moody's and Fitch. With all three rating agencies cutting Enron to junk status, suddenly Enron owed another $3.9 billion in obligations due almost immediately.

Enron was still throwing out some massive trades—large enough to indicate we were trying to close out some positions. The U.S. Treasury Department was keeping a close eye on both the credit markets and the energy markets. There was growing concern over how an Enron shutdown would impact the markets as a whole— markets that Enron once dominated. Fortunately for the U.S. economy, Enron's death had taken weeks instead of minutes, allowing enough time for trading partners and competitors to pre- pare for it. El Paso, Williams, Reliant, Duke, Mirant, AEP, and Dynegy would gladly absorb the volume and the market share. These competitors were losing a major trading partner in Enron, but they were also gaining a spectacular opportunity. On the final stretch of the Kentucky Derby, the Enron horse—which had been ten lengths ahead—had just snapped its leg and slid into the rail. It was time for one of these companies to emerge as a new front-runner.

One way for competitors to step up and take Enron's place was to grab the best Enron people—the people who carried the intel- lectual capital around in their heads. Enron résumés were flowing by the hundreds to each of these companies, and Houston-based headhunters were dancing around our building with faces painted and weapons in hand.

The stock price, the business operations, and employee morale had completely collapsed; however, the most frightening aspect of those last few weeks was the collapse of Enron's senior leadership. The atmosphere was turning to one of self-preservation. Waterston and McLainey knew as little about the future of our jobs as I did. There were no more all-employee meetings, e-mails from Ken Lay, or intranet postings. Each day we stayed glued to CNBC and the news wires, hoping for some tangible information about our own company. We had nothing to do, and no clue what the next minute would bring.

Those last few days I would ride the elevators, hoping for an important message from the Building Guy. I expected him to take off his hard hat and say, "Look, people. Enron management is doing everything they can right now. Their number one priority is taking care of Enron employees. Regardless of how this thing ends, none of you will be left out in the cold." He would then put his hard hat back on, give us a salute, and say, "That's a promise from the Building Guy. Remember, I've got your back!"

Instead the Building Guy continued to tell us about the new building's fiber optics and imported marble—like this disaster wasn't even happening.

After the death of the Dynegy deal, there were three options being discussed: Chapter 11 bankruptcy filing, Chapter 7 bankruptcy filing, or a government bailout.

Chapter 11 protects a company from its creditors while allowing time to develop a reorganization plan. This type of filing was preferred, not only by Enron itself, to preserve some portion of the business, but also by Enron creditors, who would ultimately get more money back from Enron if it continued to generate revenue.

A Chapter 7 filing is an instant liquidation of all company assets. Liquidation would mean a lot more layoffs and a lot more pain for creditors. Late November 28, we heard (again, through the news media) that new CFO Jeff McMahon was not considering Chapter 7 for Enron. As usual, we figured his statement only increased the likelihood that it could happen.

A few of us started a betting pool. Each entry would pick between the two types of bankruptcy and a filing date. I put my $20 on Chapter 11—to be filed on Friday, November 30—thinking that somehow a Friday would be easier from an administrative standpoint.

If Enron did file for Chapter 11, the critical issue for us would be debtor-in-possession (DIP) financing. The DIP financing would secure funds for Enron's continuing operations, salaries for retained employees, and severance packages for laid-off employees.

Some rumors were floating around that 85 percent of employees would be laid off; this number suggested that liquidation via Chapter 7 was more likely.

As for a government bailout, this seemed highly unlikely.

First of all, the government had shown no signs of coming to Enron's rescue at any time during the collapse in October and November. Second, the situation facing Enron was one of executive fraud and accounting scandals, not exactly a cause that taxpayers would be willing to support. Finally, no sane politicians—especially those in the White House, with record-breaking approval ratings, and despite strong Texas connections—would put reputations and reelections at risk by supporting the Crooked E.

Whatever was about to happen, we knew it would happen soon—Enron was running out of cash fast.

So we sat at our desks, and waited.

• • •

There are many words that describe those finals days of the Enron collapse, but one word somehow encapsulates the complete essence of the occasion: *wacky*.

Something happens to the "best and the brightest" when their religion turns out to be a hoax: the stunned faces, the bizarre behaviors, and the desperate measures. I looked around the trading floor and thought, "So this is what it's like when the magic space-ship doesn't show up, or when all the Kool-Aid does is kill you." It was pure wackiness, plain and simple.

Sherman the shredder was working harder than ever, grinding through documents around the clock. Also working hard was my administrative assistant. She and the other admins were scrambling to get expense reports entered into the system. Some of the members of our group had thousands of dollars' worth of business expenses on their Enron credit cards, which they would be on the hook for if Enron dried up. It was a nerve-racking rush to get expenses filed, approved, and paid before we were laid off. Lucky for me, my expenses had been paid the week before.

The business casual dress code reached a new low. Blue jeans became an everyday thing, often including T-shirts. Every now and then someone would show up in a suit for lunch-break job interviews. The résumé workshop also continued.

More than a few times those last weeks, the alarms went off on the trading floor, forcing us to evacuate Enron Center South and stand out on Smith Street. Each time it happened we wondered if it was just a trick to get us out of the building so the bankruptcy police could lock the doors. We also had a bomb threat. I turned around to McLainey and Duffy. "I bet it's an angry investor." We agreed that my theory wasn't that far-fetched.

A friend of mine decided to share with me—and I still don't

know why—a perfect example of the mind-numbing stress we were all facing. She explained that she was chewing gum (after recently quitting smoking) as she paid a visit to the women's restroom. Her mind was on other things, including the fact that she was running late for a meeting. She got rid of her chewing gum by folding it up in some toilet paper, then went ahead and used that same toilet paper for its intended purpose. Oops. Someone in the meeting actually asked why she was walking funny, wondering if she had hurt her leg or something. It was a sticky situation that she dealt with for the rest of the day.

To deal with the stress, we spent a great deal of time putting Slinky toys on the escalators (in theory, they would somehow reach an equilibrium and stay in place, but it never worked), throwing footballs across the trading floor, and taking three-hour lunches. We would even stop by unattended computers and send out instant messages to random recipients, messages like "I love you" or "You're fired."

On a visit to Middleton's desk, I found a crowd of employees gathered around his computer monitor. I thought it must be something important—perhaps some breaking news or an e-mail from senior management. When I finally saw the computer screen up close, I realized it was a listing of local movie times. The frustratingly bored Enron employees were deciding which bad action movie to go see around 1:00 P.M. that day. They asked if I wanted to join them, but I had to get back to the Slinky and the escalator.

Magazine photos began to appear, taped either to the trading-floor columns or other walls. These were usually pictures of Ken Lay or Jeff Skilling (from magazine articles that praised them as top CEO or something). Like Mimi Swartz's *Texas Monthly* article, some of these pages had been edited with black markers—to give our Enron leaders a new look of fancy facial hair and fashionable piercings.

And other makeshift signs were posted on high-story windows to warn people: "This is not an exit."

Again, the elevators and ETV were delivering the usual pro-Enron propaganda. But the attitude of the people *inside* the elevators was drastically different, where one day somebody flipped Ken Lay a middle finger.

Late in November, Liz Perry and I decided to take a morning breakfast break. It was around 9:00 A.M.

As we were walking off the trading floor, Liz asked, "So . . . where do you want to go? Energizer?"

"NO ENERGIZER. I've got to get out of this building. Someplace far away from here." I needed some air. Sitting at my desk not working was starting to get to me.

As we walked out of the Death Star, we noticed the small army of news vans and news crews. As we crossed the street, local TV news reporter Phil Archer and his cameraman approached us.

"You guys work at Enron?" asked Phil as he approached us.

I took the question in terms of what I was thinking—that I was sick of sitting there not doing anything. So I answered, "No, not now we aren't."

Phil's eyes lit up as he and his cameraman misinterpret what I had said. We veered in a slightly different direction as he yelled, "Did you just get laid off?" The chase was on, and Liz Perry and I started speed-walking as he pursued us.

The news crews had been waiting for layoffs from the outside, just as we had been waiting from the inside—and suddenly they thought Liz and I were breaking news in the flesh. They thought we were the first of the laid-off Enron employees.

"We're just going to eat breakfast," yelled Liz back to Phil Archer and his camera-lugging sidekick.

"C'mon . . . talk to us!" He gave up as our distance was increasing. We had broken through the wall of interview-hungry reporters and escaped unharmed. We slowed our pace and continued heading far, far away in search of some greasy, cheese-filled breakfast burritos.

At breakfast we discussed our job-searching situations. Liz, whose husband remained unemployed from a job he lost months earlier, was not looking forward to having zero household income with a mortgage, student loan, and car payments. She had a few leads with companies she had previously left—again, Houston-based energy companies—but nothing too exciting.

As for me, I was caught up in the possibility of developing our business plan with McLainey, Duffy, and others at a new company. I had a few headhunters working for me as well, but the jobs they called me about either lacked excitement or never generated a callback.

The job market, especially the Houston job market, was extremely thin. Liz and I agreed that if we both got laid off and couldn't find new jobs, we would open up a new bar in Houston and call it the Barking Spider.

We returned to the building after breakfast and carefully snuck past the news crews; of course, they would have little interest in people going *into* the building. They were hoping for the money shot: the first axed employee walking out of the building in a fit of rage and sadness. They wanted a victim, someone willing to go on display in millions of living rooms.

As we entered the Death Star, I noticed that the glittery Enron cow, *Moost Immoovative,* was no longer in front of the building. Had it been stolen? Was this a safety measure to avoid lipstick-wielding vandals writing hate messages across its mirrored body? Most of the CowParade cows were due to be sold at a charity auction, so that was probably the more likely explanation.

In any case, I tried to imagine that as the seconds ticked down to Enron bankruptcy, thousands of employees would gather outside 1400 Smith Street and watch the dazzling cow drop from the fifty-first floor. Thousands of partying Enron employees would yell, "Five . . . four . . . three . . . two . . . one . . . Chapter Eleven!" Streamers and balloons would fill the air, and the moment the cow hit bottom, a giant sign would light up across the side of the Saturn Ring: "Enron Bankruptcy 2001!"

How to Conquer Corporate America, Rule #7: If your company offers you a "perk," take it; one way or another you're already paying for it.

McLainey, Duffy, Perry, and I were gathered in the middle of the trading floor, sharing a common thought: "If Enron doesn't pay us when we get fired, wouldn't it be nice to take home one of the giant flat-screen TVs?" These things were enormous, picture-perfect, and brand-new. It would be a chore to get one down from the ceiling mount, but one of them would look spectacular in my house.

As we contemplated the possibilities, a woman on the trading floor came up with another approach. Each employee had a supply of stickers with our names on them. The stickers were used any time we changed desks at Enron. All we had to do was slap our stickers on equipment, boxes, chairs, or other items that belonged to us—and the moving company would be able to identify the items. Those items would then magically appear at our newly assigned location. She somehow got up high enough to put one of her name stickers on one of these giant flat-screen TVs. Her hope was that if she got canned and sent home, one day the TV would arrive at her doorstep.

As we discussed the details of our plan to sneak in over the weekend dressed up as construction workers (complete with hard hats and tool belts), I suddenly realized I had forgotten something: Back on my very first day at Enron, during the orientation class, we were told about a program called Click-At-Home. Honestly, I remembered almost nothing from orientation day except McLainey telling me I was reluctantly adopted. However, there was this one little tidbit about free computers that stuck in my mind. It was Enron's most popular perk.

Click-At-Home was a program developed between Dell Computer and Enron, with the goal of increasing employees' computer skills. The idea was that by offering free computers and Internet service to Enron employees, the company was making a worthwhile investment in the tech-savvy abilities of its workforce.

The deal worked as follows:

An employee signed up with Enron, then went to the Dell ordering website to pick out the computer. There would be a few options to choose from: mostly basic models, but with the most up-to-date software and memory. Any upgrades would cost money, but without upgrades the computer system would cost $0. If the employee left Enron before a certain amount of time after the purchase date, then the employee would have to pay back a proportional amount of money to the program.

The fine print on the Click-At-Home deal offered one exception to the payback rule: you were excused from it only if Enron was forced to terminate your employment for business reasons.

I quickly decided it was time to get a free computer.

I signed up, picked out my Dell desktop personal computer

with all the fixin's, looked over the invoice for more than $1,200, and paid $0 for my new computer.

The very next day, an e-mail arrived to all Enron employees that told us the Click-At-Home deal was being suspended. Three days later my new computer arrived at my house.

As I was walking onto the trading floor, I almost stepped in a hole. Next to the hole was a maintenance technician wearing a flannel shirt and a hard hat. He was fiddling with wires and tools.

At that moment I realized why I always felt I was on shaky ground at Enron—the trading floor was actually suspended *two feet above* the real floor. The space was used for massive clusters of cables and wires, while the carpet floor we walked on was only an inch or two thick.

Through the hole I could see a dark crawl space that headed across to infinity. As I approached the technician, I asked, "So . . . any bodies down there?"

He looked up. "Say what now?"

I stopped by the hole. "Any executives hiding down there?"

"Oh . . . HAH! Nope, just a bunch of wires." He laughed, thinking I was kidding.

"Look," I said in a serious tone, as I handed him my Enron business card. "If you find any cash, like in trash bags or something . . . or maybe some suspicious-looking documents, file folders, that type of thing . . . just give me a call."

He looked at my card, and then looked up at me with great concern. "Okay. Uhh, yes sir . . . I'll do that."

"Great. Thanks for your help." I walked on to my desk, thinking there had to be a better way to use up my business cards.

Back at my desk was an e-mail from Bickers. It had a short message with a movie file attached to it.

• • •

Cruv—
Check this out. It's safe.
—Bickers

Telling me it was safe meant that I could open the movie without concern for workplace dangers. Some of the garbage that got forwarded over and over and over to me through the Internet could have been grounds for getting fired for "misconduct"—and again, I needed to get fired for business reasons to get a severance package. Bickers knew I worked on an open trading floor where everyone could see my screen. He was letting me know that this was acceptable material; it was safe.

The movie file was a cartoon called "Laid Off: A Day in the Life" and was made by a dot-com casualty named Todd Rosenberg—a.k.a. Odd Todd.

The animated short created by Odd Todd became an instant hit across the trading floor and across America. On that day in late November, Odd Todd showed us all a preview of the unemployed world we would all soon be living in.

Sleeping in, taking naps, eating junk food, having panic attacks, living with parents, watching TV, and not being able to leave the house—because leaving the house is "hard when you have no money." Later in the cartoon, Todd decided he was going to write a movie screenplay, "but after a page or so I got kinda bored and I found out it's really hard to write a whole movie."

At one point, as the e-mail spread, I could hear Odd Todd's movie echoing across the Enron trading floor. McLainey, Duffy, and Perry gathered around my desk as we watched it a second and third time.

We also found the Odd Todd website (www.oddtodd.com),

which asked visitors to give Todd a tip. I figured he was unemployed, and I was still sitting at a desk—so I sent him $1. Besides, the situation we were in needed his humor; a laugh at Enron in November was worth *at least* $1.

The thought of unemployment was racing through everyone's head every minute of the day. During one of those minutes, something suddenly hit me. Again, self-preservation was taking over. I spun around to talk to the back of McLainey's head.

"McLainey, you got a second?"

His chair spun around. "Of course, I've got lots of seconds."

"Let's say that moment comes when we all get locked out of the building . . . or suppose they tell us tomorrow not to bother coming in." I was whispering, and I wasn't sure why.

"Uh-huh," he said with curiosity.

"What happens to the butt-load of work I have stored on my computer? What happens if our business gets bought or we need to update the business plan, and all this work is lost?" The truth is, I had hundreds of hours' worth of work stored on my hard drive that we couldn't afford to leave behind. If we did go to work for a new firm or for ourselves, it was hundreds of hours that I preferred *not* to relive.

Duffy turned around to join in the discussion. Soon we were all whispering.

McLainey, after some discussion and thought, said, "Yeah, we really need to save that stuff." He looked over at Duffy.

Duffy added, "Yup. I've been sending stuff home for weeks."

That figured, since Duffy had also been gathering his "evidence" for weeks as well. He had printed out policy documents, proof of salary and vacation time, and Enron communications that stated that the severance policy was in place and would be followed.

McLainey agreed that the three of us should play it safe and transfer our work to our home computers. As it turned out, that wasn't playing it safe at all.

I packaged up all of the computer files I needed and zipped them into a single file. I named the file "Little Big Horn," for no reason other than I'm a smart-ass. I sent the file to my wife's e-mail, since my Internet e-mail account didn't have room for it.

Later that afternoon, McLainey was called away to a meeting. When he returned, he described the events as follows:

Someone had contacted McLainey saying they were with Enron's Employee Relations department. They asked to meet with him immediately. When McLainey arrived at the meeting, the Employee Relations people began their questioning.

"You're his supervisor, right?"

"Why is he sending it to his wife? Is she in on it, too?"

"What exactly is this file, anyway?"

"What's behind the name 'Little Big Horn'?"

McLainey told them that it was related to Enron work, and that I was just planning on doing the work from home. He also agreed that he would speak to me about it.

The grilling by Employee Relations seemed to leave McLainey in somewhat of a daze. As he described it to me, I imagined his interrogators wearing black suits, while they circled around him and pounded their fists on the table. A dusty old lightbulb was swinging from the ceiling, in an otherwise dark and chilly room . . .

Anyway, I was busted. So McLainey and I sent e-mails to each other confirming what I later realized: the Little Big Horn file never made it through the Enron system. I wondered if it was the size of the file, the dubious name, or both that allowed Enron's cybercops to snag it. Whatever the reason, I decided to give up on getting my work out of the building.

Meanwhile, the Enron cybercops were dealing with other cases much dirtier than mine. A group of employees decided that some trading fundamentals—Enron's bread and butter of buying and selling, price forecasting, etc.—would be worth keeping for their own use. They attempted to steal the material by burning it to a computer CD.

Somehow they were caught. Security came down and grabbed them, escorting them out of the building and tossing them on their butts onto Smith Street.

I realized how close I might have come to such a dramatic exit myself. The thought made me gulp so hard it hurt my neck. Lucky for me, Enron didn't see Little Big Horn as being valuable to anyone but us. Our ideas and our business were not only considered "non-core" by Enron's definition, but it wasn't even a business that Enron planned to salvage or sell. The fact was that if we didn't save what we were doing, it would simply vanish— creating no value for us, no value for Enron, and no value for the business community.

On the other hand, the trading fundamentals that those poor suckers were caught stealing could have been worth thousands (if not millions) of dollars. A competitor down the street, or a completely new operation, could instantly profit from having the core secrets of Enron.

On those final days before bankruptcy, the shredding and the scrambling that took place on the trading floor highlighted one of the risks associated with Skilling's "intellectual capital." Unlike hard assets, intellectual capital could fit in someone's pocket, be sent over someone's outgoing e-mail, or be gobbled up through someone's eyeballs. This wasn't a warehouse full of inventory, cash in the bank, or a physical pipeline under the ground—these were ideas stored on chips and inside people's heads. As soon as it disappeared, or someone else got a hold of it, it would lose value.

Just like Enron had lost *its* value.

We were all accustomed to using our e-mail systems to organize meetings. Our calendars were linked together, we could see each other's schedules, and reminders would pop up on our screens or PDAs when a meeting time was approaching.

McLainey would send me a meeting request via e-mail, even if he had just spun around seconds earlier to say, "Let's meet in ten minutes." It was just habit, and we all lived by it.

Needless to say, schedules were pretty open and meeting requests were rare in late November. It was a typical workless afternoon when I decided to send out the following meeting request:

To: Greg McLainey, Jim Duffy, Liz Perry, and Vic Lazarri
Subject: get out of here, drink beer
Location: nearest bowling alley
Start Time: 1:00 p.m.

Perry and Lazarri accepted the meeting, while McLainey and Duffy just weren't up for it. Liz suggested we start with some grease and cheese, so we stopped at Barry's Pizza on our way to the bowling alley.

After several slices of pizza, more than a few beers, and thirty frames (in which Liz kicked both our asses), we decided to call it quits. I could have sworn there were other groups of Enron employees there, but I knew their faces and not their names. It was a pretty low-stress day of work, especially for a Tuesday afternoon; but we were tired, and our feet hurt from the rental shoes. We decided to take the rest of the day off.

> Thursday—November 29, 2001
> *ENE opening price: $0.47*
> *ENE closing price: $0.36*
> *ENE trading volume: 265,165,296*

The Enron Tour Guide was bringing more groups through the trading floor. This time it was clearly an issue of commercial real estate. We did our best to goof off while the tours were coming through. Stress balls, footballs, Slinky toys, and whatever else we could send flying through the air—the goal was to see how close we could come to the thirty-foot ceiling without hitting it. I'm sure the visitors were impressed.

More downgrades from Wall Street analysts came along as the Dynegy deal collapsed. Apparently, the analysts didn't think investors should buy the stock anymore, now that it was below $1. UBS Warburg and RBC Capital Markets had dropped ENE off the Strong Buy list the day before, and Goldman had dropped it off their Recommended List the week before. Some of the analysts appeared on CNBC to explain that it was only a symbolic gesture. We had a symbolic gesture for them as well.

In a way it was gutsy for these firms to draw attention to themselves with a ludicrous downgrade. Other Wall Street firms were quietly maintaining their buy ratings on ENE, while hoping that no one would notice. In fact, as of November 29, five firms rated ENE a Buy or Strong Buy.

Theories started to trickle out as to why analysts had consistently overpumped ENE for so long. Why did they maintain Buy ratings even after Skilling resigned, the SEC began to investigate, the CFO was canned, and four years of earnings had to be restated? Analysts had argued for years over whether or not Enron's business was a "black box"—which begs the question: "If you don't understand it, how can you recommend it to your clients?"

The most common theory: If they condemn ENE stock, then they risk losing (or not gaining) Enron as an investment-banking client. And, by the way . . . analysts are often close friends with company management, they might own the stock themselves, and it's hard to go out on a limb when every other analyst rates the stock a Buy. Plus, how could they downgrade the stock with all the great things Enron management was telling them? This is a publicly traded company—so they *have to believe everything they hear, right*?

The best explanation for maintaining a Strong Buy on ENE stock came from Lehman Brothers. Apparently, their firm was playing a role in the Dynegy-Enron merger deal, which meant that—by their own policy—they were prohibited from changing their rating on ENE stock. So they felt they were required to leave it at a Strong Buy.

Meanwhile, ENE stock trickled helplessly down to $.30. However, the bigger news on that Thursday was that Enron was taking other companies down with it. As the entire industry faced fears of market mayhem and nonpayment from Enron, energy stocks began to plummet. Dynegy, which at the peak of the Enron merger hype was around $47 per share, was at $34 and dropping (Dynegy would eventually hit $20 in mid-December—a 50 percent drop in less than a month).

El Paso, the energy trading firm down the street, was telling its investors it only had a measly $50 million in exposure to Enron. As for doing any more deals with Enron, a statement was released:

"New business will have to be supported by cash collateral"—cash that Enron was quickly running out of. El Paso stock took a 7 percent hit that day.

Back on the trading floor, Enron employees were frantically trying to follow the Yahoo! message boards to get news about ENE. Stock message boards were gaining popularity as a way to measure public sentiment on a stock, and Yahoo! had the most widely used boards on the Internet. Unfortunately, the message boards were mostly garbage.

Anyone could create a screen name on Yahoo! and anonymously post whatever junk messages they liked. They could bash a stock, pump the stock up, spread rumors, or just heckle other people posting proof of their own stupidity. The ENE message boards got extremely out of hand those last few days, partly because users could and did remain anonymous. Yahoo! had policies about what could and could not be posted, and in the past people had been busted for posting misinformation. But in reality, the board was automated and running full steam. Anyone could say anything and not worry about the consequences.

Most of the anonymous postings came from angry investors, desperate optimists, and a few I-told-you-so-er's. Much of the anger was directed at Andy Fastow, with messages wishing that he be incarcerated or even killed. Yes, the hatred for Enron executives was boiling over to the point of four-letter words and twisted threats. Some users even began posting personal information about executives, such as their home addresses or phone numbers.

Online anonymity was allowing for untraceable iniquity.

Then again, we must not forget the Enron cybercops.

Liz Perry and I took notice of the belligerent messages being posted by a user calling himself "utlonghornsrule." Since Liz and I were both University of Texas alums, we were particularly annoyed at the garbage being written by this individual: the foul language, the personal attacks on Ken Lay, etc.

It's not that "utlonghornsrule" didn't have a right to vent personal frustration, but Liz and I felt that such a classless display of hostility shouldn't be associated with our favorite school. Others agreed, as people began to post messages asking "utlonghornsrule" to stop, including comments like "You're an embarrassment to UT."

The real problem for "utlonghornsrule" wasn't the return hostility he was facing on the message board, but the watchful eye of the Enron cybercops. Not only did Enron find out that he was an Enron employee, they immediately fired him and escorted him out of the building, also tossing him on his butt onto Smith Street.

I later read reports that he agreed with Enron's actions, admitting that his mistake was using company equipment while on company time. In other words, if he had been bashing his employer from his home computer, the behavior would have been acceptable?

And "utlonghornsrule" wasn't the only Enron employee fired for using the Yahoo! message boards. Another employee used the online forum to tell the world about millions of dollars in retention bonuses—a secret Enron management would have liked to keep quiet. That employee was also identified and fired; but once again, the message board was automated and unfiltered—so the word was out about the retention money and the damage to Enron was already done.

Rumors about layoffs and severance packages were flying around at a dizzying rate. I literally heard dozens of different versions of rumors every day—sometimes a few different versions within minutes. McLainey, Duffy and I would spin around and share the latest, either with joy or with anger, depending on the quality of the rumor.

"No layoffs until January."

"Layoffs tomorrow, no severance packages."

"We're all going to get three months' pay!"

"A year's salary if we agree not to file a lawsuit against Enron."

Word came from our colleagues in London that the liquidation team from PricewaterhouseCoopers (PWC) had already taken over part of the Enron building there. U.S. headquarters in Houston had already cut off cash to European and Australian trading operations.

We eventually reached the point of saturation. I reached the point that I wanted to go bowling again . . . and I don't even *like* bowling.

Then came a miracle. As we all sat at our desks, we noticed a crowd forming on one end of the trading floor. Hundreds of Enron employees gathered, walking slowly toward a distant voice. Like zombies we headed toward the voice as well. When we were close enough, we saw an Enron executive named Ray Bowen.

He was standing there in the middle of the floor, giving an inspirational update on the state of the business. He told us what he believed the severance package would be (although none of us understood his explanation) and expressed his frustration with other Enron executives. He promised that he would stay and fight; that he still believed the Enron business had a future. Although we couldn't actually hear most of what Bowen said, it was nice to see someone standing up and at least *trying* to communicate with employees about what was coming. Thanks, Ray.

Meanwhile, back on the subject of retention bonuses:

Enron had decided that, in order to keep the business going after a bankruptcy filing, they needed to pay certain "essential" employees to stick around. Sometime during the last week of November, someone somewhere decided who was essential and who was not. How essential they were would determine if the retention bonus was in the millions or just the thousands.

In any case, the retention bonus would require the employee to stay for three months after bankruptcy—otherwise they would have to pay it back. Enron would not be able to survive if the key operators all bailed immediately following the bankruptcy— making Chapter 11 impossible and total liquidation unavoidable. Conclusion: Retention bonuses are a reasonable concept. Reality: Enron took the concept to the extreme.

In exchange for the promise to stay ninety days, about five hundred employees got $55 million (on top of their normal salaries). People we had never heard of got hundreds of thousands of dollars. People that we believed were essential got nothing. When the full list was later published on the Web, we looked at the list with nauseating disbelief: "Can you believe [insert name of lucky bastard] got $200,000? How can he be *essential* if his entire group was eliminated?"

And our friend Ray Bowen, who inspired us that afternoon with his courage and his belief in Enron, was given a ninety-day retention bonus of $750,000. No wonder Ray delivered that Knute Rockne speech and vowed to stick around.

> Friday—November 30, 2001
> *ENE opening price: $0.37*
> *ENE closing price: $0.26*
> *ENE trading volume: 173,511,904*

A dollar doesn't buy much these days, but on the last Friday in November it bought about three shares of Enron stock. I sat at my desk that afternoon with CNBC broadcasting through my phone, the Yahoo! message board on one screen, and my E-Trade account on the other. I was searching for a reason to buy the stock again. I guess I was out of my mind.

It was another day of roller-coaster rumors and emotional Ping-Pong. To kill time and keep our boredom in motion, we explored the Web. We checked on our friend Odd Todd, we bought and sold stock, we scanned the news headlines . . .

. . . and we looked in Jeff Skilling's backyard.

As creepy as it sounds, it's just another exciting game that can be played on the Internet. Anyone with a computer and a connection to the Web can do it.

With a few people gathered around my desk on the trading floor, the subject of Jeff Skilling was getting hostile and hot. So we searched through public records to find Skilling's home address. I then guided my audience through the property's transaction history, the property's taxable value (capped at $4.2 million), and even looked over Skilling's tax bill (which was paid in full for 2001). Then, to the amazement of my audience, I pulled up a satellite photo of the house itself.

The luscious River Oaks mansion was large enough to be easily viewed by a one-eyed satellite. I zoomed in to the point where the red roof and stucco exterior filled the entire computer screen.

Then Lazarri walked over to see what the "oohs" and "ahhs" were about.

Someone told him, "We're looking at Skilling's house."

• • •

The party on the trading floor picked up that afternoon. As I was walking back to my desk from lunch, I followed a keg of beer (in a trash can, on wheels). There were several kegs by the late afternoon, and hundreds of people walked around the floor with foam in hand.

We talked about job leads and what we planned to do next. I exchanged phone numbers and e-mails with people I knew I might not see again. It wasn't just a party; it was a *farewell party*.

"This is just incredible, hard to believe," said Duffy, as we all scanned the scene.

Liz responded, "I can't believe I clapped for Ken Lay. I can't believe I clapped for that fucker."

"This is not what I expected when I chose the Enron job; I took this job because it was safe." I said this while thinking about the choices I had made: escaping the start-up dot-com and deciding against a return to consulting.

Others responded to my comment with flashbacks of their own.

"I knew our start-up group would be risky," said McLainey, "but I always thought Enron would have a place for me."

Duffy jumped in. "Yeah. I thought, 'If this start-up fails, then Enron will have dozens of others waiting for me.' I knew that whatever happened, the upside potential was spectacular." Duffy was referring to the Enron bonus he would never get.

"I just wanted Enron on my résumé," explained Liz. We all nodded in agreement. There was a time when Enron could launch a career into many brilliant directions.

I added the old Enron cliché, "Yep . . . the 'best and the brightest.' That's us."

We just stared into space for a few seconds, trapped in that last thought.

Then Liz asked a funny question: "Do you guys think anyone is happy about Enron collapsing?"

McLainey laughed and said, "Well of course!"

Then Duffy started a list. "Let's see . . . everyone in California, all of Enron's competitors, dozens of pissed-off countries around the world."

I added, "And everyone who Skilling ever told that they just 'don't get it.' "

Liz continued. "Right . . . they don't get it because they're not from Harvard!" We all had a good laugh over Skilling's failed genius and then went to refill our beers.

As we headed over to the kegs, I asked Liz, "Does Enron have an alcohol policy?"

She answered, "Yes—you aren't allowed to drink alcohol while driving a company vehicle."

"Is that it?"

"Oh," she began with a smile, "and they also encourage us to drink heavily during SEC investigations."

Late that Friday afternoon, I began packing up a box of personal belongings. I still had no solid information about layoffs, but figured I had nothing else to do.

I also took Duffy's lead and started my own collection of "severance evidence." I assumed that an extreme state of panic and confusion was fast approaching, so I thought it was best to keep proof that I ever was an Enron employee.

Just as I was about to leave, the phone rang.

"Enron," I answered as usual, but it sounded different after a few beers.

"Dude." It was Bickers. He and I hadn't spoken by phone in several days.

"Hey Bickers . . . what's new?" I said it as if things were business as usual.

"Dude. I don't know what to say."

"About what?" I stood my ground. I wasn't going to let him off that easy.

Bickers raised his voice. "I'm sorry . . . I'm trying to say I'm sorry."

Just then it hit me. My New York friend with a New York attitude was showing a softer side. He was sorry about the mess I was in. He was sorry that he had always talked about ENE without considering how it felt for me to be part of Enron. He was sorry, because he knew I was about to get canned.

"Why are you sorry? Did you invest in LJM?"

He didn't think it was funny. He started rambling on and on about job contacts he could give me in New York. While I appreciated the offers, I had no interest in moving anywhere above the snow line.

"Dude . . . I'm sorry."

"Please stop saying that." Really, it was starting to annoy me. I liked the other Bickers better.

"You just can't seem to catch a break."

Bickers was referring to my illustrious career after business school—in which Enron was now strike three. "What can I say . . . it's a losing streak. But I can't win if I don't place a bet."

I told Bickers I needed to get out of there and beat Friday traffic. We agreed to talk the next week.

As Friday came to a close, I realized that I had lost on my bankruptcy pool entry—my $20 guess for a Friday filing had expired.

The loss in the pool was a reminder of when I was back in college and I spent all my spare time betting on sports. One of the more popular axioms among our gambling gang was, "If the favorite can't cover the point spread, then they deserve to lose the game."

As I walked out of the Death Star that day, I wondered if that was how investors were feeling. Enron had burned them for such a huge financial loss that they probably felt a twinkle of satisfaction watching Enron crash and burn.

I shook my head as I passed an E logo on the wall. Once a symbol of pride for all of us, it was now a symbol of distrust and disdain. Everyone had a reason to hate Enron—customers who felt they were ripped off, competitors who had always been stepped on, analysts who were now looking foolish, investors who had lost their lunch, and employees—like me—who were about to lose their livelihood.

That last Friday in November, I took one last look at the big banner in the lobby: THE WORLD'S LEADING COMPANY.

All I could do was shake my head.

I thought that someday soon, that banner would need to be taken down, perhaps by Skilling and Fastow—perhaps dressed in state-issued orange jumpsuits. They would climb up on stepladders, with Lay down on the lobby floor directing them.

Then I pictured Fastow, on the right side, slipping on a $100 bill and falling from his ladder. He would then grab the banner on the way down, ripping it in half.

And all that would remain of the banner:

THE WORLD'S LEADING CON

8

Parade of Victims, Parade of Villains

"I've worked myself up from nothing to a state of supreme poverty."
—*Groucho Marx*

I n the state of New York, a license is required to hang clothes on a clothesline. In the state of Texas, a license is required to possess a dead alligator. Beyond that, the laws of the two states are pretty much the same, right?

On December 2, 2001, Enron Corp. filed for Chapter 11 reorganization with the U.S. Bankruptcy Court in the Southern District of New York.

That night Bickers called.

"Sorry dude . . . game over."

His call was the first I was hearing about the bankruptcy. "On a Sunday? Are they saying if I need to go to work tomorrow?"

He ignored me and continued, "They're suing Dynegy for $10 billion, and they're keeping the pipe."

Bickers was referring to a lawsuit filed in conjunction with the bankruptcy filing. The suit alleged Dynegy had wrongfully terminated the merger agreement and that only a valid termination should allow Dynegy to exercise the option to acquire the Northern Natural Gas pipeline.

"Nice. Let's take everyone down with us. At least the lawyers will be happy." I cared more about that Sunday's football games. "Your Jets choked! They were up thirteen to zero against the spineless Patriots, and ended up losing by a point."

"Dude . . . New England is actually pretty good. They're at least going to be a playoff team!"

I responded sharply, "Okay—now *you* are on crack!" Bickers was being an idiot. New England had no chance of making the play-offs—they'd be lucky to finish with a winning record.

Monday—December 3, 2001
ENE opening price: $0.29
ENE closing price: $0.40
ENE trading volume: 165,778,800

Nobody won the bankruptcy pool, and we would each get our $20 back. Who would have guessed Sunday?

Monday morning came slowly. I called McLainey on my way into the office, hoping for some concrete information. He told me that the word on the trading floor was heavy on the side of Wednesday layoffs. Three more days of employment: I did the math on how much of a partial paycheck that would give me on the fifteenth.

When I arrived at the Death Star, news vans were *everywhere*. They had surrounded the building, and each reporter was well lit and well positioned in front of the main entrance. With the giant chrome E logo in the background, they would deliver to the world frequent updates on "The Enron Debacle" or "The Collapse of an Energy Trading Behemoth." Those headlines and more were staring at us from the television screens throughout Enron head-quarters. We were inside the building, looking at live video of the outside of the building. I wondered what would happen if I held a TV up to a camera that was filming a live shot of the TV.

Sparked by boredom, some Enronians ventured outside for camera time or even interviews. I got calls from people telling me to watch over the shoulder of a certain reporter on a particular channel. All day long (on recorded replays) I would see them on CNN, MSNBC, or CNBC, walking by with cell phones at their ears.

Enronians giving interviews brought stomach-aching laughter to the trading floor. One woman declared to the world, "It's business as usual." I watched as hundreds of people on the trading floor cheered and applauded and rolled on the floor in hysterics. Did she even work for Enron? What planet was her department on?

Some people preferred still photos. One analyst from our group ended up as the main photo for Bethany McLean's *Fortune* magazine article "Why Enron Went Bust," holding his Enron mug in one hand while biting his fingernails on the other. If only the photographer had a bottle of artificial tears handy: now *that* would have been an award winner.

Meanwhile, back inside the fishbowl, I was handed a flyer for a new website—www.1400smith.com—which was being thrown together as a way for Enron alumni to stay in touch. Even though I was not yet an ex-employee, I went to the website and added my contact information.

In the bland and often mechanical world of investment lingo, the term *dead cat bounce* just brings a smile to my face. The phrase refers to a slight and temporary rise in a stock (or market) after a significant or steep decline, as in "Even a dead cat will bounce if it is dropped from high enough." The trick is not to confuse the dead cat's gravitational rebound with a sudden return to life.

At around $0.30, Enron was hardly even a dead fur ball.

But I sat there looking at my E-Trade screen, and I couldn't think of a reason *not* to take the chance. ENE had dropped from so high that maybe bankruptcy, layoffs, or whatever could give it a small pop. All I needed was a pop up to $0.60 and I could double my money.

Just as I was about to pull the trigger on a trade, Waterston asked all of us to gather around him for a meeting. I decided the trade could wait.

Standing next to Waterston in the middle of our trading area was our Human Resources representative. This was the first time I had seen him since my first day at Enron. Everyone in our group was present that morning, and everyone formed a half circle around the two of them. Waterston began the meeting:

"Well . . . I guess we all knew this was coming."

He and the HR rep continued to talk, but it was a blur. We all just stared in a state of dreamlike disbelief. McLainey, Duffy, Perry, Lazarri, and two dozen other assistants, analysts, traders—we were all being sent home.

"You have half an hour to leave the building," the HR rep continued.

Waterston looked at his watch. "Okay, so that's eleven-thirty we need to be out of here." I was amazed at how cool and professional Waterston was being. He was getting canned with the rest of us.

I looked around the massive trading floor to see four or five other groups having the same meeting. It was peaceful and quiet, like each cluster of employees was conducting a study group at a library.

I turned back to Waterston and the HR guy. None of us said a word or even looked at each other. We hung on every moment.

"Make sure I have your contact information," continued the HR guy, "so I can let you know if we want you to come back in."

Yeah, right.

Without a word about severance, final paychecks, expense reports, or paperwork—it was over. The HR guy then asked, "Any questions?"

Of course there were questions! Our group started firing away at him:

• • •

Q: "What about severance packages?"

A: "Don't know."

Q: "What happens to my expense report?"

A: "Don't know."

Q: "Do we get some kind of pink slip or notice? Something we can use to file for unemployment?"

A: "Not that I know of."

Then the questions were stopped, as it became clear there would be no answers. "Look, I'm in the same boat as you are." It was almost a fair statement from the HR guy, except that *he wasn't getting laid off.* "I have to do a dozen more of these meetings today, so I need to get going. Again, e-mail me your contact information and I'll be in touch."

Waterston wrapped it up like it was just another meeting. "Okay guys," he lightly clapped his hands together, "we've got half an hour."

There was no riot, no panic, and no outburst of emotion. We each returned to our desks like robots and began packing. Our questions would have to wait—for now, we had half an hour to pack up our Enron careers and get the hell out.

A stack of empty boxes, which I hadn't noticed before, was sitting in the corner. I pointed them out to some people around me. I didn't need a box, since I had been slowly packing one for days.

I looked across the trading floor to see hundreds of people doing the same—packing quickly to meet their thirty-minute deadline. The phone was ringing off the hook, as people called to share their fate. I noticed a handful of Houston police officers taking their positions around the trading floor. They each stood calmly with their arms folded, scanning the enormous room.

The news broke as well. I could see our building up on the TV screens as the first groups of ex-Enronians poured out of the building with cardboard boxes in hand.

Our thirty minutes seemed like thirty hours, but I still made my "take or leave" decisions at lightning speed.

Take: anything that we may need to start up a new business, anything that proves how much severance money Enron owes me, anything that had sentimental value like a football, Slinky, or Enron memorabilia.

Leave: my Enron laptop computer, my chair, and my Enron *Code of Ethics* handbook.

I was all ready to go as others continued to pack, and I spun around to soak in my last few moments at Enron. The scene was spectacular and tragic at the same time—all those lives, changing in an instant.

McLainey would return home to his family, a family he had just relocated to Houston from California. He would pull up in his minivan to be greeted by his wife, two daughters, Pumpkin the pet hamster, and their two lizards, Squiggles and Zippy. He would explain to his young girls that he had lost his job; and they would respond with remarkable accuracy: "Well, you better get another one!"

Duffy would go home to his family as well, just a few weeks since their relocation and purchase of a new home. His children would be much too young to understand, already facing the adjustment of new schools and new environments.

Liz Perry would arrive home to her husband, and they would figure out a way to survive off two unemployment checks. They would contemplate moving, perhaps to a new part of the country, just to get a fresh start. Luckily, they had only their fat little dog Pecos to support—but even he would have to cut back on the doggie treats.

Lazarri was the one person with a look of confidence. It was no big deal; it was business. He had a look on his face like his next job was already lined up.

A young marketing analyst in our group found out her husband was being laid off at the exact same moment. They would go home together that day, having lost their income and their benefits, just a few days after finding out she was pregnant with their first child.

International employees went into crisis mode. People in our group were displaced across oceans, with no means of returning home. Employees in London were given just a few hundred pounds and locked out of the building, with no relocation assistance to get back to the United States. Conversely, our group had people from France and Central America who were stuck in Houston—with useless work visas and no means of relocating back to their home countries.

And then there was Waterston, who had taken a chance on our new start-up group. He watched as his vision faded into a landscape of empty chairs and blank computer screens. I could only imagine the magnitude of his loss—not just the financial loss from stock options or 401(k) savings—but the professional loss of an Enron future now in ashes. To my amazement, Waterston's greatest concern continued to be all of us. He was concerned about our futures ahead of his own, arranging others' job interviews, sharing his contacts and serving as a reference, and telling us everything he could during the collapse. He apologized constantly, as if any of this was his fault. He was the selfless captain of our sinking ship.

Next time you come across an anthill, give it a little kick. Within a few seconds, you will see *exactly* what Enron headquarters looked like on December 3, 2001.

After hugs and handshakes and short good-byes, we headed out of the building as the thirty-minute deadline approached.

The elevators were packed, so I took the stairs. When I reached the halls, they were packed as well. I suddenly found myself in a thick line of laid-off people I didn't know. Each person had his or her hands full, with boxes and bags and even a few small plants. As the line of people struggled to move forward, I noticed a distinct separation in behavior: male and female. There were several males acting like complete idiots—making obscene noises and yelling out obnoxious commentary. It reminded me of a high school fire drill, except they weren't acting quite that mature. Meanwhile, the women were doing one of three things: either they were getting pissed at the men for acting like jackasses, they were crying, or they were doing both. As for me, I just kept to myself and tried to keep moving.

When I reached the main lobby, I noticed the street was filled with news crews and cameras. I walked out in front of the main entrance, put down my cardboard box, and picked up my wireless phone.

Bickers answered. "Can you see me?" I asked.

"Dude . . . what channel?" He had television screens scattered across his trading floor as well.

"I don't know." I looked around the front of the Death Star. "All of them."

There were too many people and too many channels for him to spot me, but he got the point. I was laid off, along with four or five thousand other people. We all went home, with our Enron careers crammed into a box and a head full of unanswered questions.

"Dude . . . what are you going to do?" asked Bickers.

"What else? I'm going home."

• • •

There was hardly any traffic. I called my wife and we talked about the day's events. She was astonished, as was I, at the way we had been laid off. She had expected an individual meeting, one that included an exit interview, paperwork, and some helpful resources. But this wasn't that kind of layoff—this was a complete disaster.

There are three other things I remember about the drive home that day. First, the radio stations were breaking the news and immediately turning to the subject of a future name for the baseball stadium . . . oh, please—*not again!* I switched to some light classical music. Second, a pebble kicked up out of nowhere on the Interstate. I watched in slow-motion as it found a soft spot in the middle of my windshield (within twenty-four hours the crack would be ten inches long). Finally, I remember it was a perfectly cloudless day, with the temperature in the low seventies, relatively low humidity for the Gulf Coast, and a gentle breeze around 10 mph. I remember thinking it was a beautiful day to lose my job.

In New York, the Honorable Bankruptcy Judge Arthur Gonzalez was approving Enron's "First Day Orders":

> *Enron's financial and operational stability going forward were enhanced through the granting of the following motions: Payment of pre-petition and post-petition employee wages, salaries, business expenses and benefits, including medical, for current employees, during the company's voluntary restructuring under Chapter 11; and approval for immediate use of the first $250 million of the proceeds of the debtor-in-possession (DIP) funds to continue operations, pay employee salaries and wages, and fulfill post-petition vendor obligations. The Court also approved an initial payment of $4,500 for each employee who might become severed.*

> Kenneth L. Lay, chairman and CEO of Enron, said, "We are pleased with the Court's prompt approval of all of our 'first day orders.' These first day orders will enable the company to continue operating and take care of our remaining employees as we commence what will be an orderly and intensive strategic restructuring process."
>
> A final hearing to consider approval of the DIP financing is scheduled for Jan. 7, 2002.

The word of the $4,500 for each laid-off employee spread fast, and no one was happy about it. The standard severance plan—the one that would have paid my bills for a few months—was canceled. Employees that had given Enron *decades* of their working lives would also get $4,500. Employees that were eligible for a year's salary would get $4,500. Across the board, it was considered a slap in the face. It was an insult. It was a joke.

By the time I arrived at my home in redbrick suburbia, I felt exhausted and overwhelmed. I took a quick look at the injury to my windshield and realized it was already beyond simple repair. I left my Enron belongings in my trunk and went into the house.

It was a tough day for me, but it was even tougher for Bailey and Harry, our two boys. They were shocked to see me at home, and they sensed something was very wrong. They knew it was more than just a half day at work—it was a schedule change, and it would take them weeks to adjust.

Bailey, our 120-pound rottweiler "puppy," quietly followed me around the house, tilting his head and staring whenever I stopped. Harry, our enormous gray monster of a cat, followed me around as well, jumping up on furniture and counters to stare at me from eye level. I changed clothes, retrieved the mail, fixed myself some lunch, and turned on the TV. The mail consisted entirely of utility bills, I couldn't eat anything, and the TV stations were discussing the future name of Enron Field. I gave Bailey and Harry my lunch (the cat eats first, while the dog waits for whatever is left), and I fell asleep on the couch.

It was one of those dreams that you just don't forget—so vivid, so clear, and so extreme. If only I could explain it.

I was being calmly washed away by a flood of crystal-clear water. As the water carried me along, I tried to grab for things to hang on to. With one attempt, I reached up only to see my left hand get chopped off. As I continued along the path of the floodwaters, I saw various Enron executives dressed in Santa suits beating the crap out of each other. Finally, I grabbed onto a hole in the water and climbed through. After passing through this opening, I found myself eating at a restaurant called Tako Bell (*tako* is Japanese for octopus). I was enjoying my *tako* while sitting across from a polar bear. Then things started to get weird . . . .

I woke up to a ringing phone.

Bailey was resting his dog chin right by my face. Harry was sitting on my chest. They were both staring at me again. I politely yelled, "Back off!" as I got up to answer the phone.

It was a call from Mr. Blue. He and I had agreed to keep in touch after our meeting a few weeks before at the Four Seasons.

"Oh, I'm fine," I told him, suppressing a yawn and clearing my eyes. As we talked, I couldn't help but picture him in a Santa suit. "It's not like this came as a surprise. You were right about the Dynegy deal."

"Yep . . . and now we get dueling lawsuits." Mr. Blue was referring to Dynegy's decision that day to sue Enron on two fronts: one to gain control of the Northern Natural Gas pipeline, and another for damages to the DYN stock price (which had taken about a 10 percent hit each day since the merger failed). As the *Houston Chronicle* described it, the lawsuits were purely "tit for tat."

Mr. Blue continued to predict the future, mostly in terms of who would take most of the blame for the mess.

I asked him, "Who do *you* think deserves the blame?" I thought it was a simple question.

"Well, the executives should have kept the hype machine under control. This never should have been an eighty-dollar stock—it should have grown steadily in the thirty-dollar to forty-dollar range. At the same time, analysts perpetuated the hype by not asking real questions, not raising issues sooner, and by generally keeping their heads up their asses." He was rattling off his answer, like he had given it hundreds of hours of thought.

"And the board was *always* clear about their unilateral support for management. Each member accepted his or her three hundred thousand dollars a year while the books were being cooked for more than a decade . . . and of course Andersen just did what their client told them to do."

Just when I thought he was finished, he said, "Even the investors themselves should have known better than to dump all of their nest eggs in one basket; people who lost *everything* must have had *everything* tied up in ENE stock." He paused to catch his breath. "The SEC—too little too late. They've been looking at Enron's filings all of these years; what were they *doing*? Accounting standards— I mean *really*! Ninety-nine percent of this off-the-books bullshit is perfectly acceptable. It's time for FASB to wake up and smell the unconsolidated coffee."

Finally I got a word in, "So . . . "

"So it's all about conflict of interest," he cut me off. "It's about perception versus reality or money versus responsibility. The government regulators get campaign funding from the same companies they are supposed to regulate; the analysts are recommending companies that are clients or that they own stock in themselves; the board gets paid to shut up, or they're off the board; the auditors and lawyers get paid to sign off on everything, or else they lose a client."

He was more fun when he was drinking expensive Scotch.

Back at the Death Star, the employees left behind were feeling just as miserable as those who were fired. The place was empty, the future was uncertain, and the executives were in the midst of a firestorm. At least the people who were laid off got a head start on landing the few jobs that were out there.

Another intranet Q&A appeared inside Enron for those people remaining at the battered company. The questions seemed somewhat more direct than those posted for the Dynegy deal.

Q: Will this filing affect payroll? When do I get my paycheck? Will there be any reductions in employee salaries?
A: This week's payroll is already funded and we expect to receive court permission shortly to continue to meet payroll on an ongoing basis, and in the usual manner. We have no plans to reduce employee salaries.
Q: Will there be further employee layoffs as a result of the filing? If so, how many layoffs are planned, and when will they be announced? What about severance programs? Will there be retention plans offered to those employees asked to remain with Enron?
A: In light of our current financial situation and the uncertain economic outlook, Enron has initiated a thorough evaluation of all aspects of our business operations with the objective of achieving significant

cost savings wherever possible, including staff reductions. This process will result in the disposition or elimination of non-core activities, sales of non-core assets, and a reduction in workforce. Following a bankruptcy filing, a company must seek approval for certain activities, including distribution of severance payments. Enron has an amended severance pay plan and will petition the bankruptcy court for an appropriate severance plan given our current situation. We are awaiting the court's decision. Enron also intends to develop retention plans to ensure that it keeps key employees. When decisions are made affecting Enron, our operations, and our people, we will let you know as quickly as possible.

Q: Will employees continue to receive performance bonuses?

A: Enron has not determined whether bonuses will be paid for 2001. Enron is exploring several alternatives, which include the payment of regular bonuses and/or retention bonuses for people critical to maintaining its value.

Q: What happens to the 401(k) plans?

A: 401(k) investments are in trusts separate from Enron and are protected by federal regulations. Shares of Enron stock held in employee 401(k) plans are subject to the same market conditions as regular common stockholders. If you own shares of Enron stock, you should consult with a financial or tax adviser to assess your personal situation.

Q: What happens to Enron's stock now? What will be its value moving forward?

A: The New York Stock Exchange (NYSE) has suspended trading of Enron stock pending this announcement. The ultimate value of Enron stock, if any, will be determined through the Chapter 11 process. If you own shares of Enron stock, you should consult with a financial or tax adviser to assess your personal situation.

Q: Is Enron going out of business?

A: No. The purpose of Chapter 11 is to preserve and strengthen our business so that we can best meet our financial obligations to our creditors. We expect to do just that. As part of this process, however, certain businesses and operations will be sold or wound down in an orderly fashion.

Q: Have other companies filed for, and successfully emerged from, Chapter 11 in the past?

A: Yes. Many companies, among them such well-known enterprises as Continental Airlines, Texaco, and Macy's, have successfully gone through the Chapter 11 process in the past.

Q: Why has Enron filed a lawsuit against Dynegy? What are the details of the lawsuit?

A: Enron has filed suit against Dynegy Inc. (NYSE: DYN), seeking damages of at least $10 billion, in the U.S. Bankruptcy Court for the Southern District of New York (the same court in which we have filed for Chapter 11 reorganization). Enron alleges, among other things, that Dynegy breached its Merger Agreement with Enron by terminating the agreement when it had no contractual right to do so; and that Dynegy has no right to exercise the option to acquire the entity that indirectly owns Northern Natural Gas, because that option can only be triggered by a valid termination of the Merger Agreement. The Dynegy lawsuit alleges that the reasons offered by Dynegy for its termination of the Merger Agreement were mere pretexts to provide legal and public relations cover for its decision to renege on a binding contractual obligation. This conduct has torn a hole in Enron's business, and caused it to suffer billions of dollars in damages.

Q: Will there be changes to the senior management team or the Board of Directors?

A: We do not expect any changes to the Company's board of directors or management team.

Q: What are our debt obligations?

A: That information is in our bankruptcy filing, which is available on our web site.

After my conversation with Mr. Blue, the phone kept ringing the rest of the day. I had the same conversation—over and over—with family and friends, former and current Enron employees, and a handful of telemarketers who thought they had a chance of selling me a dream vacation or a cemetery plot.

The conversations were all about the parade of victims and what it felt like to be a victim myself. But I didn't feel like a victim—I felt lucky. I was lucky to be young and to have a career that seemed recoverable.

I thought about those who might never recover: anyone who, like Mr. Blue said, had put all of their nest eggs in one basket.

I began my own personal recovery that day by watching twenty minutes of Jerry Springer. It was enough to help me realize that things could have been a lot worse: I could have been pregnant with an alien baby.

On CNN, CNBC, and other television stations, the story was Enron. They were putting images of the victims (including a few shots of me on my phone call to Bickers) up against images of the villains. In early December, those villains were partnership puppeteer Andy Fastow, rosy-cheeked leader Ken Lay, and the deal breakers at Dynegy. It was a short list of wrongdoers, compared to the list in my head. Where was Skilling's name? What about Pai, Sutton, Mark, White, the Andersen partners, or the board members?

How to Conquer Corporate America, Rule #8 ("The Accounting Rule"): The numbers are all related; if one is wrong, they are all wrong.

As reality was just starting to sink in for Enron employees, the well-groomed perception of Enron's financial condition was being unraveled.

On June 28, 1999, the Enron board of directors had a special meeting to approve the splitting of Enron stock. During the hour-long meeting, the board also heard a proposal from Andy Fastow to create a special-purpose vehicle (LJM1) whose purpose was to move Enron's debt off the financial statements. Fastow disclosed that he would serve as the general partner and would also receive management fees. In order to approve Fastow's role within the partnership, the board would need to waive Enron's Code of Conduct.

So they did.

When the board met again at the Four Seasons Hotel in October, and approved LJM2 following Winokur's recommendation, they were again agreeing to put aside Enron's Code of Conduct. Part of that agreement to allow these Fastow-controlled entities was a promise to have an annual review of their transactions. Such a review would be conducted by the audit committee.

The first of such reviews came in February 2000. At that meeting, Enron's chief accounting officer, Richard Causey, told the committee that, in his opinion, the transactions were proper and negotiated at "arm's length."

And so LJM1 and LJM2 continued to spin a wicked web of transactions. The devastating billion-dollar loss that Enron posted on October 16, 2001, was substantially linked to LJM2; the crushing earnings restatement in mid-November 2001 was tied to LJM1 and Chewco (another partnership, run by Michael Kopper).

The half-dozen Enron employees who participated in the LJMs and Chewco made significant amounts of money from the deals, including Fastow making at least $30 million and Kopper making at least $10 million.

The accounting rules were stretched and broken, the details of

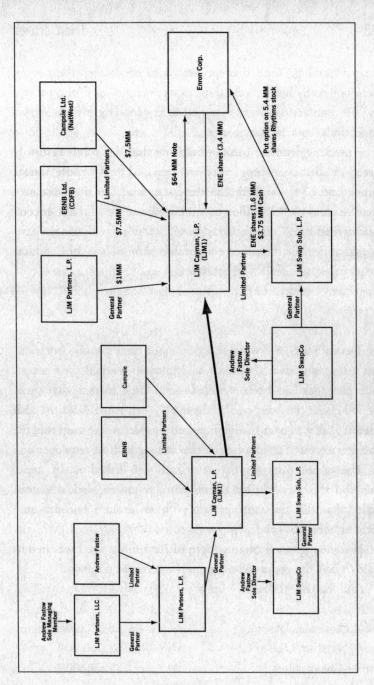

Structure of LJM1 (left) and structure of an LJM transaction (right) —from the Powers report

the partnerships were misrepresented to the board, the hedges were not really hedges (the third party was just an Enron party), and the transactions were designed to improve the results shown on Enron's financial statements.

Anyone defending Enron would say that the rules were followed and that everything Enron was required to put in the Annual Report and 10-K was there for everyone to read. The line items *were* there, such as the $20 billion in liabilities listed for Enron's "unconsolidated affiliates," shown in the year 2000 filing with the SEC.

What the line items never accurately showed was the complex structure of the deals—structures that led to Enron's cascade of repayments, structures that were ticking like a time bomb.

On December 6, the word was out about the retention bonuses. Just a few long days after laid-off employees learned their severance packages had been canceled—and after hearing that their $4,500 check (less tax) was "in the mail"—we heard about the $55 million that was paid to five hundred people before bankruptcy. The news created an absolute uproar among laid-off employees.

The so-called stay-on payments had been dished out by some uninhibited jackass who sat around one day and decided "who gets what." Was this the same person who sat around one day and decided "who stays and who goes"?

No one expected these people to turn down the money; but again, who's the genius who came up with these numbers?

And for *just 90 days*!

Lavorato, John	$5,000,000
Kitchen, Louise	$2,000,000
Fallon, James	$1,500,000

McMahon, Jeffrey	$1,500,000
Bowen, Raymond Jr.	$750,000
Haedicke, Mark	$750,000
Hickerson, Gary	$700,000
Colwell, Wesley	$600,000
DiMichele, Richard	$600,000
Hughes, James	$500,000
Nowlan, John Jr.	$500,000
Hayslett, Roderick	$400,000
Maxey, R. Davis	$400,000
McClellan, George	$400,000
Muller, Mark	$400,000
Piper, Gregory	$400,000
Racicot, Paul Jr.	$400,000
Butts, Robert	$375,000
Rogers, Rex	$375,000
Beck, Sally	$350,000
Gonzales, Eric	$350,000
Seeligson, Stewart	$350,000
Bradford, William	$300,000
Dietrich, Janet	$300,000
Faldyn, Rodney	$300,000
Hermann, Robert	$300,000
Joyce, Mary	$300,000
Leff, Daniel	$300,000
McGowan, Kevin	$300,000
Rieker, Paula	$300,000
Schuler, W.	$300,000
Tawney, Mark	$300,000
Walls, Robert Jr.	$300,000
Webb, Jay	$300,000

• • •

Some people who received retention bonuses would later say the money wasn't necessary—that they would have stayed at Enron without it. Some friends of mine who remained at Enron, but did not get retention money, were lied to by their bosses: "They told us they didn't get bonuses; that they got nothing just like the rest of us. Later, when the list showed up on the Internet, we saw that they had lied to us." "We ended up calling special meetings to ask them, 'What the fuck!' "

Enron spokesman Mark Palmer, who only got a wimpy $200,000 for his ninety days of continued employment, told the media, "To protect and maintain the value of the estate, we wanted to retain key employees in critical business." Okay, Mark—I have to ask one more time—if an entire line of business is eliminated (for being non-core or noncritical), then why would some employees from that group be paid as "key" to protecting the "value of the estate?"

Just three days after bankruptcy, the stock closed above $1.00 and even peaked at $1.26. If I had just bought ENE stock at $0.30 right before the layoffs, I could have *quadrupled* my money! In any case, we couldn't figure out who was buying the stock. Why was the price going up?

After a few days of misery, I decided to start job searching.

Fortunately, I had my new computer, compliments of the Enron Click-At-Home program, to get me started. I put my résumé up on Monster.com, and sent out a few e-mails. I followed up with the headhunters and corporate recruiters I knew. But with the holidays approaching, and with corporate budget approvals waiting until January, the job market just flat sucked.

I paid a visit to Odd Todd again, just to see if he could recommend a good soap opera. I was having trouble deciding between *Guiding Light* and *All My Children,* and I knew my brain simply didn't have the capacity to follow them both. Odd Todd didn't have a recommendation on soaps, but he did recommend Gold Toe socks.

I then went to the 1400smith.com website, which offered me a good summary of news headlines, useful links, and a way to reach other ex-Enronians. They were officially calling us Enron Alumni at that point, which I decided was pretty pathetic. We didn't graduate! We weren't proud of our association with the Crooked E.

It dawned on me that I might have e-mails sitting out in cyberspace, lost after being sent to my Enron e-mail address. I went to the Enron server on the Web and was able to log in and check my messages. It was easy—just like I was never really fired. I figured they just needed a few days to delete my account.

The most interesting e-mail was from the Office of the Chairman. Such e-mails once had names attached to them, like Ken Lay or Jeff Skilling—but not this one. There was no name, as if the computers had taken over and were shutting down life-support.

——Original Message——
From: Enron Office Of The Chairman
Sent: Fri 12/7/2001 3:10 PM
To: DL-GA-all_enron_worldwide1
Subject: Update
To Enron Employees:

We want to take this opportunity to update all current employees of our ongoing plans for bringing our company out of bankruptcy.

First, to be clear, there are valuable businesses at Enron. We intend to restructure the company and emerge from Chapter 11 as a healthy, albeit smaller, company.

In evaluating each Enron business or asset, we have been asking ourselves two key questions: "Is the business or asset more valuable to the creditors as a going concern that generates positive cash flow, or is it more valuable being sold and turned into cash?"

We have completed our preliminary analysis and have concluded that the majority of the U.S. assets are more valuable as a going concern. These include pipelines, power stations, and oil and gas properties to name a few. Many of our emerging market assets are not generating adequate cash and, thus, may be more valuable being sold and turned into cash.

The wholesale trading operation is clearly only valuable with a strong balance sheet behind it. Unfortunately, Enron does not currently have a strong balance sheet. Therefore, we are negotiating a transaction whereby Enron would contribute this business to a third-party joint venture with a high credit rating while retaining a residual interest in its profit stream. We believe this is the best alternative to preserve the value of the wholesale business and maintain a cash flow for the remaining businesses of Enron.

We know that everyone is concerned about the recent retention payments made to certain employees. Let me try to explain our rationale. As you know, Enron is an intellectual capital business. Without key people, we go into liquidation. The wholesale natural gas and power business has been the most profitable business at Enron for the past several years. It was this business that Dynegy was most interested in acquiring. Therefore, in early November as the proposed merger was being negotiated, approximately 75 employees related to this business received retention bonuses. These retention bonuses were paid to employees that were essential to the ultimate success of the merger.

Last week, we took the additional step, related specifically to our bankruptcy filing, of offering payments to approximately 500 employees who are critical to operate our company. These payments came with the condition that the employees receiving such payments stay employed at Enron for a period of at least 90 days. Seventy-five percent of employees who received these payments were below the vice president level. The payments must be repaid, with a significant penalty, if the employee leaves the company early. With these people in place, these businesses have substantially greater value, which will enhance our ability to pay creditors and provide the greatest benefit to all of Enron stakeholders.

The next step will be for us to work with creditors to agree to a retention plan strategy for the remaining employees. The goal is for this program to provide you with an incentive for you to stay with us while we work our way out of Chapter II. We also intend to see if we can work with creditors to develop more generous severance for current employees who involuntarily lose their jobs in the future.

This is an extraordinarily difficult time for all of us at Enron. With the constraints of bankruptcy and the deluge of reports from the media, it is difficult for any employee to feel certain of our situation. However, our previous and near-term actions are intended to preserve as much of the value of our businesses as possible so that we remain a viable company both in the short and long term.

Thank you for your patience, your understanding and your continuing hard work and contributions.

Office of the Chairman

I read the damn thing four times. The e-mail referred to retention "incentives" for remaining employees, plus "more generous" severance for employees laid off in the future. As for those forty-five hundred of us laid off the week before, all we heard was, "It's in the hands of the bankruptcy court. We can't help you."

As I was forwarding the e-mail to McLainey, Duffy, Perry, and a few dozen other ex-Enronians, an instant message popped up from Carrie Mills at Arthur Andersen.

carriemills: hey—you okay?
briancruver: never been better
carriemills: this place is nuts right now, everyone is freaking
briancruver: my place is nuts too, the dog and cat are freaking
carriemills: ha! at least you still have a sense of humor
briancruver: barely
carriemills: let me know if i can do anything, and send me your resume
briancruver: thanks, really i just want the weird dreams to stop
carriemills: oooh! i love that stuff, and my mom is an expert—details please?

Despite my better judgment, I told Carrie all about the floods, the sushi, the Enron execs in the Santa suits, the amputated hand, and the polar bears. Our IM session ended with her promise to get back to me.

An hour later she sent me an e-mail, summarizing what my subconscious was trying to tell me.

Polar Bear—Due to its color, a polar bear in a dream is a good omen signifying an improvement in your circumstances.

Okay, so the bear was trying to tell me I was better off without Enron.

Eating Tako (Octopus)—If you are eating an octopus, you have recently put a period of romantic turmoil behind you.

Octopus was my least favorite sushi item. But in this case, it was pointing out the fact that post-Enron, I would actually get to see my wife more than twice a week.

Santa Claus—This corpulent symbol of good cheer is a warning in disguise. Like the song says: "You better not pout, you better not cry." It's time to make a list and check it twice: You're about to get what's coming to you.

Fascinating.

Hand—A broken hand or the loss of a hand is a warning that you need to pay closer attention to your own personal affairs.

Fair enough.

Flood—If the flood was gentle and the water clear, your troubles will be short-lived. If the water was muddy and/or the flood a raging destructive force, you can expect to have to hoe a long hard row. If you were swept away in the flood, it is a warning that someone of the opposite sex whom you trust is actually trying to use you. If you escaped from the flood, you will be helped to overcome your obstacles.

So my flood was clear and gentle, and I escaped from it. Great! The unemployment thing was going to be a breeze.

What a load of crap.

Back in the real world, the blame game was heating up.

Congressional leaders were starting to chime in. In mid-December, the House Financial Services Committee opened its investigation. Ken Lay declined an invitation to appear before the committee, claiming he had Enron bankruptcy issues to deal with.

The SEC filed an action to get Fastow to produce documents and testimony under oath—as part of their investigation into Enron and Andersen's auditing procedures.

Rumors that Fastow had booked flights to Israel and rumors

that other executives were moving personal assets offshore began to stir up rage among plaintiffs' attorneys.

Fastow's attorney, Craig Smyser, responded to the reports. "He's here. . . . He is not going anywhere. . . . He was in my office. . . . He receives death threats. . . . It doesn't behoove him to be any more visible than he has to be."

The SEC itself came under fire from congressional leaders as well. The question was put to SEC chief accountant Robert Herdman why the dumping of Enron executives' stock didn't raise a red flag in the early part of 2001.

Meanwhile, Andersen CEO Joseph Berardino told the House committee that it was Enron executives who misled his accounting firm. "Important information was not revealed to our team," he said. The mistake Berardino did admit to—leaving LJM1 off the consolidated financial statements—was described by Berardino as an error that "did not cause Enron's collapse" and was "a very small item relative to total assets and equity."

Others bashed Andersen, saying it had failed to stand up to its client, in hopes of keeping its largest Houston account.

Berardino explained that Enron "was not a simple company to audit." Enron paid Berardino's firm $52 million in fees in 2000, which demonstrates how "not simple" the audit must have been.

Anatomy of an Enron Partnership—Part II

Like a lot of people, I keep a list.

It's a list of all the things I want to experience—at least once—before I die. Most of it is pretty standard: places to travel, things to learn, books to read, books to write, etc.

Nowhere on my list is anything *even close* to going on a hunting trip. But December 2001 was a special time. I felt like shooting something.

Mind you, I'm the type of guy who runs his car off the road just to avoid hitting a little birdie drinking from a puddle.

So, I didn't *really* want to shoot an animal—especially not a Disney character like Donald Duck. But the in-laws were comin' to town, and they were bringing their shotguns. I decided to go along on my first-ever hunting trip. The target: millions of ducks and geese flapping around Southeast Texas.

By the time the trip was organized, it included nine heavily armed, well-camouflaged males (seven family members, two hunting guides). We headed out into a pitch-black field at 4:00 A.M. The temperature was hovering at zero degrees, and the field was covered in twenty inches of water. My entire body was completely numb after five minutes, with only ten more hours to go.

The nine of us—two experienced hunters and seven clueless idiots—were lined up on our backs, each in our own floating plastic tub. As the sun started to come up, the moment came when several thousands ducks and geese were flying above us.

"Git 'em, boys," the guides screamed without warning.

With a thick mass of thousands of birds overhead, all nine shotguns blasted off three or four rounds each, with each round containing dozens of steel pellets . . .

. . . and not so much as a feather fell from the sky.

"We suck," I said to the group. Everyone agreed, and we discussed ordering a pizza instead. It would be a while before another duck came by.

Just as icicles were starting to form under my nostrils, my brother-in-law asked me a question. "So what exactly is all this off–balance sheet stuff?"

"Are you serious? We're duck hunting right now."

He laughed. "No, really. It's all I hear about in the news, but nobody ever explains it."

"That's because no one has the *patience* to explain it." At that moment, with my ass frozen to my plastic tub, I realized we had nothing but time. "Okay, let me think of an example . . .

"Let's say you need a personal loan of $100,000, but your credit is borderline problematic and you're worried about how the loan will affect your credit report. You want the loan so you can pay bills, buy Christmas presents, and install a new sprinkler system—but going straight to a bank is not the best option."

He cut me off. "I don't need a sprinkler syst . . . "

"Shut up. Instead of getting the loan yourself, you create a new legal entity to get the loan for you." Just then, a duck flying toward us saw nine people sitting in plastic tubs and reversed direction. "Let's call that new entity 'Mallard.'"

"That's it? I just decide I want to create Mallard to get a loan for me?"

I sneezed, clearing my nostrils of icy mucus.

"Not quite done yet. In order to create Mallard and have it be considered separate from you, you'll need to get some outside investors to put money into it—at least three percent of the total funding. You need three percent because that's the rule created by FASB [Financial Accounting Standards Board]."

"Okay. Will you do it?" He was starting to like the idea.

"Sure—but only because it's imaginary," I responded as my plastic tub started taking on cold water. "So I put three thousand dollars into Mallard for you, which allows Mallard to get another ninety-seven thousand dollars from a bank. Mallard agrees to pay back the bank loan, and your own credit report doesn't even show that Mallard exists."

"Sort of like when I was sixteen and needed someone else to buy me beer?"

I was surprised at the accuracy of his analogy. "Right."

"So that's it? I take the money from Mallard?" He was starting to get it, except that I wasn't even close to finished.

"You don't just *take* it . . . you need to sell something. How about the furniture in your house?"

He disagreed. "I can't just get rid of . . . "

"No no no . . . just because you sell it to Mallard doesn't mean it leaves your house. You will still have all of your furniture, you just won't own it." I could see a smile appear on his face.

"So how much do I sell it for?"

"Well, since you control both sides of the deal . . . sell it to Mallard for one hundred thousand dollars." I started to wonder who owned Andy Fastow's furniture.

The hunting guides then told half of us to walk over to another area. Our group was splitting up, but my brother-in-law and I stayed together to continue our conversation.

"But everything in my house isn't worth half of that," he said as we both slung our shotguns over our shoulders.

"Exactly . . . you are selling assets to Mallard at whatever price you want. In fact, that's why you are doing this deal with an entity you're in control of—you get to name your price . . . and as the guy who put in three thousand dollars, I don't care."

"Why wouldn't you care—you're getting ripped off." We both knelt down behind a large blade of grass, as if it could serve as a duck blind.

"I'm willing to risk my three thousand dollars on any kind of deal because you backed up my investment with your entire house. If the deal works out, you repay the loan to the bank, and you fulfill a promise to me to *buy back* the furniture—for a price of nine thousand dollars, tripling my initial investment."

He squinted and asked, "Wait . . . where do I get the money to pay the bank and buy back the assets?"

"Easy. To get *that* money, you'll need to set up Mallard II with someone else."

A lightbulb came on, just above his head.

He was starting to get the picture. "So that's what Enron was doing that caused all this trouble?"

"Well, maybe in a very simplified nutshell. There were actually thousands of these deals, each slightly different in size and shape and timing. The interesting thing is, almost all of it was perfectly legal and followed the accounting rules just fine. The problems began when Enron's own people started putting their own money into the deals, seeking personal profits."

He jumped in, "Like if I was to put the three thousand dollars into Mallard myself."

"Right, and the other problem was that some Enron entities fell below that three percent threshold of outside investment needed for them to be considered 'non-Enron.' "

"Because if Mallard isn't really a separate entity from me, then the debt that Mallard has should show up as my responsibility." He had a grin on his face.

"Exactly. This is exactly the kind of deal you're going to hear about in the news for the next ten years. Names like Raptor, JEDI, Chewco, Southampton . . . "

I was interrupted by a shotgun blast from fifty yards away. We heard a whizzing sound go by and were all transfixed.

"Holy shit!" My brother-in-law was referring to the fact that steel pellets had just missed our small group.

Missed everyone except me, that is.

The stinging in my left hand was colossal. The pain traveled up my arm and into my brain, causing me to open my mouth without actually emitting a sound. I had been hit by a steel shotgun pellet, and my hand instantly started to change colors and ooze fleshy goop from a growing welt.

I later learned that the guide in the other group was shooting at a duck in the water; without realizing our group was in front of him. The guide—the experienced professional who was leading us on this manly expedition—had just shot me.

From the warning on a box of shotgun shells:

> *To avoid serious injury / death to shooter and bystanders . . . Keep firearm pointed in a safe direction at all times. Do NOT shoot at hard surfaces or water, to prevent ricochet . . . we disclaim all liability for damage, injury, or death that may result.*

The waiting area for Dr. Muckenberger's office was *absolutely packed*. When it was finally my turn, he addressed the group, "Mr. Cru-vay?" I stepped up, around, and into his office. I decided to sit in a different chair. I was tired of looking at the Monet.

I decided it was my $100 per hour, so I would run this meeting, "So, it looks like you are pretty busy these days?"

Dr. Muckenberger responded, "Yes, well, with the holidays . . . and with the Enron thing . . . it's been a great month for me."

"You know, I worked for Enron, too . . . and I got laid off." As I said it, he flipped through his notes to find my information.

"Ahh," he looked up at me, "and how is that going?"

"Like I said, I got laid off."

"So what are you feeling abou . . . "

"I also turned thirty years old . . . and I got shot." Again, I decided this was my meeting; plus, I sort of enjoyed interrupting him. "All of this in a matter of weeks."

He responded, "That's a lot to deal with. Do you suppo . . . "

"The crazy thing is I feel better than ever. It's like the pressure is off, I'm sleeping better, I have more time to spend with my wife, I can watch *Oprah* now . . . " I thought back to the dream I had on layoff day, " . . . and the polar bear is telling me that everything is going to work out better than before."

"Hmm . . . Polar bear . . ." He pulled out his prescription pad and started to write.

"Oh, I'm sorry," I said, looking at my watch. "We've run out of time."

That was my last visit to Dr. Muckenberger.

9

Laid Off, Laid On

"May the forces of evil become confused on the way to your house."
—*George Carlin*

With the holidays approaching, the plan was to have job interviews lined up for the new year. My résumé needed to be polished, my suits needed to be dry-cleaned, and I needed to come up with the best way to spin my Enron situation.

The first test of the new job search: an Enron-sponsored job fair on December 14. The job fair would be at the baseball stadium, which was still hanging on to the name Enron Field.

Meanwhile, McLainey and Duffy and I were pushing the potential buyers of our business. While they worked with consulting firms and other interested companies, I was hitting up venture-capital firms.

I made contact with several, and three were really interested. Normally it would take a miracle to get a quick meeting with a VC firm, but I had something going for me: I had a piece of Enron. With all of the negative, scandalous outrage swirling over the Enron hype machine, there were still some who saw the Enron mess as an opportunity. Enron had collapsed into thousands of pieces, and some of those pieces still had untapped value. For post-Enron opportunists, the trick was sorting through that pile, finding the right pieces, and acquiring them at a deep discount.

The VC firms cut right through the standard procedure for submitting business plans and were willing to meet with us on short notice after just a few phone calls. McLainey and Duffy and I were keeping each other in the loop on our different fronts. We were all cautiously optimistic that our business plan would lead to new jobs and new income. This was kind of important, since we were all left without severance and we were starting to burn through our personal savings.

I had been watching the 1400smith.com message boards for information about the $4,500 checks from Enron—and some people were saying that they had received the payment. According to those ex-employees, the payments had been sent by mail and included termination forms—but nothing showed up in my mailbox. I was getting nervous.

The night before the Enron Field job fair, I checked my bank balance. There it was—an automatic deposit. I called my wife to tell her the good news: that Enron had sent me my $4,500 bankruptcy payment . . .

. . . only the deposit didn't add up. The math was just wrong, and the check hadn't come by mail. Even with extreme assumptions about tax deductions and extra money for vacation days, there was *no way* the payment was . . .

Holy cow! This is a paycheck!!

My mind was racing. Somehow the bankruptcy gods were smiling down on me. Enron—caught up in a blender of lawsuits and layoffs—had accidentally left me on the payroll.

I called Liz Perry.

"Did you get your forty-five hundred dollars yet?"

"No!" She answered like she had been pulling her hair out over it.

"Do me a favor—check your bank balance and call me back."

Liz confirmed it. She had received an automatic deposit in her bank account as well. But without paperwork attached to it (like a pay stub or a letter), we were only guessing about what this money was.

We agreed that the approach to take, until we had more information, was to just shut up about it.

Enron Field was only two years old. As an Astros season-ticket holder, I had the place memorized. The sparkling new stadium was a perfect venue for baseball fans: a variety of hot dog toppings, beer vendors every few feet, a home-run-friendly playing field, and a retractable roof for the muggy days of summer.

But on December 14, it was the site of the Enron Death March.

The scene was outrageous. Thousands of recently fired Enronians, all dressed up with no job to go to. We piled into the ballpark like eager fans on opening day. Outside the stadium, the circus was fully operational: news vans, camera crews, helicopters, and even a small airplane towing an advertising banner for Jack Daniels.

An ex-employee, John Allario, was selling T-shirts to mark the occasion of the world's leading bankruptcy:

"Thanks—Ken, Jeff & Andy"

"I Got Lay'd by Enron"

"The Execs that Stole Christmas"

"My Boss Got a Retention Bonus, All I Got Was This T-Shirt"

John's goal—according to his website, Laydoff.com—was to become "The World's Leading Active AngryWear T-Shirt Company." That same day on CNBC's morning *Squawk Box* program, David Faber and others held up Allario's T-shirts and plugged his website.

At the entrance to the stadium, news crews were pissed that they couldn't get in. Enron welcomed the media attention outside the stadium but wouldn't let the cameras inside. On my way in, a TV news guy asked me, "C'mon, how 'bout an interview?"

No thanks—the last thing I wanted was to be on TV.

Inside Enron Field, the job fair was a joke. About a hundred companies were there to show their sympathy and support for the community (and were probably pissed that the news crews were being kept out). In conversation, many of the companies with booths admitted that they weren't planning to hire anyone. Some companies, in the midst of layoffs themselves, just offered a smile and said "b-bye" with the sincerity of an airline flight attendant. A large percentage of them told me to submit a résumé on their website, to which I thought, "Gee, I could have done that from home."

The Enron-sponsored job fair was an unbelievable waste of time. It looked and smelled like a corporate PR stunt.

There was a bright spot, though: the day turned into a reunion. Layoff day earlier that month had happened so fast that we really didn't get a chance to say good-bye to anyone. I ran into several Enron colleagues and friends at the job fair, including McLainey and Liz Perry.

"This sucks."

McLainey agreed, and we both looked at Liz.

"I got one job lead, I *think*," she responded.

"I say we get out of here," McLainey said as we veered toward the exit. "Let's go grab a beer."

The bar across the street from the stadium was *packed*. It was the center of the reunion for the Enron alums (although many people at the job fair were still working at Enron, and some others had *never* worked at Enron). People were exchanging stories, trading job leads, and getting hammered. The bar was quickly becoming a much more useful place to be than the inside of the stadium.

McLainey, Perry, and I nabbed a table by the sidewalk. The bar was partially outdoors, and our table faced the streets filled with news crews and T-shirt buyers.

The Jack Daniels plane flew over again; the three of us laughed.

"So Greg, did you get your $4,500 check from Enron yet?"

"Yep . . . I called my bank this morning and it was there." He wasn't that happy about it. It was a slap in the face for everyone, but more so for him. Considering his salary and his extensive two-year career at Enron, he was getting screwed out of a *huge* severance payment.

"Did you get any paperwork with it? Any notice that you were laid off, or an explanation of the deductions?" I was trying to get him to draw his own conclusion, secretly hoping it would be the same conclusion I had drawn.

He answered, "No . . . no, but Enron could take weeks or months on that."

With Liz looking at me like I was still a bit nutty, I somehow got the three of us to discuss the details of the payment amounts. Sure enough, we had received different sums of money the night before. Although we didn't know what one another's salaries were, the differences seemed pretty clear. This was definitely *not* the $4,500 bankruptcy payment.

Once again, the Jack Daniels plane flew by.

I looked at them both, and then looked to see if anyone at the bar was listening. I whispered, "*I can't believe it! Those assholes left us on the payroll.*" McLainey was stunned as he realized it must be true. Liz still had her doubts. But it made sense. We were all shocked, and didn't know what to say.

Everything added up nicely: We had access to e-mail, our Enron mobile phones were still working, and on the night before the mid-month payroll, our direct deposit paychecks had shown up.

And we agreed there was only one thing to do: We decided to just shut up about it.

With political eyes slowly turning toward Houston, the investigations into Enron started to heat up. In addition to the lawsuits filed by shareholders, creditors, and Dynegy, Enron had instantly become the subject of eleven federal government inquiries:

In the U.S. House of Representatives:

The Education and Workforce Committee—Looking into the laws that control (or fail to control) employee stock and 401(k) plans

The Energy and Commerce Committee—Focused on investigating the implosion of Enron's financial condition, with a special bone to pick about the destruction of evidence (shredding of documents)

The Financial Services Committee—Targeting Arthur Andersen and the accounting goofs

In the U.S. Senate:

The Banking, Housing, and Urban Affairs Committee—Examining the problems facing the investment community, including flaws in the accounting system and the lack of safeguards for investors

The Commerce Committee, Consumer Affairs Subcommittee—Looking at Enron retirement funds . . . with a magnifying glass

The Energy and Natural Resources Committee—Reviewing the effects of Enron's bankruptcy on the energy industry as

a whole; in about two years, the committee will likely con-
clude that the industry was set back about two years

The Finance Committee—Has Enron been abiding by tax
laws? Of course it has—the tax laws of the Cayman Islands

The Governmental Affairs Committee—Enron's influence on
the Bush administration energy policy; this has nothing to
do with the actual collapse of Enron—but, hey! everyone
else gets to do an investigation

The Governmental Affairs Investigations Subcommittee—Who
knew what, when did they know it, and what exactly they
didn't do about it . . . and why

Federal Agencies:

The Department of Justice—A criminal investigation that
includes the Federal Bureau of Investigation (FBI) and
U.S. attorneys from coast to coast

The Department of Labor—The same thing as the Senate
Commerce Committee

The Securities and Exchange Commission—"We are actively
and aggressively investigating the entire situation and its
ramifications on future regulatory actions. We are also
examining how we can improve our current disclosure and
accounting systems to make disclosures more meaningful
and intelligible to average investors."

Fortunately for me, there was no government agency or congressional committee looking into Enron employees who had
accidentally been left on the payroll, at least not yet.

I decided to stick to the "just shut up about it" plan as best I
could (which would get harder and harder the longer they kept
paying me). Justification for accepting the payments was easy—

"Enron owes me!" I even calculated the exact amount that Enron owed me. That amount included the standard severance plan, plus the agreement not to sue Enron, plus the vacation days I had saved up. I then deducted each paycheck as I got it. At the suggestion of my wife and the advice of my attorney, I planned to notify Enron when the accidental payments eventually added up to the amount of my claim.

Oh yeah, my claim. As long as Enron was still paying me, I deferred submitting a bankruptcy claim form to the court in New York. Employees who were left without severance money, or lost their deferred compensation money, became unsecured creditors along with everyone else who was stiffed by Enron. This means that individuals were left with no option but to file with the bankruptcy court just like Dynegy, the big banks, Enron suppliers, and any other company that Enron owed money to.

The Enron website was generous enough to provide the forms that people needed. I also looked at the list of Enron's largest unsecured claims—claims that the screwed employees would be filing in competition against. Citibank loans added up to $3 billion, although a spokesman for Citibank indicated that much of this amount had been syndicated (passed on) to other banks. Chase Manhattan had a big fat note on the list for more than $1.9 billion, and Bank of New York (which in reality was serving as a trustee for bondholders) showed more than $2.4 billion. These were some pretty big numbers compared to the severance-related claims of an employee, which might have averaged in the tens of thousands of dollars.

And it was the big banks that got behind a fight to keep the case in New York, where only three hundred of Enron's creditors (compared to twenty-two hundred in Texas) were located.

The severance claims were one thing, but the deferred

compensation plans were a much *bigger* thing. About four hundred senior Enron employees built up nearly $400 million in deferred compensation, which had turned out to be just another losing bet on Enron. For most of these employees, the deferred comp plan represented a blissful retirement, but they suddenly found themselves in line with the rest of the unsecured creditors, looking to grab a piece of what was left of Enron.

The plan was to meet McLainey and Duffy at the burrito place across from the Death Star, where we could grab lunch and go over our notes before meeting with the venture-capital firm nearby. I drove downtown, falling into my old pattern, and it wasn't until I reached Enron headquarters that it suddenly hit me: "Oh shit, where am I going to park!?"

Just as that revelation hit me, habit led me to the Enron parking garage, where I hadn't parked since the day I was canned. My Enron remote was still on my windshield, so I decided to give it a shot.

Bingo! It was as if I had never left. My e-mail, my mobile phone, my voice mail, the paychecks . . . and now parking privileges.

The Enron garage welcomed me with open gates, and I even nabbed a prime space on the first level, the "Bold" level. It was a truly amazing parking experience that I would remember for a lifetime.

Then I got out of my car, realizing that the garage was *half empty*. Suddenly, getting a "Bold" parking space wasn't so special anymore. Believe it or not, when a company gets rid of 60 percent of the people in the building, there aren't as many cars in the lot.

I entered the burrito place, still grinning about my unexpected garage access. After passing through the burrito line, I sat down with the two former Enron directors. McLainey and Duffy had arrived early.

"So, did you guys park in the Enron garage?" I asked with a smirk.

"Are you serious?" was the instant reaction from Duffy, while McLainey didn't seem at all surprised. Duffy continued, "How the hell did you pull that off?"

"I just figured since I'm still on the payroll . . . " I said it in a matter-of-fact way, thinking we had all figured it out by then.

"WHAT!" Duffy spun to look at McLainey, who still had no reaction. McLainey and I both sat expressionless as we realized Duffy was out of the loop. Somehow he had been excluded from the TV sitcom goof that the rest of us had been enjoying for the previous few weeks.

Duffy always seemed laid-back, in high spirits, and curiously content. I had never, *ever* seen him angry.

But now his face was turning beet-red, with steam blowing out of his ears.

McLainey finally spoke. "I guess you haven't figured it out yet: that direct deposit I got . . . it wasn't the $4,500. . . it was a paycheck."

Duffy turned to me, and I nodded. Then the pain spread across his forehead as he revealed the biggest career mistake he had ever made: "I didn't sign up for direct deposit."

Oops.

We tried to keep Duffy calm by discussing the situation logically. It made sense that he should be included in the accidental paycheck fun. After all, we worked in the same Enron group, fell into the same cost center, and had the same HR guy. In fact, everyone we knew of in our group had received their Enron paycheck . . .

. . . except for Duffy—the only person on the *entire planet* who decided not to sign up for direct-deposit.

We filled Duffy in on the situation, and then he explained the obvious process for getting his usual paychecks. It was the prehistoric way: Enron would put his paycheck in an envelope and mail it to . . .

" . . . to your house, *right?*" I said it with the word jackass barely held back on my tongue.

His voice switched to a low mumble. "No, to my desk!" Duffy was screwed.

McLainey and I both rolled back with a moan.

Duffy then attempted to defend himself. "Hey, look, I wasn't expecting to get fired and then keep getting paychecks!" He was making a good point, but still . . . *jackass.*

"You know," I said with a baiting tone, "if the parking remotes still work, and e-mail and voice-mail still work, then I'm sure your building access badge still works."

Then came one of those rare moments when you get to see a person change, in an instant, right before your very eyes. Duffy looked at me, face still red, and then looked at McLainey. He checked his watch. We had only fifteen minutes until our meeting with the VC firm. He would need to get through three layers of Enron security. He would need to do it in a hurry, and somehow seem calm and cool. It was risky. But he had no job, no severance package, a wife and two kids, a new house, *and two weeks' worth of a six-figure salary sitting in an envelope somewhere inside the Death Star.*

Without saying a word, Duffy stood up from his half-eaten burrito, walked outside, and headed across the street to the Enron building. McLainey and I watched as Duffy jaywalked across the honking traffic at a heedless pace. McLainey then sighed and said to me, "You know, he's about to fuck this up for all of us."

I agreed. But without him getting his money, it would have been impossible to get Duffy to agree to our "just shut up about it" strategy.

McLainey and I discussed the worst case: that Enron would do an automatic withdrawal of the money they had just deposited in our accounts. We agreed that it was a possibility and decided the money needed to be moved. McLainey called his wife to have her open a new account at a new bank immediately. I decided I would move mine using the Web that afternoon.

Then, after about ten minutes, Duffy returned to his cold, half-eaten burrito. He smiled and removed an envelope from his coat pocket. The angry Duffy was gone, and the Duffy we all knew had returned with a beautiful paycheck.

As we headed to the meeting with the VC firm, Duffy detailed his adventure:

As he approached the building, his confidence built up. If his badge didn't work, and the lights turned red, he wouldn't panic or run; he would just act confused and surprised. By the time he reached the main lobby, he was carrying himself like he owned the place.

The badge worked at the first checkpoint, which made check-points two and three a breeze. The Death Star was nearly empty, and when he reached our trading floor it was almost *completely* empty. He arrived at his old desk to find a layer of dust and some untouched piles of mail several feet high. He quietly sorted through the mail looking for paychecks. He didn't find anything.

As he was giving up and starting to feel sick, he decided to log in to his old computer and check e-mail and the Enron Intranet. It turned out to be a very wise move, because the first e-mail he read was from another employee telling him, "Hey, I have your paycheck."

He located the employee's desk, but no one was there. He thought about it for three seconds, and then looked around the trading floor to see if anyone was eyeing him. In a casual manner, Duffy began searching through the guy's desk drawers. Some of the drawers were locked, but he found a key. Finally, inside one of those locked drawers, Duffy found an envelope containing his paycheck.

Mission accomplished.

• • •

The same day Duffy was sneaking into the building for a paycheck he wasn't supposed to get, other Enron ex-workers were rallying in front of the Death Star. It was an event organized through the 1400smith.com website. About two hundred laid-off employees gathered in the grassy park across the street from Enron, as HPD officers on horseback watched in close proximity. Like all of the laid-off ex-Enronians, the group was insulted by the $4,500 payments—angered that the company suddenly dropped the severance policy that had been used for the previous fifteen years. The group signed a letter to Enron executives demanding answers to their questions.

Also nearby, the state of Texas had provided us with a taxpayer-funded program called The WorkSource. Using empty Enron office space—of which there was an endless supply—the center was made available to ex-Enronians and contract workers who needed new jobs. The center included computers, Web access, and top employers looking to interview Enron's abandoned talent.

For McLainey, Duffy, and me, the meeting with the VC firm went pretty well. They seemed genuinely interested in our ideas and our financial projections for the launch of our credit-risk business. On the flip side, they expected it would take several months to get funding lined up, and none of us could afford to wait that long. Venture capital firms like to invest in entrepreneurs that are willing to make sacrifices themselves, which was fine, except that we would have to live out of cardboard boxes while we waited for the initial funding.

After the meeting, the three of us went our separate ways. McLainey went home to make sure his new bank account was in place, Duffy went straight to his bank to deposit the newly discovered paycheck, and I decided to pay a visit to the Death Star.

Part of me did it just to see what it was like after bankruptcy; but most of all, I wanted to update my computer passwords. For security reasons, Enron passwords expire every sixty days—and they could not be updated from home. By changing my password from my desk, I would be able to continue tracking my Enron e-mail for another couple of months. McLainey gave me his old password and asked me to update his password as well.

I tried to do just as Duffy had described and cruised into the lobby like I owned the place. I nodded at my favorite security guard as I passed the main checkpoint—the badge worked fine. I took an empty elevator and had a reunion moment with the Building Guy, who was cracking his usual canned jokes. The place was like a ghost town, so I didn't think for a second that I would run into anyone I knew.

"Cruver?"

For a moment I considered not stopping, while acting as if he was confusing me with someone else. Then I realized it was a friend of mine from my old trading firm who was still stuck at Enron.

"Wow, I didn't realize you were still here," I said as we stopped in the middle of the Saturn Ring.

"Yeah, but I should be getting laid off in the next week or two."

"Cool," was my response, thinking that was good news. "What exactly have you been doing the last few weeks?" He was a financial genius in one of the power trading groups.

"Let's see," he said with a smile. "Lugging boxes around the building, watering plants, that kind of thing."

"Hmmm . . . good stuff for the old résumé."

"Oh, yeah."

We started to peel apart, indicating the conversation was ending; but I had to ask, "Retention bonus?"

"Nope."

"That sucks," I responded, although I would have completely

lost my chicken right then and there if "watering plants" had been deemed critical to preserving Enron's core business.

The conversation ended and I had avoided any questions about why I was there.

I arrived at my old desk and saw just what Duffy had described: a layer of dust and piles of mail. It was like a science-fiction movie in which everything human had been vaporized. My computer was still on, and I was still logged in to the system. My laptop computer was still sitting there. Nothing had been touched. Every desk in our old section of the trading floor was in the same frozen state. EnronOnline was completely deserted. The glass offices around the exterior were completely empty.

Only two things had changed about my desk: huge mountains of unopened mail (that Duffy had sorted through) and a uniformed Houston police officer sitting a few feet away. He was right next to Sherman the shredder.

And he was sound asleep.

He looked a bit like the cop who gave me the speeding ticket on Louisiana Street, but I wasn't about to wake him up and find out. I quietly went about my business, wondering if he had orders to shoot me on sight. Fortunately, with his arms tightly folded and his chin resting solidly on his chest, nothing could have interrupted his midday doughnut dream.

I updated my password and checked the Enron intranet. I went to my Internet bank accounts and started moving money around. I decided that I would drain the account each time Enron put a paycheck into it. I thought perhaps the Enron cybercops would detect my presence, but then I realized that the system would identify me as a current employee.

McLainey's password had already expired, so I couldn't help him. I sorted through the mail piles and found a few bills for my mobile phone and my Enron credit card—and decided to leave them there.

As I left I took one last look at the sleeping policeman. If only I had a blanket to cover him up.

I stopped by the men's restroom on my way out of the building.

How to Conquer Corporate America, Rule #9: If you're going to use the toilet stalls at work, don't wear shoes that other people may recognize.

I was quietly minding my own . . . uh-hum . . . business, when the guy next to me started talking. Was he talking to me? Was he talking on his mobile phone?

I was suddenly *very* uncomfortable as I realized he was talking *to himself*. Mr. Brown-Shoes-With-Blue-Jeans was talking about staying calm, trying to convince himself that he needed to relax—even as he was madly tapping his left foot at 1,000 tpm (taps per minute).

Now, in the thirty short years of my life, I have honestly *never* spoken to someone through a bathroom stall divider—it's just not something normal people do. But this was a special situation.

"Hey man, you okay?"

He suddenly stopped talking and his left foot stopped moving. Had he not seen me there? In any case, I was now Mr. Black-Shoes-With-Khaki-Pants, and I was asking him a question.

"I think I'm losing it," he said in between deep breaths. "My department had hundreds, now we have ten, and I'm one of only two that *didn't* get a retention bonus."

"Well you're getting a paycheck, right?"

He snapped back, *"Fuck the paycheck!"*

"Okay, then." It was time for me to flush and leave. "Hang in there. Good luck."

I speed-walked out of there. If this guy was about to go postal, a bathroom stall would be a bad place to hang out.

Just when the day couldn't get any stranger, I passed by a small conference room and accidentally caught a scene from *A Few Good Men*. That's right, the same movie that Mr. Blue told me was a favorite on the Enron corporate jet; and it was being acted out by a handful of jaded Enron employees. The only differences: their version of the movie was the Enron version, and Jack Nicholson wasn't playing his role of Colonel Nathan R. Jessep—he was playing ex-CEO Jeffrey K. Skilling.

A Few Good Enron Men
(adapted from the original Aaron Sorkin screenplay)

Lt. Daniel Kaffee (played by Tom Cruise, acting like Tom Cruise):
(continuing to address Jeff Skilling)
"Fastow ordered the code red, didn't he? Because that's what you told Fastow to do."
Capt. Jack Ross (played by Kevin Bacon, acting like Kevin Bacon):
"Object!"
Judge Randolph (played by J. A. Preston, acting like a judge):
"Counsel."
Kaffee will plow through the objections of Ross and the admonishments of Randolph.
Kaffee:
"And when it went bad, you cut Fastow and Kopper loose."
Ross:
"Your Honor—"
Randolph:
"That'll be all, counsel."
Kaffee:
"You refused to sign your name, but you knew *all about* these deals—"
Ross:
"Judge—"

Kaffee:

"You shredded the documents that showed you were involved."

Ross:

"Damnit Kaffee!!"

Kaffee:

"I'll ask for the fourth time. You ordered—"

Ex-CEO Jeff Skilling (played by Jack Nicholson, acting a lot like Jack Nicholson):

"You want answers?"

Kaffee:

"I think I'm entitled to them."

Skilling:

"You want answers?!"

Kaffee:

"I want the *truth.*"

Skilling:

"You can't handle the truth!"

And nobody moves.

Skilling:

(continuing)

"Son, we live in a world that has financial statements. And those financial statements have to be managed by men with superior intellect. Who's gonna do it? You? You, Lt. Weinberg? I have a greater responsibility than you can possibly fathom. You weep for shareholders and you curse the executives. You have that luxury. You have the luxury of not knowing what I know: That Enron's rise and fall, while tragic, poured trillions of dollars into the global economy. And my existence, while grotesque and incomprehensible to you, helped to create the modern markets."

(pause)

"You don't want the truth. Because deep down, in places you don't talk about at parties, you want me cooking the books. You *need me* cooking the books."

(boasting)

"We use words like respect, integrity, communication, excellence. We use these words as the backbone to a life spent creating Enron. You use 'em as a punch line."

(pause)

"I have neither the time nor the inclination to explain myself to a man who rises and sleeps under the blanket of the very energy industry I created, then questions the manner in which I created it. I'd prefer you just said thank you and went on your way. Otherwise, I suggest you pick up a dry-erase marker and design your own off-balance sheet partnership. Either way, I don't give a damn what you think you're entitled to."

Kaffee:

(quietly)

"Did you order the code red?"

Skilling:

(pause)

"I did the job Wall Street expected me to do."

Kaffee:

"Did you order the code red?"

Skilling:

(pause)

"You're goddamn right I did."

Silence. From everyone. Randolph, Ross, the M.P.s, they're all frozen. Demi Moore and Kevin Pollack are likewise. Skilling seems strangely, quietly relieved. Kaffee simply takes control of the room now.

Kaffee:

Please the court, I suggest the jury be dismissed so that we can move to an immediate Article 39a Session. The witness has rights.

Silence.

• • •

My continuing access to e-mail allowed me to see the following
internal update:

——Original Message——
From: Enron Office Of The Chairman
Sent: Tue 12/18/2001 5:11 PM
To: DL-GA-all_enron_worldwidel
Subject: Organizational Announcement

As things begin to calm down somewhat after events of last week,
we wanted to update all employees of certain organizational and personnel changes that have occurred recently.

Organizational Matters

The Creditors' Committee was formed last week by the United States
Trustee. This committee is comprised of 15 individuals representing various creditor groups including: banks, bondholders, insurance companies, and employees. The Creditors' Committee will be the key point of
contact as we reorganize the company and emerge from Chapter 11. Initially, they will send financial advisers to our offices to monitor any asset
liquidations as well as review our cash flow projections. Ultimately, they
will be responsible for approving our reorganization plan as to which
assets or businesses we sell and which ones we retain.

From an Enron perspective, the plans for reorganization have
already begun. Overhead has been reduced dramatically, certain
employee retention programs have been put in place, and a wider retention program is currently being developed. We hope to share the wider
retention program with you in the very near future. Furthermore,
detailed cash flow projections are in their final stages of preparation
and will be reviewed by senior management this week. This will be the
critical first step in formulating our reorganization strategy to emerge
from Chapter 11 as a healthy company.

By now, you must have heard of "NETCO." This company was

formed as a means to maximize the value of Enron's most valuable business, the wholesale energy business. Certain Enron North America employees have been assigned to NETCO to rebuild the North American gas and power business under different ownership. We will be filing with the bankruptcy court this week proposed auction procedures to allow bidders to bid for NETCO. It is our expectation that Enron would retain a 49 percent (or perhaps less) noncontrolling interest in NETCO. The NETCO employees would become employees of the winning bidder. We anticipate this process to reach closure sometime in January.

As for the remaining businesses of Enron, they are all under review as to which ones will be proposed for sale and which ones will be proposed for retention. This review process will take time as it will require approval of the Creditors' Committee. We will update you periodically on our process.

Personnel Matters

As a result of our current situation, we have made many personnel changes over the past several months to maximize the value of the organization.

Office of the Chairman—Enron Corp.

Jeff McMahon, Executive Vice President and Chief Financial Officer, has been added to the Office of the Chairman of Enron Corp. along with Ken Lay and Greg Whalley. Among other things, Jeff has been working on the business plan for reorganization in Chapter 11 and is the primary contact with the newly formed Creditor's Committee.

Treasurer—Enron Corp.

Ray Bowen was elected to Executive Vice President, Finance and Treasurer of Enron Corp. recently. In this role, Ray is responsible for all finance activities of Enron Corp. Ray also has the lead role in managing the cash activities of the company on a day-to-day basis.

Management Committee Departures

Unfortunately, due to the current financial condition of the company, the following members of the management committee have left the company or will be leaving the company by the end of December:

Michael Brown

Mark Frevert

Steve Kean

Mike McConnell

Jeff Shankman

Additionally, John Lavorato and Louise Kitchen have resigned from the Management Committee to arrange for the joint venture energy activities of NETCO.

We know as employees the uncertainty surrounding the future of the company is unsettling. Unfortunately, that aspect will not change in the near term. We ask for everyone's patience and continued support as we move forward through the Chapter 11 process. We are committed to reorganizing into a strong company once again and will need the help of all the employees to achieve that goal.

The five Management Committee members who were listed under "Departures" were each noticeably absent from the list of those who received retention bonuses. Lavorato and Kitchen, the two biggest beneficiaries of the retention bonuses, were being put in charge of NETCO.

The eventual winning bidder of the NETCO business was UBS Warburg, the same firm that was one of the last to downgrade ENE stock.

UBS bought the business from Enron for exactly $0 up front, with an agreement to pay Enron 33 percent of future profits from the operation. They leased two trading floors from Enron Center South and renamed the venture UBS Warburg Energy. Most of the group consisted of several hundred former Enron employees.

With the trading unit now in the hands of UBS, the hope of generating income for Enron creditors had shifted to the power plants and the pipes. Many were targeted to be sold off, but any assets that fetched a reliable cash flow would help creditors collect more Enron debt.

The Northern Natural Gas pipeline—all 16,500 miles of it—remained the central matter in the Enron-Dynegy merger failure litigation. Even if Enron lost that battle and gave up NNG, allowing Dynegy to take control of it, Enron would still be left with another 9,000 miles of pipe to operate and draw revenue from.

As the Enron reorganization continued, and as the dozen or so investigations were gaining traction, Ken Lay began to cut his losses. In addition to putting several real-estate properties up for sale, he resigned from his director positions at Compaq Computer Corp and Eli Lilly and Company. The resignation from the Compaq board of directors included a stock sale of 124,000 shares for about $1.2 million. Lay also cashed out when he left the board of Eli Lilly, with proceeds of more than $750,000. Lay had served on the pharmaceutical giant's board for nine years and was reported to have left "voluntarily" to focus on Enron issues. For both Compaq and Eli Lilly, Lay still held a significant number of shares (at the end of 2001)—about $3 million in each company.

On a related note: Eli Lilly is the company that makes the drug Prozac, an effective treatment for depression with over 40 million prescriptions worldwide. It's not quite as potent as crack, but it would be slightly easier for Mr. Lay to get his hands on.

Another e-mail was sent to all Enron employees, which I guess included me? Whatever. They're paying me, so I might as well read these things.

• • •

——Original Message——
From: Enron Office Of The Chairman
Sent: Thu 12/20/2001 3:52 PM
To: DL-GA-all_enron_worldwidel
Subject: Bankruptcy Management Committee

In an effort to better organize the activities and minimize the expenses related to the Chapter 11 filing, we have formed the Bankruptcy Management Committee. There are many outside firms representing multiple parties that will be requesting, among other things, certain tasks to be performed, filings with the bankruptcy court, financial analysis, and general business information. To ensure these activities are coordinated, the Bankruptcy Management Committee will now be responsible for overseeing this process. The following is a list of some of the parties that may contact you directly. If anyone from these firms, or other firms, contacts you related to the bankruptcy, please notify a member of the committee to ensure the efforts are coordinated. All outside firms will be requested to notify a member of the committee prior to contacting other Enron personnel or outside parties, including the court and Creditors' Committee.

Bankruptcy court (i.e., motions, etc.)
Creditors' Committee
U.S. Trustee
Ernst & Young—Accountants for the Creditor's Committee
Houlihan, Lokey, Howard & Zukin—Financial advisers for the Creditors' Committee
Blackstone—Financial advisers for Enron
Batchelder & Partners—Financial advisers for Enron
Weil, Gotshal & Manges—Bankruptcy attorneys for Enron
Milbank Tweed—Attorneys for the Creditors' Committee
Andrews & Kurth—Attorneys for Enron Corp.

• • •

Enron's "independent auditor," Arthur Andersen, and "outside" law firm, Vinson & Elkins—whose own actions in the Enron collapse were being examined—were conspicuously absent from the list.

Across the street from the Death Star, the New York Pizzeria was dealing with a 40 percent drop in lunchtime revenue. Other nearby restaurants, dentists, barbershops, and retailers were suffering as well. One economic researcher estimated that the Enron mess would cause more than six thousand jobs to be lost at other Enron-dependent companies.

Local charities that had always benefited from the generosity of Enron and its executives were also in deep trouble. Hospitals, museums, nature programs, disease research programs, and universities garnered several million dollars from Enron and its employees each year. Future years were looking bleak.

In 2000, the United Way received more than $5 million from Enron, including over $100,000 from Ken and Linda Lay. Enron also created a cancer prevention clinic at the M. D. Andersen Cancer Center to the tune of $2 million.

Enron money had sponsored numerous museum and theater programs—including the recent *Star Wars: Magic of Myth* exhibit—as part of more than $2 million given to the arts over the previous few years.

Houston's two major institutions of higher learning would also be taking a hit. More than $13 million had been given to Rice University and the University of Houston for libraries, education centers, and professorships. High schools had been provided $1.4 million for scholarships, and the Enron Kids program always donated thousands of dollars' worth of Christmas gifts to local elementary-school children.

Dozens of other organizations were losing their biggest donor. The YMCA (with a Ken Lay–named center funded by a $1 million

Enron grant), the Enron Boys and Girls Club, the Jewish Community Center, and the University of Texas Health Science Center reading program knew that the Enron collapse threatened their continued existence. Most of these organizations had already seen a drop in donations after the September 11 terrorist attacks.

At the end of 2001, Houston's small businesses and nonprofits were facing an enormous void due to the Enron bankruptcy, as well as the financial wounds dealt to Enron employees.

The Enron Field job fair yielded nothing, except for a few letters saying, "Thank you for stopping by our booth, wasting your time, and kissing my ass." The headhunters had far too many heads to disperse among just a handful of jobs, and the listings on Monster.com required ten years' experience in some new technology that had only existed for five years.

The good news for Enron employees in December was that we had endless sympathy from family, friends, and fellow Houstonians. Not that we wanted it or needed it, but it was nice to know that people didn't blame us—the average Enronians—for what had happened. I was bombarded with symbolic offers of financial assistance and contact information for possible jobs. More important, we were being viewed as victims of the culture, rather than designers of it—a distinction that spared us all a lot of personal trauma. We also felt the relief of shedding our Enron skin, as our time with the company moved farther into the past. "Enron" was gaining staggering momentum as the newest bad word, and we wanted no part of it. We were extremely lucky to break away from the lie, cheat, and steal stereotypes, especially considering the outbreak of twisted revelations about the Enron mentality. Aside from the big stories about the partnerships, overhyped businesses, and fraudulent accounting, the media microscope was bringing a number of wild Enron tales to the world's attention.

Most notorious was an incident in 1998, in which a visit from dozens of Wall Street analysts included a tour of a bogus trading floor. Ex-employees recall the maneuver as an attempt to fool analysts into thinking they were looking at a thriving Enron Energy Services operation, one that in reality did not exist. With Skilling, Lay, Lou Pai, and Tom White all in attendance, the analysts were brought through the trading floor, which included secretaries posing as traders, computers that weren't plugged in, and a system to track all of the deals in "real time." According to one former VP from EES, there were "less than two deals" actually done at the time; and according to other ex-EES employees, the list of potential customers was doctored and the people on the floor were urged to "look like they were putting deals together."

Enron had gone to extremes to create the perception that EES was a huge, thriving, profitable business by dumping hundreds of thousands of dollars into a ten-minute performance for the visiting analysts.

Bickers told me that when he heard the news of the fake trading operation, he came frighteningly close to pushing his desk through his thirtieth-floor window.

The world was also getting wind of the reality that surrounded mark-to-market accounting. The public was stunned to learn that long-term deals were booked however Enron wanted them to be booked (a reality that I and everyone else from Enron already knew about). To add clarity to the news, former Enron traders were starting to speak to the media. They confessed that they were continually pressured to meet targets and show "as much profit as possible." Surprise, surprise.

With unusual commodities, lacking standard measures and

regulations, being traded for such unusual periods of time, Enron was often the only source of a market price. Therefore, Enron had the freedom (and the talent) to book the trades at the *extreme edge* of what they could get away with. Arthur Andersen was responsible for overseeing the fairness aspect of these deals—booking them safely away from this *extreme edge,* and more toward middle-of-the-road conservativeness. But in reality, Arthur Andersen simply didn't have the market expertise to do this. *They didn't know the difference between pushing the limits and playing it safe.*

I also began to hear rumblings of a connection between Enron and Michael Milken. When I first heard about it, I quickly grabbed my copy of James Stewart's *Den of Thieves* off my bookshelf and found a reference to Enron in the 1991 book. The passage on page 158:

> *In April, Cecola [analyst at Lazard Freres, an investment bank] tipped Wilkis [investment banker at Lazard] that Houston Natural Gas had retained Lazard to handle a merger with Internorth [the deal that created Enron]. . . . Wilkis passed the information on to [Dennis] Levine, who again bought through Meier [a banker in the Bahamas], indiscreetly characterizing the as-yet-unannounced transaction as a "sure deal."*

The section revealed how the Enron deal in 1985 was actually part of one of the greatest insider-trading rings in Wall Street history. Milken and Levine, who headed up the notorious investment bank of Drexel Burnham Lambert in the '80s, both ended up in prison for these dirty deeds (Levine was sentenced to two years in 1987, Milken to ten years in 1990).

After the merger of Houston Natural Gas and InterNorth in the mid-'80s, Lay became a Milken client as well as a close friend. As a customer, Lay used Milken's advice in accumulating mountains of debt for the young Enron (the debt was a staggering 73 percent of its total long-term financing). As a friend, Lay would later compliment his ex-convict pal (in an interview with *The Economist*) as "innovative" and "aggressive." These were the same primary traits that Lay had firmly inculcated throughout his Enron culture, the same two traits that fed Enron's demise.

And the amassing of debt in the early days of Enron? Apparently Lay was starting an Enron tradition.

The year ended with another paycheck from Enron. This time there was no discussion about it with McLainey or Liz Perry—that wouldn't fit our "just shut-up about it" strategy. I called Cingular Wireless to switch my Enron mobile phone service into my own name, *but they wouldn't let me!* They forwarded me to a special customer service representative for ex-Enron employees, who told me that they couldn't do anything until arrangements were finalized with the bankruptcy court. I decided not to push it and made several expensive calls around the world. Since I was technically still an employee, I also had medical benefits intact, and it seemed like a great time to get some overdue dental work done. In addition, Enron was paying for my home Internet access (on my free Enron computer).

In exchange for all these perks as a fully employed laid-off person, I decided I would do my part as a highly productive employee—I checked my e-mail at least once a week.

——Original Message——
From: Enron Office Of The Chairman
Sent: Fri 1/4/2002 4:45 PM
To: DL-GA-all_enron_worldwidel
Subject: Northern Natural Gas

Yesterday, Enron settled a procedural dispute with Dynegy over Northern Natural Gas. Our settlement allows Dynegy to exercise its option to acquire the pipeline, dismisses their Texas lawsuit, and extends Enron's right to repurchase until June 30. We reached this settlement as part of our efforts to bring Enron out of bankruptcy. While we would like to keep Northern Natural, we still have some 9,000 miles of safe, profitable interstate pipelines as a base to rebuild our core businesses.

The settlement provides the best opportunity to resolve the pipeline issue quickly and pursue our $10 billion damage claim against Dynegy. It also allows us to avoid the very substantial costs and distractions from protracted litigation in state courts.

We want to see a positive future for the employees working with Northern Natural Gas.

Ken

10

The Enron Garage Sale

"It's good to shut up sometimes."
—*Marcel Marceau, world-renowned mime artist*

With the new year came a new angle on the Enron story. The news vans were no longer parked just in front of the Death Star, but in front of the White House in Washington, D.C. The Enron news was no longer limited to the business section—the Enron saga had become front-page political headlines; those looking to take shots at the Bush administration were happily licking their chops.

For those familiar with Enron's political ties, the Washington media blitz was a surprisingly delayed reaction. Enron, specifically Ken Lay, had been firmly attached to leaders of both state and federal administrations since the company's inception. Those attachments came in the form of campaign contributions, shared initiatives, the ownership of ENE stock, and executive positions at Enron.

At one not-so-extreme end of the spectrum was the call for a special prosecutor, as well as a push to label the scandal Enrongate. Some believed that there was no way the Department of Justice could conduct an independent and thorough investigation of Enron—not when the Bush administration seemed "indistinguishable" from the Enron top brass.

From 1993 to 2000, more than $550,000 was given to George W. Bush by Enron and Ken Lay, making Bush their top political recipient.

Beyond Enron, the firms Arthur Andersen and Vinson & Elkins gave Bush another $560,000 combined for his gubernatorial and presidential campaigns; this included Andersen managing partner D. Stephen Goddard Jr., one of the Bush "Pioneer" fund-raisers who gave $100,000 or more. Goddard was put on leave by Andersen following the shredding scandal. The connection to Bush went well beyond contributions. His top advisers and associates, such as Karl Rove, Tom White, and James Baker, were linked to Enron as major shareholders, former executives, or former board members.

Bush and his staff took a number of steps to distance the administration from Enron. For one thing, they pointed to Lay's support of Texas democratic governor Ann Richards, before George W. Bush took the state house. They also pointed to contributions made across the country to *both* parties, which accurately reflected Enron's pursuit of favor and influence in the most lucrative markets. For example, over $430,000 went to California politicians, including $97,500 to Governor Gray Davis. In all, nearly $2 million had been spread across twenty-eight states since 1997 in a systematic manner. Enron even had a computer program to calculate the political cash flows: it was called the Matrix. As part of an operation based in Washington, the software was used to calculate business costs based on the quantitative elements of deregulation, such as lobbying costs, inflation, and growth factors. It was simply a cost-benefit analysis relating campaign contributions to pro-Enron legislation. Enron was playing the political money game as it related to the future of the energy industry, in the hopes it would pave the way to free-market bliss.

Anyone who insisted that Lay or Enron had a personal "bond" or overlapping interest with the Bush administration, or any other political entity, was stretching a bit. These were paper-thin relationships, linked only by egos, greed, and the price of a favor. In late 2001, the favor that Enron needed was quite simply out of reach, so expensive that even Enron couldn't afford it. As the company tumbled down the liquidity mountain, the government *could* have stepped in and backed Enron's debt. In late October 2001, the thought of a Chrysler-type bailout was hot on everyone's rumor list. But the Bush administration avoided political suicide, and when push came to shove, no favor was given. Ken Lay called Treasury secretary Paul O'Neill, Commerce secretary Donald Evans, and Federal Reserve chairman Alan Greenspan—all during the last two weeks of October—perhaps hoping for some prepaid support . . . *Not a chance.*

Enron's closest friend in Washington was Tom White, the former EES executive who had left in May to become Secretary of the Army. A few days after taking his new position in Washington, White gave a speech about how his experience at Enron would benefit the military: "I spent eleven years in corporate America with Enron Corporation, an energy company. . . . It is very, very clear to me that there is enormous potential to improve the basic business practices of this department." White made more than a dozen phone calls to Enron during that same crucial month of October 2001, the same month he sold nearly $3 million worth of Enron stock.

And when the Bush-whackers pointed angry fingers at Enron's key involvement in formulating the new administration's energy plan, the question was begged: "Why not?" At the time this was the world's leading energy company. Still, the pressure to release documents related to Dick Cheney's actions and the formation of the energy plan was intense. Meanwhile, the Bush team was compelled by court order to release eleven thousand pages of heavily redacted material from Energy secretary Spencer Abraham's department. The big scoop from that pile of paper was that Abraham had met with 109 energy industry leaders, practically ignoring consumer or environmental groups. Those same groups were overlooked when

Bush named his first two appointments to the Federal Energy Regulatory Commission (FERC), both of whom were on a list that Ken Lay submitted to the administration in January 2001.

So as the search for Enron dirt continued, that search seemed to get farther and farther away from the collapse of the company, while getting closer and closer to *anything else.* Investigators seemed willing to pursue whatever leads created problems for the Bush administration, and I immediately began to sense that politics would interfere with the search for relevant truths and meaningful reform.

How did the Whitewater investigation end up becoming a story about oral sex, anyway?

Which reminds me: Another countermeasure dropped on the inventors of Enrongate was the long history between Enron and the Clinton administration. Enron's staggering growth from 1993 to 2000 was aided by more than $1 billion in subsidized loans provided by the Clinton gang (compared to zero loans from the previous Bush and Reagan administrations). The loans were used to finance Enron's international power plant and pipeline projects. During those same Clinton years, Enron dumped more than $1 million into the Democratic Party, and Lay played in a golf foursome with Clinton, President Gerald Ford, and golf legend Jack Nicklaus.

When compared to flying around with George W. Bush on the Enron corporate jets, I would definitely choose the golf outing—Clinton wins.

Major news sources began fighting over the facts about Ken Lay's stay in the Lincoln Bedroom. Was it during the Clinton years? Was it during the Bush Sr. years? And who is feeding these falsehoods to the media? *Who cares?*

By turning their backs on Enron in 2001, and because of a well-documented history of Enron simply playing the favorite, the Bush White House was building up immunity to political attack. Bush even pointed out that his mother-in-law, Jenna Welch, lost over

$8,000 in trading ENE stock because "she did not know all the facts" (she bought 200 shares at $40.90, sold them at $0.42). In addition, Bush could also fall back on more powerful issues: "Congress . . . needs to stay focused on the American people. We're in a war. We've got to make sure our homeland is secure and we've got to make sure that people can find work."

As Bush defended his relationship with Enron, and as the political combat intensified, many investigators decided to take a big step back.

U.S. attorney general John Ashcroft, who received $57,000 in campaign money from Enron as he battled to keep his Missouri senate seat in 2000, recused himself from the investigations. In the Justice Department, Ashcroft's chief of staff, David Ayres, also recused himself from the Enron inquiry. Back in Houston, many of the prosecutors in the U.S. attorney's office had family ties to former and current Enron employees—so the entire office decided to recuse itself. At the Texas state level, Attorney General John Cornyn ($193,000 in campaign money from Enron) reluctantly decided to recuse himself as well: "No matter how earnestly I want to fulfill the duties entrusted to me by the voters of Texas, I have decided to withdraw from participation in the Enron investigation." In 2002, Cornyn was campaigning to fill Phil Gramm's shoes—the Republican Texas senator who was retiring—albeit without Enron contributions.

And SEC chairman Harvey Pitt, who had once battled the SEC as an attorney for Arthur Andersen, bucked the trend and decided to stay the course. Pitt stated that suggestions that he had a conflict of interest were "an attempt to politicize the workings of an independent agency."

As his retirement neared, Senator Gramm was also not budging from his Enron-related investigation seat. Criticism was heavy surrounding the fact that his wife, Wendy Gramm, was a member of Enron's board. He decided he would not take part in the investigations specific to the Enron collapse, but would continue to participate in "issues that are relevant to all business." Wendy Gramm, in addition to losing more than $680,000 in retirement funds from the bankruptcy mess, was viewed as a potential witness with "some serious explaining to do." Phil insisted that there would be no conflict of interest, as the couple avoided conversations about "work" when at home. Phil explained, "We talk about my taking out the garbage and Texas A&M football."

Uhh . . . Phil? Maybe it's time you and Wendy did some shopping at your local Victoria's Secret.

Signing up for direct deposit would have been too risky for an employee laid off weeks before. So in the early days of January, Jim Duffy got dressed up for a visit to Enron. His plan was to be there for fifteen minutes tops, collect his paycheck, and get the hell out.

The second time was harder than the first; his emotional run from the burrito place had been backed by pure adrenaline and financial pain. It was an act of impulse. Round two would be harder because he had only one thought: "What if I run into the HR guy?"

He barely ran into anyone, although when he reached the trading floor, he did run into a flying Nerf ball from a touch football game. His paycheck wasn't in the mail pile, but after trading e-mails with the guy whose desk he previously raided, the check was found. Whew.

Two weeks later, Duffy would get dressed up for another fifteen minutes of Enron work. The third time was even luckier than the first two: he caught up to a mail collector (Enron was starting to get a *little* more organized) and managed to rescue his check from being sent back to HR.

My state of unemployment—or my "no money situation," as

described by our friend Odd Todd—was getting tougher as each day passed. As the Enron scandal heated up outside of Houston, and as word of Enron's deceitful ways spread around the globe, companies began squealing at the idea of buying our "Enron business." That opportunity was quickly fading away, so McLainey, Duffy, and I began to focus harder on other options.

This is not to say that Enron businesses weren't popping up everywhere. After all, there's no telling what the *best and the brightest* from the *most innovative company in America* could come up with, especially when they were getting desperate. In addition to John the T-shirt guy and the Web gurus who created 1400smith.com and Enronx.org, plenty of other ex-Enronians were building new careers from scratch. An investment bank, called Stoneworth Financial, was kicked up by former Enron deal men Evan Betzer and Charles Harris; a group of ex-Enronians led by Glenn Dickson (from EES) started Complete Property Services, a property management business; and another group of former Enron computer geeks had rapidly introduced to the market a software application called "Time & Money"—two things that Enron could have used a little more of.

And another ex-Enron employee—a guy named Jeffrey Skilling—whipped up a new company of his own. It wasn't very long after leaving Enron (for personal reasons) that Skilling incorporated "Veld Interests" (for business reasons). The new venture, which Skilling's spokeswoman described as "a company looking for a business," was apparently starting slowly due to his hectic legal schedule. In addition to having Skilling as CEO, Veld Interests started up with other ex-Enron talent: Skilling's wife, Rebecca Carter, and personal assistant, Sherri Sera. Whatever business Veld eventually went into, I decided it might be fun to send them a résumé . . . if the investigations ever cooled off.

On the regular job front, it seemed that anyone who had been making more than $100,000 at Enron was having a hard time, unless they were from a trading group.

In the first few months following the bankruptcy, energy trading companies like Duke and Reliant had hired between fifty and seventy ex-Enron employees. No less than twenty-seven firms in the city of Houston alone had hired Enron casualties into their trading operations. In the words of one placement administrator at The Work-Source, "If you don't come from an Enron trading floor, there just aren't any jobs."

Unless . . .

—It was just a matter of time before it came to this—

. . . you are willing to take off your clothes. *Playboy* magazine announced it was preparing a "Women of Enron" issue for release in the second half of 2002. All female employees of Enron were invited to send in their pictures to qualify for a spot in the magazine, as well as some hard-earned cash. At first I was just a bit disappointed that the "Men of Enron" were excluded, until *Playgirl* followed suit with a similar announcement.

Meanwhile, the woman referred to earlier as "Tina" in our credit group—the one with the 5 on her redeployed résumé who Liz Perry hired for a few days, before she was redeployed *again*—began her new career. She had "a friend" take some pictures, which she sent to *Playboy*. Tina was then selected as one of fifty women to meet *Playboy* executives at a Houston hotel. Her instructions were to bring a bikini and high heels. When she arrived, she saw that other young Enron women were wearing much less. After forty-five minutes of photos and questions like "What's your favorite color?" Tina began her nervous wait for the big news.

The following week, she found out she had been eliminated by the photo editors. She had missed her chance at the $15,000 per body that *Playboy* was paying the Enron women. Tina was back to square one in her job search.

How to Conquer Corporate America, Rule #10: Always ask the person interviewing you, "How did you become so smart?"

As the pace of job interviews picked up for me, I was given a choice: energy company, consulting firm, energy company, consulting firm.

Job interviews are a bit different when the interviewer knows *exactly* what your situation is. They knew when I got canned, why I got canned, and how impossible it was to going to be to get a job— and they did their best to let me know they knew all of this.

I would explain that I was part of the first mass layoff, and the interviewer would respond with a comment like, "Gosh, that must be tough to get only forty-five hundred dollars to last you the past couple of months. Have you filed for unemployment yet?"

Did you bring me here to hire me, or just to torture me?

After my Enron experience, it was hard to consider other jobs. In a strange way, Enron was *still the best place I ever worked*. At Enron, the business world turned faster. In my first two months at Enron, I learned more than I did in *two years* at other companies after business school. The challenge, the push for creativity, the pressure—Enron years were like dog years when compared to anywhere else.

So when interviewers would ask my opinion about Enron, I could only guess what they were looking for:

"Well, sometimes meeting expectations means cutting a few corners."

Wrong answer.

"Cash is king, but the right amount of debt can take over the universe."

Another wrong answer.

"By keeping things complicated, no one will understand how to ask the tough questions."

Of course, I would *never* be able to say those things with a straight face, so I stuck with how I really felt:

"Enron had a wealth of creative energy, but a shortage of manageable means to develop it."

"Cash *is* king."

"Intellectual capital can disappear if you oversleep."

Some interviewers wanted a suspicious amount of detail about what Enron was up to, leaving me to wonder about their reasons for bringing me in.

In any case, I found myself comparing everything to Enron: too much like Enron, not interested; not at all like Enron, not interested.

It's not like I was traumatized or something like that—I was just looking for something that compared to the best job I ever had. I was caught up in finding something that resembled my Enron job (with people that resembled the Enron people), but with a company that wouldn't slit my throat or its own.

I couldn't find it.

And since Enron was somehow still paying me—weeks after my pink slip—I decided not to just settle for something less.

Lawsuits, lawsuits, lawsuits. However the story ends (if it *ever* ends), the only victories in the Enron saga will be won by the attorneys. Firms from Houston, Dallas, New York, and all across the country are swarming to the Enron mess. Even O. J. Simpson attorney Johnnie Cochran is involved, hired to represent some ex-Enron employees: *"If the 401(k) goes to shit, you must not acquit!"*

Only Enron's chief law firm Vinson & Elkins is forced to sit on the sideline—as they are being sued by shareholders themselves for their involvement in creating the off–balance sheet deals. Enron represented 7 percent of V&E's revenue, compared to Enron representing just 1 percent of Arthur Andersen's revenue.

As the lawsuits spread like wildfire, anyone who might have known anything became a target. Beyond Enron itself, the list includes executives who sold stock, board members, auditors, lawyers, and banks.

One lawsuit involves a broker who was fired from UBS PaineWebber (part of the same UBS that recommended ENE down to $4, and the same UBS that purchased Enron's wholesale trading business for $0). The broker, Chung Wu, sent an e-mail to his clients in August 2001 recommending that they sell the stock. The e-mail, which came just a week after the Skilling resignation, was sent to a list of recipients that included Enron executives.

One of the Enron executives, namely Aaron Brown who was the head of Enron's stock-option program, were extremely "disturbed" by Wu's message. Brown sent an e-mail to UBS PaineWebber asking that they "please handle this situation."

Three hours after the Enron e-mail was sent to Wu's supervisor, Wu was fired.

As he should have been! For one thing, Wu had no real basis for his sell recommendation (at least he didn't provide one). He referred to liquidity issues and shrinking margins, which demonstrated nothing more than his lack of knowledge about the industry. The owner-of-a-Chinese-restaurant-turned-broker [no kidding] was also going against the recommendation of the firm (Ron Barone had ENE rated a Strong Buy at the time), which is a cardinal sin on Wall Street. In addition, no broker is supposed to send out a mass communication without first clearing the message with management.

In a letter sent to Congress, PaineWebber offered details about the termination of Chung Wu:

> *Any financial adviser who sends an e-mail in the middle of the night to dozens of firm clients urging them to take an action contrary to [UBS] Warburg's research recommendation, without informing the clients of that recommendation or obtaining the necessary review and approval, would be treated the same as Mr. Wu.*

Again, I completely agree with the decision to fire this guy. I mean, what was he thinking? Did his experience selling dumplings give him some special expertise that allowed him to override Barone? It didn't make sense. His sell recommendation was unrelated to the eventual reasons Enron collapsed, so it can't be said that he was really *right* about Enron. My gut tells me that—with Enron executives on his client list—perhaps he knew something interesting about Enron's future, something that was too delicate to put in his clumsy e-mail.

Great Moments in the History of Paper Shredding

The urban legend goes like this: "Swedish business consultant Ulf af Trolle labors thirteen years on a book about Swedish economic solutions. He takes the 250-page manuscript to be copied, only to see it reduced to fifty thousand strips of paper in seconds when a worker confuses the copier with the shredder."

I'm not sure about that one, but the following events are well documented—so here is a selective history of the paper shredder, long before our mechanical friend Sherman went on a rampage across the Enron trading floor:

The automatic paper shredder is invented in 1935 by a Bavarian guy named Adolph Ehinger. Some say he comes up with the idea from watching pasta-making machines; others say it was Adolf Hitler who "requested" the invention.

It's not until almost four decades later that shredding makes big news. In June 1972, the morning after the Watergate break-in, Nixon aide G. Gordon Liddy begins "shredding stuff left and right" (his words). The shredding takes place at the office of the Committee to Reelect the President (CREEP) and aims to cover up details of the scandal that eventually will lead Nixon to resign.

In 1979, radical members of the Iranian National Guard storm the U.S. embassy in Tehran, taking fifty-two Americans hostage. During the siege, the Americans shred as many secret documents as they can, only to have the paper strips glued back together. As a result, shredders are invented that dice paper into thousands of tiny bits rather than long strips.

In the mid-'80s, Oliver North and his secretary, Fawn Hall, testify that they had shredded evidence related to the Iran-Contra scandal. Air Force major general Richard Secord later tells Congress that he has also destroyed documents—his were related to the Nicaraguan Contras.

Despite the high-profile destruction of evidence in Washington, the Supreme Court rules in the 1988 case of *California v. Greenwood* that businesses (such as banks and law firms) are responsible for unshredded documents that are stolen from their trash.

Could the scandal-laden Clinton years go by unshredded? Nope. Around the time the Whitewater investigation begins in 1994, White House counsel Vince Foster commits suicide. A pair of students employed at Foster's old law firm in Arkansas—where Hillary Clinton also worked—testify that they were ordered to shred documents with Foster's initials on them.

In 1996, a race-discrimination lawsuit against Texaco is settled for $176 million, based on recordings in which Texaco employees use racial slurs and talk about shredding evidence. Lawyers for Texaco claim to have accounted for ten missing documents. Note to reader: Only lawyers are capable of accounting for objects that do not exist.

In a lawsuit against Coca-Cola in 2000, plaintiffs claim that the company used a shredder to destroy important employee records. Coke defends itself, saying that no shredder was ever purchased—until lawyers come up with the invoice from Staples.

If only Coke had bought that shredder for Unilever. In 2001, Procter & Gamble (P&G) pays Unilever $10 million to settle a lawsuit alleging that P&G spies went through Unilever's garbage. P&G also agrees to allow a third-party assessment of stolen product ideas.

All of which brings us to the Enron shredding festival. Checking my e-mail from home in January 2002, the following message arrived from James Derrick, Enron legal counsel and former V&E attorney:

——Original Message——
From: Legal - James Derrick Jr.
Sent: Mon 1/14/2002 4:02 PM
To: DL-GA-all_enron_worldwidel
Subject: Retention of Documents
    This is to remind all employees that, as earlier instructed, in view of the pending and threatened legal proceedings involving the company, no company records, either in electronic or paper form, should be destroyed. In the event of an office closing, please contact Bob Williams at (713) xxx-xxxx to arrange for storage of any records.
    Please call Bob with any questions.

• • •

The "as earlier instructed" was referring to an e-mail sent to Enron employees on October 25, in which we were asked to keep all materials such as "handwritten notes, recordings, e-mails and any other method of information recording." The October e-mail further explained that employees could be "individually liable for civil and criminal penalties if [they] fail to follow these instructions."

Long after the October e-mail, in the months of December and January, Enron called in mobile shredding trucks—including one with the name Shredco on the side—to destroy documents. The trucks are capable of destroying more than seven thousand pounds of documents per hour. On the Shredco website, an animated graphic explains why one might hire their services: "You threw it away—Or so you thought—Now you're being sued—Don't just throw it away—Destroy it!"

Enron claimed the shredding was unrelated to the investigations, but plaintiffs' attorneys were furious.

Attorney William Lerach made an appearance on the news walking around with a box of paper strips. He claimed the strips included information about "phony partnerships," which I assume was a reference to the very *real* partnerships Enron kept off the consolidated books. Lerach added his view that it's "better to live with whatever the facts are" than shred the evidence of those facts. I think a lot of people who have fed paper into shredding machines would disagree.

In any case, Enron claimed it was doing all it could to prevent more shredding, including the placement of guards on the nineteenth and twentieth floors of Enron Center North, and allowing the FBI to enter the Enron building. With these preventative steps tightly in place, anyone needing to destroy documents at Enron would be forced to use machines on one of the other forty-eight floors.

Around the corner from the Death Star is the South Tower of Pennzoil Place, where Arthur Andersen was facing its own ragged reality.

An investigator for one of the congressional panels revealed that an Andersen attorney gave employees assigned to the Enron account the "green light" to destroy documents. The internal message came just a few days before the infamous October 16 earnings release that opened the floodgates. The shredding of Enron-related materials continued through October 23, when Andersen partner David Duncan called an urgent meeting to *speed up* the destruction. Duncan's meeting came *after* the SEC began to gather accounting information from Enron, and led to Duncan being fired by the firm.

In addition to Duncan, Andersen also took action against seven other auditors and partners from the Houston office.

The shredding at Andersen continued until November 9, when Duncan's assistant sent out an e-mail to the Enron team: "Stop the shredding." It was the day before, November 8, that the SEC delivered its subpoena to Andersen.

Andersen CEO Joseph Berardino began spinning in his public statements and on talk-show appearances, realizing that the Enron mess could bring his firm—one of the world's Big Five accounting firms with eighty-five thousand employees—to a quick and painful demise.

What exactly *is* a whistle-blower, anyway? *Merriam Webster's Collegiate Dictionary* tells us that the name is given to "one who reveals something covert or who informs against another." The term itself implies that a noise is made; that anyone within range will hear the sound.

In mid-January, the term *whistle-blower* became permanently attached to the name Sherron Watkins. Nearly five months after her memo and visit to Ken Lay, Watkins was shrouded with the title of Enron heroine: the one who "spoke out when no one else would."

But did anyone stop to consider that she "spoke out"—or should I say "blew her whistle"—inside the soundproof walls of Enron's fiftieth floor? Does telling *only* Ken Lay about what she knew qualify as heroic?

The ultimate whistle-blower (although he hates when the term is bestowed upon him) is a guy named Jeffrey Wigand. Played by Russell Crowe in the movie *The Insider,* Wigand is a former tobacco exec who revealed the addictive and lethal truth about cigarettes. He backed it up in the courtroom. He did it all based on loyalty to "a higher order of ethical responsibility."

Watkins gave *Ken Lay* the information. He said thank-you and proceeded to do nothing about it, although he did grant Watkins her requested transfer. Watkins went back to her business—which included selling her own ENE stock and keeping quiet again.

Wigand, who initiated the wave of truth about Brown & Williamson Tobacco Corp. (at the time the tobacco industry's #3) and other tobacco companies, has said that Sherron Watkins was no hero, that her actions didn't merit the credit she was given. "She turned around, sat back down, and shut up. . . . I don't think what she did was right," said Wigand, in an interview with *Fast Company*'s Chuck Salter.

The memo she wrote *was* spectacular—incredibly detailed and insightful. But the letter surfaced five months after it was given to Lay—the shareholders and employees were never able to benefit from it. Of course, the argument was that Lay should have acted on her warning. She saw him as a guiding force that would fix the problem.

In testimony before Congress, Watkins would defend Lay and claim he was "duped" by Skilling and Fastow. I think *duped* is the perfect word—except that the *entire world* was duped, and Ken Lay was part of the duping. Watkins, who was slammed by Skilling and his lawyer in a Larry King interview for coordinating her high-profile accusations with a supposed book deal, was essentially blowing the whistle in a void.

There she was, riding in the getaway car with the rest of us, telling the bank robbers, "Hey, that's wrong what you did to that bank back there." After getting no response, she decided to sit back and go along for the ride. Just like me. Just like thousands of others who knew *something,* but not *everything.*

So who are the Enron whistle-blowers? So many others—past and present—found themselves in the same backseat as Watkins.

How about Jim Alexander, a former president of Enron Global Power, who tried to cry foul about aggressive financial dealings to both Ken Lay and former Enron president Richard Kinder? Not only did he get less than a response, he created a bumpy career path for himself. Still, he kept his job and went along for the ride.

Even Jeff McMahon, the replacement CFO after Fastow was removed, had registered complaints. He once expressed his discomfort with the Fastow deals and the fact that Fastow was on both sides of the table. McMahon took a new assignment, and went along for the ride.

Jordan Mintz testified that he delivered repeated concerns to Skilling about the Fastow deals as well. Mintz even hired an outside law firm to review the transactions from a distance, because he felt V&E was just too close. In a memo to Skilling in May 2001, Mintz notified Skilling of the LJM approval sheets, which "provides for

[Skilling's] signature." The Mintz memo also promised to deliver documents to Skilling for him to "then sign at [Skilling's] convenience." Skilling never signed.

Mintz may have been genuinely concerned about the conflict-of-interest issues surrounding the partnerships, and he may have expressed those concerns to chief executives. But did he blow any whistles? In April 2001, Mintz sent a memo to Andy Fastow regarding the public disclosure of Fastow's involvement with the partnerships: "[W]e need to continue to be cognizant of this issue [LJM2 disclosure] as the year progresses and continue to consider some of the safe-harbors provided under the SEC rules from having to disclose related party transactions . . . I, of course, will continue to examine other alternatives as well." Mintz was doing his job, which included pushing disclosure rules to their limits.

Other media-hyped whistle-blowers like Jan Avery and Margaret Ceconi—who decided to spill their guts to Wall Street analyst Carol Coale only *after* they were fired by Enron—went along for the ride for several years. Avery had been involved in Enron deals for eight years, part of an Enron team that admittedly bullied Arthur Andersen into getting what they wanted.

No heroes. No whistle-blowers. No happy ending.

Movies will someday be made about the Enron collapse, but Hollywood will need its best screenwriters to spin heroes out of a game that had no winners. There are dozens of "I told you so" analysts, journalists, and whateverists, each of whom knew something but none of whom knew everything.

No one had the power to save us from, or even warn us about, the impending doom.

Not even Ken Lay had *that* much power.

• • •

Wednesday—January 16, 2002
ENRNQ opening price: $0.29
ENRNQ closing price: $0.31
ENRNQ trading volume: 53,341,600

Enron stock hadn't traded above $1.00 since the week after bank-ruptcy, so the New York Stock Exchange said good-bye to the symbol "ENE" forever.

Inside Enron, an e-mail went out to all employees plus at least one nonemployee:

———Original Message———
From: Enron Office Of The Chairman
Sent: Wed 1/16/2002 8:45 AM
To: DL-GA-all_enron_worldwide1
Subject: New Stock Symbol

Enron announced today that its common stock will now be traded as an Over-the-Counter (OTC) equity security under the symbol "ENRNQ." This follows a decision by the New York Stock Exchange (NYSE) to file an application to delist Enron's common stock, which means that Enron's common stock and related securities are sus-pended from trading on the NYSE. Enron is considering whether to appeal the NYSE's decision.

The NYSE has standard criteria for listing stocks, which can be found on their website at www.nyse.com. Enron recently fell below the following listing criteria: average closing price of a security less than $1.00 over a consecutive 30 trading-day period. Quotation service for Enron's stock will now be provided by the National Quotation Bureau, LLC "Pink Sheets."

Enron chose not to appeal the decision.

Back at the Death Star, the occasion of ENE's departure from the NYSE was celebrated with another keg party.

The scandal was so hot in mid-January that *anything* related to Enron or the Crooked E logo was increasing in value. Even Enron stock was skyrocketing—the certificate, that is.

As something of a business historian, I collect old stock certificates: Walt Disney, Chase Manhattan, RJR Holdings, U.S. Steel, AT&T, and all four of the Monopoly railroad companies—just to name a handful. Now my ENE stock certificate, signed by Chairman Kenneth Lay, CEO Jeffrey Skilling, and Secretary Rebecca Carter, was worth $90.

When the news came out that Enron "memorabilia" was being sold on eBay, I just laughed. Then I checked my bank balance, and stopped laughing.

I ran around the house gathering everything I had related to Enron. When I finished, I had a big pile of junk. The pile included commemorative pens, mouse pads, retractable modem cords, a cooler bag, golf tees, and a baseball from the first game ever played at Enron Field.

Okay, so I kept the baseball—complete with its Crooked E logo.

But all my other Enron trinkets were listed on eBay within an hour—I wanted to get it on the site before the story faded. Instead of going through the pain (and expense) of listing each item, I put it all up as "All my Enron stuff at once—17 items—LOOK!" The eBay listing included a nice color photo of the items arranged like prizes on a game show.

Not only did *thousands* of people view the listing, but bidding was hot. I suddenly realized the junk pile was headed for hundreds of dollars. I knew it would fetch a few dollars, but this was ridiculous.

So I scrambled around the house looking for more Enron. I looked at the baseball again—no, I'm keeping the baseball.

Then it hit me: I had something that was rare, interesting, marketable, and easy to deliver. There would be no shipping cost, and I could sell *as many as I wanted!*

E-mail. I decided to sell my still-growing collection of Enron e-mail.

In hindsight, it was the best stupid idea I've ever had. I gathered all the Enron e-mails I had from Lay, Skilling, and others that were related to the collapse. I put them in a single document that also included the intranet Q&As and other memos. Then I put half a dozen listings for the item up on eBay:

"Enron: E-mails etc from Lay, JS, others 64pgs"

It was pure genius. Bidders started in on the document, which I promised would be delivered by e-mail as soon as payment was received. The item was red hot, and it started getting media attention as well.

That evening I told my wife about my little business venture. She was certain I would be sued by Enron or go to jail or something. I insisted that Enron's legal team was too busy to worry about eBay and my little packet of papers. And if other ex-employees can sell their training manuals or their *Code of Ethics* booklets, then certainly my e-mails were harmless.

Even Enron seemed to approve. Enron spokeswoman Karen Denne talked to the media about the eBay madness: "The whole situation is unfortunate, and we've always had resourceful, innovative employees. This is just the latest demonstration."

Just as my wife was about to be convinced my little venture was safe, the phone rang. As I raced to answer it, I said, "I bet that's the *New York Times* wanting to do a story about my eBay item." We both laughed.

The phone call was from the *New York Times*.

With an agreement *not* to use my real name—only my eBay user name "cruvdog" (credit Bernie Bickers with that obnoxious handle)—I shared the sixty-four pages with a *Times* reporter named John Schwartz. In return, Schwartz said there was a chance my eBay item could get some exposure by way of a few column inches in the *Times*—a paper with a seven-digit circulation.

The night before the possible *Times* story, I checked my eBay items. The "64pgs" was doing fine at over a hundred bucks. The "All my Enron stuff" was also building momentum.

The next morning, I got a call from Bernie Bickers:

"Dude . . . the *New York* fucking *Times*! You're going to be rich!"

I was certain that my little blurb in the *Times* would generate thousands of dollars per eBay listing. I would sell as many as I could, as other newspapers and TV stations flocked to the story and the momentum grew. CNN would speculate on what the "64pgs" contained, and as I sold more and more, I could start planning my monthlong vacation in . . .

Suddenly, they were gone, vanished, nowhere to be found. My "64pgs" had disappeared from the eBay website. I was stunned.

For Auction Online: Enron's Memos

By The New York Times

HOUSTON, Jan. 17 — A former Enron employee was selling a 64-page cache of internal **Enron** Corporation memorandums on eBay today.

One memo from the company's chairman at the time, Kenneth L. Lay, read, "Our growth has never been more certain." In another, Mr. Lay and Jeffrey K. Skilling, then Enron's chief executive, discuss "values of respect, integrity, communication and excellence in the workplace." The going auction price this evening was $18.27.

"I decided to throw it up there and see if somebody's willing to pay for it," said the former employee, who goes by the online name cruvdog.

An e-mail was immediately sent from eBay, which explained the disappearance:

Dear Brian R Cruver,

eBay appreciates the fact that you chose to list your auctions . . . [list of items] . . . with us. However, we have determined that your items are inappropriate for listing on eBay. Therefore, we have ended these auctions and all fees have been credited to your account. Please do not relist these items.

Though Enron is going through bankruptcy, the sale of possibly proprietary information related to internal communication from a corporation is protected at this point.

Also, selling this information would be in violation of the terms of service in the User Agreement, section 6.2.

IMPORTANT NOTICE: Please be aware future incidents of this nature can lead to the suspension of your account. We value you as a member of our community and wish to continue this relationship, so we must ask you to refrain from any violations of the Listing Policies or User Agreement in the future.

We thank you in advance for your cooperation.

Regards,

Kirsten (ended@ebay.com)

e.Bay

So much for my latest get-rich-quick scheme. At least my collection of junk, the "All my Enron stuff at once—17 items—LOOK!" was still on the auction block.

The mouse pads, cooler bag, golf tees, pens, and other trinkets eventually made $260.

And I still have the baseball.

Overall the eBay madness was a huge success for Enron employees in search of a few bucks. When I first heard the story, there were only a couple hundred Enron items on eBay. By the end of that week, there were *several thousand* items.

Back inside the Death Star, remaining employees reportedly ran around the deserted office spaces and collected Enron junk to sell. From clothing to clocks to coffee mugs—everything Enron was being disposed of via a virtual garage sale.

On January 18, Enron fired Arthur Andersen as its auditor. It was just the beginning.

Within weeks, companies rapidly dropped Andersen, including Waste Management, Dynegy, Freddie Mac, Merck, Delta Airlines, SunTrust Banks, Calpine, Centex, and Pennzoil. More than a hundred clients in all left Andersen during the first few months of 2002, flocking to the rest of the Big Five (the other four being Deloitte & Touche, Ernst & Young, KPMG, and Pricewaterhouse-Coopers). The mass exodus was precipitated by an indictment of Andersen for obstruction of justice (shredding) and the resignation of CEO Berardino.

With the indictment, the SEC no longer accepted Andersen audited financial statements, and companies still tied to Andersen were given sixty days to have their financial statements reviewed by another firm. Later, shredding team leader David Duncan would plead guilty to a single-felony obstruction-of-justice charge, as part of a deal to cooperate with the government in its criminal case against Andersen. Arthur Andersen was starting to gasp for air.

An Enron press release:

FOR IMMEDIATE RELEASE: Wednesday, January 23, 2002
HOUSTON—*Enron (ENRNQ) announced today that Kenneth L. Lay*

has resigned as Chairman of the Board and Chief Executive Officer of Enron Corp. Mr. Lay, who will also retire as an Enron employee, will remain on the company's Board of Directors. The Board, in cooperation with the Creditors' Committee in Enron's bankruptcy, is in the process of selecting a restructuring specialist to join the company who will assist in Enron's efforts to emerge from bankruptcy and, on an interim basis, serve as acting chief executive officer.

"This was a decision the Board and I reached in cooperation with our Creditors' Committee," said Mr. Lay. "I want to see Enron survive, and for that to happen we need someone at the helm who can focus 100 percent of his efforts on reorganizing the company and preserving value for our creditors and hard-working employees. Unfortunately, with the multiple inquiries and investigations that currently require much of my time, it is becoming increasingly difficult to concentrate fully on what is most important to Enron's stakeholders."

Lay would resign from the Enron board of directors within two weeks.

Ken's wife, Linda, appeared on NBC's *Today Show* just a few days later. Linda delivered a tearful tale of a couple teetering on the brink of personal bankruptcy.

"Virtually—other than the home we live in—everything we own is for sale."

I checked eBay to see if I could find the items she was referring to.

"There's some things [Ken] wasn't told." Linda pointed to Arthur Andersen and Vinson & Elkins as examples of those who had failed her husband.

"Everything we had mostly was in Enron stock."

"We've been poor and we've been rich, and we were happy when we were poor and we were happy when we were rich."

It was hard for most viewers across America to feel sympathy for Linda or Ken, especially as she spoke from their multimillion-dollar high-rise penthouse (the one that is *not* for sale).

Soon after the tearful display, the world learned of the Lays' $25 million worth of real estate properties and $8 million worth of non-Enron stock. The quote is worth repeating: "Everything we had mostly was in Enron stock."

After spending the week prior to the interview working with a media coach, you would think Linda could have come up with something better. You would think she could avoid assertion of fact that could be so easily disproved.

And although I never found any Lay family items on eBay, Linda Lay soon announced her intentions to open a secondhand store called "Jus' Stuff," which would sell some Ken and Linda memorabilia. Mark Swindler, one of Linda Lay's first customers, emerged from the store saying, "It's just stuff alright . . . stuff they got by ripping off other people."

The following week, Jesse Jackson came to town. He announced plans for a rally across the street from Enron headquarters—at Antioch Missionary Baptist Church—to get ex-employees fired up about a trip to Washington. The bus caravan from Houston would focus on the need for government relief for Enron's former workers. In the words of Jackson, "The burden must be shared by the government and Enron."

Other forms of employee relief were created as well. The Enron Ex-Employee Relief Fund Account (EERFA) was formed, and a few politicians donated dirty dollars they were given by Enron. The Severed Enron Employees Coalition (SEEC) was also created, looking to get a valuable seat at the bankruptcy table in support of ex-Enronians.

• • •

Friday—January 25, 2002
ENRNQ opening price: $0.45
ENRNQ closing price: $0.49
ENRNQ trading volume: 21,692,700

It was another impossibly warm January day in suburban Houston. After checking for neighbors, I stepped outside into eighty degrees of fresh air, and slowly wandered to the mailbox. It was 2:00 P.M. on a weekday, and I was still in my boxers. I had a lot of time on my hands; a trip to the mailbox was the highlight of my day.

A letter had arrived from Enron:

> *This letter is to inform you that the Company has decided to terminate your employment effective January 15, 2002, due to a Company business restructuring and the recent filing for relief under Chapter 11 of the U.S. Bankruptcy Code.*

The letter came almost two whole months after telling me to go home—what a joke. All I could do was ruefully shake my head. Oh, well. It was fun while it lasted.

The phone rang. My boxers and I dashed back into the house.

It was a call from McLainey. His call, and the next eight phone calls, were about Cliff Baxter, the former Enron vice chairman who resigned from Enron in May 2001.

The news was breaking that he'd been found dead early that morning—behind the wheel of his Mercedes S500, at 2:23 A.M. on Palm Royale Boulevard in Sugar Land, a Houston suburb. He was found shot to death; it was a gunshot wound to the head, and a .38-caliber revolver was inside the locked car.

The moment I heard that news, the Enron story mushroomed into a horrific tragedy. Lost savings and lost jobs were one thing, but lost life took us all into a nightmarish world, deeper and darker than we could have ever anticipated.

Phone call number ten was from Bernie Bickers.

"Holy . . . "

"I know. This is out of control."

Bickers read me headlines that suggested Baxter's death may be more than just a suicide. Many believed he was a key figure in the investigation; he was even mentioned in the Sherron Watkins memo to Ken Lay: "Cliff Baxter complained mightily to Skilling and all who would listen about the inappropriateness of our transactions with LJM." As the hearings were beginning, the timing of his death was significant.

The police in Sugar Land declared the death a suicide, long before the autopsy was actually performed. When the autopsy was finished, the experts also concluded Baxter's death was a suicide; however, questions were raised about the evidence in the report. First, the fatal shot was not a regular bullet, but a pellet-filled cartridge commonly called rat shot, which is not easily traced to a specific gun. Second, Baxter had "recent" wounds on his left hand, described in the report as "discontinuous superficial abrasions with a trail of black material." The black material was never tested, but experts suggested the material could be asphalt, and the wounds consistent with Baxter breaking a fall to the street. Baxter also had "small shards of glass" on his shirt. The police failed to bag his hands, and failed to take photos until after the gun and body were moved. There was blood outside the car. It was unclear if fingerprints were taken from the car.

Beyond all that, all indications at the scene were that it *was* a suicide. There was even a note to Baxter's wife that spoke of lost pride and overwhelming pain.

But the mystery surrounding Baxter's death would continue long after January, and the question of what he knew about Enron would remain unanswered for eternity.

CAROL,

I AM SO SORRY FOR THIS. I FEEL I JUST CAN'T GO ON. I HAVE ALWAYS TRIED TO DO THE RIGHT THING BUT WHERE THERE WAS ONCE GREAT PRIDE NOW IT'S GONE. I LOVE YOU AND THE CHILDREN SO MUCH. I JUST CAN'T BE ANY GOOD TO YOU OR MYSELF. THE PAIN IS OVERWHELMING.

PLEASE TRY TO FORGIVE ME.

CLIFF

J. Clifford Baxter

I looked back at Baxter's resignation press release from Enron. Included was a statement from Skilling:

"Over the past 10 years, Cliff has made a tremendous contribution to Enron's evolution, particularly as a member of the team that built Enron's wholesale business. His creativity, intelligence, sense of humor, and straightforward manner have been assets to the company throughout his career. While we will miss him, we are happy that his primary reason for resigning is to spend additional time with his family, and we wish him the very best."

As Bickers and I continued to talk, we were amazed at the intensity of the Enron vortex. It wasn't stopping. It wasn't even slowing down.

Cliff Baxter's death came only days after Ken Lay resigned from Enron and just after Andersen executives started appearing before

Congress. Bickers and I were shocked when Enron hit rock bottom as a business, but now we were floored by the enormity and reach of it all.

After a few moments of not knowing what to say, Bickers finally spoke. "Dude . . . I remember calling you that first week you were at Enron. That was *less than a year ago!*"

"I know. It's nuts. It's just wild crazy nuts." I had a hard time focusing on a single thought. The roller-coaster ride had shaken me. "I can't believe I sat there—right in the middle of it—and watched the whole thing crumble around me. Unbelievable."

Bickers responded, "Yeah, you and me both." He paused. "One of us should write a book."

11
Lights Out

> "Nearly all men can stand adversity, but if you want to test a man's character, give him power."
>
> —*Abraham Lincoln*

After Enron stopped paying me, I became a real unemployed person. In between job interviews, I studied a number of different logic models related to common interview questions, such as "Why is a manhole cover round?" (there are several reasons) and "How many golf balls are in the air at this moment?" (hint: it's a lot more than you think).

Okay, so I didn't *really* study for interview questions.

What I *did* do was spend a lot of time searching the Internet for insignificant crap to do; and there's a lot of that to do on the Internet.

There's eBay, where a person can buy and sell anything, from old Russian submarines to used underwear. Unfortunately, I ran out of Enron stuff to sell, and I didn't have any money to buy other people's junk. Besides, my eBay account was "at risk" based on the creepy warning they had sent me earlier. So trying to sell a $3 brass whistle and calling the item "Enron: Actual Whistle Used by Sherron" wasn't an option.

Once I had exhausted the eBay possibilities, it was time to move on to one of the Internet's many name generators. They're quite simple: All the user need do is enter a few items of personal information and click a button, instantly revealing the user's new "name." Popular name generators include the Sopranos "Mob Name" generator, the Pirate Name generator, several Rock Star Name generators, and a couple of *Star Wars* Name generators.

I played around with some key Enron executives, and managed to spend *days* on that. The *Star Wars* generators required information about prescription drug use, so I couldn't get accurate results.

Here are some of the key figures of the Enron saga and their alternative names (to make the next ten years of testimony easier to watch):

Ken's wife Linda Lay, courtesy of the Porn Star Name generator: "Holly Thong"

The balance sheet boys, a.k.a. the guys who "managed" Enron's accounting statements, courtesy of the Oz Prison Bitch Name generator:

Andy Fastow, ex-CFO: "Towelboy"
Michael Kopper, ex-Treasurer: "Ass Executioner"
David Duncan, Andersen Partner: "Stubby"

And last but most certainly not least, Jeff Skilling. His name and vital statistics come from the Pokémon Name generator:

Original Name: Jeff Skilling
Pokémon Name: Bertbar
Profile: You live in the frigid tundra of Kamchatka, and your diet consists mostly of berries, meatballs, and water.
Characteristics: You can breathe Dr Pepper. You can walk on jet fuel. You can resist salt spikes. You can throw force bolts. You have a winning smile. You can shoot lava. You can resist 8-track tapes. You can spit Mr. PiBB.
Enemies: Your natural enemy is Kofu.

• • •

Speaking of names—the use of *Star Wars* trademarks by Enron financiers received an unfavorable response from *Star Wars* creators. George Lucas and his company, Lucasfilm, expressed their displeasure with the names Chewco Investments LP (named for the furry Chewbacca), JEDI LP, Kenobe Inc., and Obi-1 Holdings LLC. A Lucasfilm spokeswoman said, "Lucasfilm was unaware of any possible use of our protected trademarks by Enron, and any actual use by Enron of such trademarks was without our permission."

The statement from the *Star Wars* people came on the heels of two other name-sensitive battles being fought by Lucasfilm. In one case, Lucas had taken the makers of "Starballz" to court, attempting to halt sales of the X-rated cartoon. The pornographic adventure, which detailed the adventures of "Wank Solo," was allowed to remain on the shelves by a federal judge. In the other case, Lucasfilm was able to stop a medical devices company from naming their new surgical beam the "Light Saber."

Perhaps these trademark violations were the sleeper case against Enron, sort of like the tax evasion case against Al Capone.

When William Powers Jr., Dean of the University of Texas law school, was named to the Enron board of directors in October 2001, he faced severe criticism. The move was intended to enhance Enron's credibility, but it only raised new conflict-of-interest questions. Powers had been named head of a special committee to conduct an internal investigation into Enron's questionable financial deals.

The questions and criticism revolved around Enron's ties to the University of Texas. Over the previous few years, Enron had made substantial donations to both the UT law school (more than $300,000) and business schools (more than $3.5 million). In addition,

Enron's general counsel, James Derrick, held various fund-raising positions for the law school, including a trustee position with the Law School Foundation and a leadership role with the alumni association.

Critics of the Powers appointment claimed he would be unable to objectively investigate Enron, specifically Derrick— who was among the executives named in shareholder lawsuits. Derrick sold nearly $7 million in ENE stock during the first eight months of 2001 and had within his domain the formation of partnerships, the approval of deals, and the release of financial information. Opponents of the decision said Powers was not independent, that he had a substantial connection with Enron management, and that he was therefore the wrong person to conduct an investigation.

Then on Saturday, February 2—the day before the Patriots won Super Bowl XXXVI—Powers released his investigative report.

The 218-page document *blasted* Enron executives, auditors, and attorneys, instantly neutralizing much of the criticism. The report detailed Enron's inflation of earnings through partnerships, the masking of debt, and the excessive enrichment of insiders.

Anatomy of an Enron Partnership—Part III

From the Powers Report:

> We have prepared a Report that explains the substance of the most significant transactions. . . . We were not asked, and we have not attempted, to investigate the causes of Enron's bankruptcy. . . .
>
> Certain former Enron employees who (we were told) played substantial roles in one or more of the transactions under investigation—including [Andy] Fastow, Michael J. Kopper, and

*Ben F. Glisan Jr.—declined to be interviewed either entirely or
with respect to most issues.*

*We have examined the specific transactions that led to the
third-quarter 2001 earnings charge and the restatement. We also
have attempted to examine all of the approximately two dozen
transactions between Enron and these related-party entities.*

The report then continues to summarize the findings:

*Enron employees involved in the partnerships were enriched, in the
aggregate, by tens of millions of dollars they should have never
received—Fastow by at least $30 million, Kopper by at least $10
million, two others [Ben Glisan and Kristina Mordaunt] by $1 mil-
lion each, and still two more [Kathy Lynn and Anne Yaeger Patel]
by amounts we believe were at least in the hundreds of thousands
of dollars.*

Fastow and Kopper had offered the investment opportunity,
named Southampton Place after the neighborhood they lived in, to
the four other Enron employees. Glisan, an Enron accountant, and
Mordaunt, an Enron lawyer, would later be in the position to
"negotiate" with Fastow partnerships—*after* their financial windfall
from the Southampton deal. The Powers report didn't draw any
conclusions as to why Glisan, Mordaunt, Lynn (a finance
employee), and Patel (another finance employee) were offered
part of the deal.

As the investigations unfolded, the world wondered which of
these Southampton participants would get a second deal—as an
accommodating witness for the prosecution.

Whatever the reason these six were included, the payout from
the deal was spectacular, especially for Fastow ($30 million) and

Kopper ($10 million). The Southampton Place deal, which was an investment in a transaction between Enron and LJM (the termination of a hedge), returned Glisan and Mordaunt their million bucks off of just a $5,800 investment (in investment terms, that's a risk-free return of over 17,000 percent—unless you consider the "prison risk"). The terms of the transaction between LJM and Enron were very generous to the LJM investors, and went directly against the best interest of Enron and Enron shareholders. In the words of the report:

> These investors walked away with tens of millions of dollars in value that, in an arm's-length context, Enron would never have given away.

And those dollars that Enron was giving away came in the form of management fees to Fastow and Kopper (as compensation for brilliantly running the highly efficient partnerships) and in the form of money taken out of Enron's pockets. The cash paid to these employees came as part of transactions that Fastow negotiated with Enron, which means that their gain was the shareholders' loss.

Each of the investors—other than Fastow—failed to get permission from Enron to own interest in the outside partnership. Fastow had permission, but the extent of his ownership and his gains were misrepresented to the Enron board.

Again, the Powers Report didn't speculate as to why the investment returns were so high for Fastow's friends. A return of 17,000 per cent may seem a bit high but that was probably right for what has turned out to be a deal with the devil.

The report continued to cover other issues—perhaps much bigger issues—beyond the Southampton scheme and Fastow's little investment club:

Many of the most significant transactions apparently were designed to accomplish favorable financial statement results, not to achieve bona fide economic objectives or transfer risk. . . .We believe these transactions resulted in Enron reporting earnings from the third quarter of 2000 through the third quarter of 2001 that were almost $1 billion higher than should have been reported.

Wow—a billion dollars' worth of fuzzy math! Surely the world-renowned accounting geniuses at Arthur Andersen had nothing to do with that.

In virtually all of the transactions, Enron's accounting treatment was determined with extensive participation and structuring advice from Andersen. . . . Enron's records show that Andersen billed Enron $5.7 million for advice in connection with the LJM and Chewco transactions alone [two of the partnerships that led to the restatements], above and beyond its regular audit fees.

In reference to Enron's public disclosures (Annual Reports, 10-Ks, etc.), the report recognized that factual references *were* made about the partnerships and transactions. However . . .

. . . these disclosures were obtuse, did not communicate the essence of the transactions completely or clearly, and failed to convey the substance of what was going on between Enron and the partnerships.

• • •

The Powers Report also described the "ever-increasing" set of proce-

dures that management told the board of directors it was implementing—as a measure to control the related-party transactions:

> *These included . . . review and approval of all LJM transactions by
> Richard Causey, the Chief Accounting Officer; and Richard Buy,
> the Chief Risk Officer; and, later during the [investigation] period,
> Jeffrey Skilling, the President and COO (and later CEO).*

The report offered more specifics about the individual pieces of
the approval and control process. Some specific highlights
regarding key parties:

The Powers Report on Ken Lay:

> *As CEO, he had the ultimate responsibility for taking reasonable
> steps to ensure that the officers reporting to him performed their
> oversight duties properly.*

The Powers Report on Jeff Skilling:

> *As the magnitude and significance of the related-party transac-
> tions to Enron increased over time, it is difficult to understand why
> Skilling did not ensure that those controls were rigorously adhered
> to and enforced . . . it appears that Skilling did not take action
> after being put on notice that Fastow was pressuring Enron
> employees who were negotiating with LJM.*

The Powers Report on Rick Causey:

> *Causey was and is Enron's Chief Accounting Officer [later
> dismissed as a result of this report]. He presided over and par-
> ticipated in a series of accounting judgments that, based on the*

accounting advice we have received, went well beyond the aggressive.

The Powers Report on Rick Buy:

Buy was and is Enron's Senior Risk Officer [later dismissed as a result of this report] . . . he apparently saw his role more narrow than the Board had reason to believe, and did not act affirmatively to carry out . . . a careful review of the economic terms of all transactions between Enron and LJM.

The Powers Report on the Board of Directors:

After having authorized a conflict of interest creating as much risk as this one [allowing Fastow to control partnerships dealing with Enron], the Board had an obligation to give careful attention to the transactions that followed. It failed to do this.

The Powers Report on Arthur Andersen:

. . . did not fulfill its professional responsibilities in connection with its audits of Enron's financial statements. . . . Andersen participated in the structuring and accounting treatment of the Raptor transactions, and charged over $1 million for its services, yet it apparently failed to provide the objective accounting judgment that should have prevented these transactions from going forward.

Although Andersen approved the transactions, in fact the "hedging" transactions did not involve substantive transfers of economic risk. The transactions may have looked superficially like economic hedges, but they actually functioned only as "accounting" hedges.

The Powers Report on Vinson & Elkins:

> . . . *as Enron's long-standing outside counsel . . . Management and the Board relied heavily on the perceived approval by Vinson & Elkins of the structure and disclosure of the transactions.*

The Powers Report had exceeded expectations, and William Powers himself escaped further criticism for his conflicting interests. Although the report's findings were perceived as too soft on Ken Lay and the board of directors, the 218 pages would ultimately serve their purpose as a sturdy foundation for future Enron inquisitions.

The concluding remarks from the report's executive summary:

> *The tragic consequences of the related-party transactions and accounting errors were the result of failures at many levels and by many people: a flawed idea, self-enrichment by employees, inadequately designed controls, poor implementation, inattentive oversight, simple (and not-so-simple) accounting mistakes, and overreaching in a culture that appears to have encouraged pushing the limits. Our review indicates that many of those consequences could and should have been avoided.*

Just a few days after the Powers Report was released, reporters from the *Los Angeles Times* did some comparisons between the report's findings and the records of executive stock sales.

They found that Skilling, Fastow, Causey, and Buy were involved in sorting out the major problems facing Enron's Raptor partnerships—between August 2000 and March 2001—while they sold a combined $35 million of their personal ENE stock. The Raptors (there were eventually four of them) had been created to hold Enron losses off the public books. As the Raptors' "credit capacity" was filling up, new Raptors were created and the entities were restructured. As the stability of these birds became more and more questionable, these four Enron officers continued to cash out their Enron stock.

Without my Enron paychecks, it was time to pay a visit to a casino. No, not a *real* casino—a virtual casino. The World Wide Web offers hundreds of them (or maybe thousands), and the key is finding one that will actually pay you if you win. I spent countless mind-numbing hours of computer blackjack with a digitized dealer, feeding me virtual cards from a software program based some-where in the Caribbean. Would they pay me if I won? Who knows?

Since the collapse of the free-music dreamland called Napster, the Internet is left with only a *zillion* other ways to download free music. My top choice was BearShare, and during the months after Enron fired me I managed to triple the size of my CD collection. Free is good, especially when you ain't got a job.

My wife did have a job, and each day she would come home to see that I was hard at work sending out résumés and pursuing job leads. She mercifully chose to ignore the growing stack of freshly burned CDs and the occasional mumble of "hit me" or "stay" while I played blackjack in my sleep.

Harry (the cat), Bailey (the dog), and I would spend our spare time watching TV, flipping between their favorite channel (Animal Planet) and the Enron hearings.

The hearings were great theater, as congressional representa-tives from across the country (each with thousands of dollars' worth of Enron campaign money in their pockets) acted out their dramatic disciplinary diatribe. In truth, the hearings would have been a monotonous parade of zipped lips if not for Jeff Skilling. As other executives, including Lay and Fastow, exercised their Fifth Amendment right to shut the hell up, Skilling decided that he (again, as the smartest human being on the planet) had nothing to hide. Skilling raised his right hand, swore to tell the truth, and faced countless hours of not-so-sharp questioning.

Using the Powers Report and testimony from other witnesses as a guide, the lawmakers of the House Energy and Commerce Committee had the first crack at Mr. Skilling. I watched for hours, in complete awe that he was actually answering questions.

Bickers called during the early part of Skilling's testimony.

"Dude . . . is he nuts?"

I responded, "He's not nuts, he's the smartest human being on the planet. He's confident he can beat these people."

"Yeah, but even if you know *absolutely nothing* you are better off taking the Fifth!"

I agreed. I know nothing . . . *and I would take the Fifth!*

In any case, Skilling's testimony provided plenty of thrills and spills—enough to keep me away from the online casino for a while.

"Mr. Chairman, I would like to answer the committee's questions, but on the advice of my counsel, I respectfully decline to answer questions based on the protection afforded me under the Constitution of the United States."

These were the words of Andy Fastow as spoken to Congress on February 7; similar words were spoken by Kopper, Causey, and Buy. Ken Lay would later take the Fifth as well, but offered the panel a touching opening statement as he sat amusingly low behind the microphone: "I come here today with a profound sadness, about what has happened to Enron, its current and former employees, retirees, shareholders, and other stakeholders." His remarks were followed by ninety minutes of scolding from the politicians he once donated money to.

Again, Skilling saved the show.

In a room filled with anger and tension, Skilling defended Enron and the business he had created: "We were . . . helping to resuscitate an ailing energy industry; and by bringing choice to a monopoly-dominated industry, we were trying to save consumers and small businesses billions of dollars each year. We believed *fiercely* in what we were doing.

"The financial statements of Enron, as far as I knew, accurately reflected the financial condition of the company. . . . at the time I left the company, I fervently believed that Enron would continue to be successful in the future."

James Greenwood, Republican from Pennsylvania, had a long response to Skilling's claim of miraculous unawareness. Greenwood listed the events of the Enron saga since Skilling's surprise departure:

> [Enron] . . . declared bankruptcy . . . fired its auditor . . . discovered massive insider dealings by its CFO and other employees . . . fired its CFO, treasurer, and one of its general counsels . . . saw Ken Lay's resignation as President and CEO . . . laid off over 4,500 employees, and has since reneged on its promise to pay them a severance . . . is under investigation by both houses of Congress, the DOJ, and the SEC . . . had to restate its earnings from 1997 to 2000 in the amount of $586 million . . . had to announce an equity write-down of $1.2 billion . . . not to mention likely additional earnings adjustments in excess of a billion dollars, that indicates that Enron was not even profitable while you were at the helm as CEO.

Skilling responded:

> On August 14, the date that I left the company, I believed that the company's financial statements were an accurate reflection of its financial condition.

For me, the highlight of the show was when Skilling couldn't remember the details of a board meeting (in October 2000 in which Fastow said Skilling approved the partnership deals) because the power had gone out, leaving the room dark.

Billy Tauzin, Republican from Louisiana, led the questions about the dark meeting. "You never heard Mr. Fastow say that you would approve all these transactions?" asked Tauzin.

Skilling answered, "I don't recall."

Tauzin again, "You just don't recall?"

Skilling again, "I do not recall."

Clifford Stearns, Republican from Florida, gave Skilling a fierce look at one point and said, "You are practicing plausible deniability."

I wanted him to say it. I stared deep into my television and *begged Skilling to say it.* C'mon Jeff . . . do it . . . say it . . .

You can't handle the truth!

Mr. Blue called to see how I was holding up and to ask if I had found a job. We talked and laughed about the hearings, and he shared his view that Skilling had "some serious balls" for agreeing to answer questions in such a hostile setting.

"So what do you think of what he is saying—that he didn't know the company was in trouble," I asked.

"C'mon . . . this guy's a control freak. Nothing went on behind his back."

I responded, "But like he said—it's a big company and there's no way . . ."

"If Skilling paid attention to *anything,* it was managing earnings," said Mr. Blue, interrupting me. "He was in charge, and the stock price was falling on his watch. No . . . he may not have been able to keep his hands on everything, but you bet your ass he was focused on the financial statements."

"What a mess." I was trying to back the conversation away from the heat, as I could sense Mr. Blue was ready to blow another gasket.

He took a deep breath and got philosophical on me: "Enron is about risk and control—and once they got addicted to the risk and the money it generated, the control part . . . well it just spun *out of control.*"

I quickly agreed, as if I was hearing that theory for the first time.

He changed the direction of the conversation and aimed it at me: "You're lucky Enron ended. You're lucky you got out when you did."

Huh? I sat there quietly, trying to decide if I felt "lucky" about recent events.

Mr. Blue continued, "Enron would have tested you—just like they tested me. If you passed that test, proving you could lie, cheat, and steal with a straight face, then you would have crossed that line and gone on to make millions like I did."

I thought about his millions, and how much he lost (he later told me it was just a *few* million). Did *he* lie, cheat, and steal to get there? Where exactly was that line? I didn't think Waterston or McLainey were on the bad side of that line. I decided it was just a few dozen people . . . okay, maybe a *few hundred* people that had passed that test and crossed the line.

But that still left more than twenty thousand honest, hardworking Enron employees, thinking they were part of something special, thinking they were part of a legitimate operation, and the next

"World's Leading Company."

He jumped back in. "By the way . . . the pipeline explosion in San Juan . . . the bankruptcy has put a hold on paying the victims." The way he randomly brought it up, it was clearly an incident that continued to be on his mind.

Sure enough, Enron's bankruptcy had halted the settlement negotiations between Enron and more than seven hundred plaintiffs with pending claims. These remaining plaintiffs (another eight hundred had already been paid a combined $60 million from Enron) hoped to be paid through Enron's liability insurance, but the future became uncertain when the cases were frozen. The victims' claims included financial loss, personal injury, post-traumatic stress disorder, and wrongful death.

Then I wondered: Had Mr. Blue been a whistle-blower when he tried to draw attention to that flawed pipeline in Puerto Rico? In terms of putting a noisy stop to a quietly developing problem, he was unsuccessful. But like Watkins and McMahon and Alexander and Mintz and perhaps hundreds of other high-minded employees, he had taken a *huge* risk and tried to deliver bad news to senior management, which continually sent the message: *No bad news!*

I asked Mr. Blue what he thought should happen to those who were guilty of greed. He was angry at the people who got out early enough to avoid facing the music.

"Eventually I'd like to see Rebecca Mark, Joe Sutton, Tom White, Lou Pai . . . " His long list continued, and he had it memorized. What he wanted was to see these people face the music and be forced to cough up some of their hardly earned cash.

Then he summed it up. "*Somebody* should go to jail." The way he said it, it was clear he didn't really care *who* went to prison, as long as it was somebody.

Our conversation came to a close with some projections for our own futures. He was retired, until something interesting came along.

In any case, he could no longer afford the retirement he had planned.

I told him about the dilemma I was facing in my job search: If the company was *too much* like Enron, I didn't want the job; if the company wasn't *enough* like Enron, I didn't want the job.

He laughed, "Why don't you just take a break from corporate America for a while."

Good idea, but how could I afford it?

Shortly after Enron realized its mistake and took me off the payroll, it sent me the $4,500 it should have sent me two months earlier. On top of the accidental paychecks, I thought that was a nice gesture.

Then, because Enron terminated my employment after the new year (instead of trying to lay me off retroactively, and possibly be forced to explain it), I qualified for new vacation days. That's right—as soon as January 1 came along, employees instantly qualified for three weeks of vacation all at once. So shortly after the $4,500, Enron sent me a paycheck for those three weeks of vacation I never used. How could I have taken the time off—I didn't work there anymore? Then the court approved another $1,100 for each laid-off employee.

In all, I got six weeks' worth of goofy paychecks, another three weeks of "earned" vacation pay, and $5,600 in "slap-in-the-face" severance compensation. The total *almost* added up to what my regular severance package would have been under the scrapped Enron plan. The total *almost* added up to me being less pissed-off about the retention bonuses.

Then the court approved *another* set of retention bonuses for remaining employees—this time to the tune of $140 million. Again I was livid, but realized Enron's foul-up with the payroll had left me better off than most.

As Enron continued to finance my unemployment (which naturally prevented me from collecting unemployment checks from the state of Texas), I continued to ponder my future and follow the televised Enron hearings.

Skilling had another chance to take the Fifth on February 26—and didn't—in front of the Senate Commerce Committee.

The focus of the panel was on earlier testimony by Skilling, Sherron Watkins, Jeff McMahon, Jordan Mintz, and material from the Powers Report. Watkins had expressed her opinion that Skilling was "well briefed" on the questionable transactions. McMahon had testified that he and Skilling discussed the partnerships, including McMahon's concern about Fastow's self-enrichment. Mintz testified he had sent Skilling documents pertaining to the partnerships, which for some reason Skilling chose not to sign.

Byron Dorgan, Democratic senator from North Dakota, was very direct as he "asked" a series of nonquestions. "Mr. Skilling says, 'Ms. Watkins is wrong, Mr. McMahon is wrong, the Powers report is wrong, the market is wrong.' You know, Mr. Skilling, I have great difficulty believing your testimony."

Skilling responded, "I have not lied to Congress or anyone else."

Barbara Boxer, Democratic senator from California, took the hearing to a more productive and purposeful level when she presented a huge blue poster displaying her favorite Skilling quote: "We are the good guys—we are on the side of angels." The quote, which came from a Skilling interview on PBS's *Frontline* regarding California deregulation, had nothing to do with the issues facing the committee—but Boxer seemed to enjoy the moment.

I watched for hours as Senate lawmakers told Skilling they didn't believe him, Watkins offered her opinion without supplying any facts,

Skilling denied that he knew anything about anything . . .

. . . and for some reason Bailey the dog would bark every time they showed Skilling's lawyer.

"It's my expectation that I will probably spend the next five to ten years of my life battling those lawsuits," said Skilling of his pending legal battles.

If his legal battles involved the same prattle as heard in the Senate that day, it'll be closer to twenty years.

Wednesday—February 27, 2002
ENRNQ opening price: $0.28
ENRNQ closing price: $0.27
ENRNQ trading volume: 7,740,500

A handful of friends remained at Enron in February, so I made occasional visits to the Death Star. After getting laid off *for real,* I lost access to the garage and the building. It felt strange to park as a guest and actually pay for parking at an Enron lot.

It felt even *stranger* to see how empty it was. The old security company had left, replaced by a new one. The plants were gone. The big disco E logo was dark and had stopped spinning. Even the news vans were gone, at least until the next big headline came along.

From the outside of the building I could tell Ken Lay wasn't there. The place just felt different. The chrome wasn't as polished, the mirrored glass didn't reflect as brightly, and the logos looked like even they were humiliated.

Lay had been replaced by business restructuring specialist Stephen Cooper. New CEO Cooper had twenty-five years' experience trying to rebuild such companies as Polaroid, Trans World Airlines (TWA), and Boston Chicken (later called Boston

Market). Cooper immediately began looking to Enron's future instead of looking back at its chaotic past: "The good news is not only do I not know what went wrong, it is literally of no interest to me."

UBS had moved into my old trading floor to run the business they had adopted. As I waited in the lobby to meet friends, I was lucky to count five people at any given moment—and this was at *lunchtime*.

In the news, Enron Corp. had expressed a preference for getting a new name, sending "Enron" into the history books forever as part of the restructuring plan. Bickers had some ideas on what that new name could be—believe me, you don't want to know.

That day at Enron, I overheard the breaking news that Enron Field was finally getting a new name. Unfortunately, speculation would continue as Astros Field was only temporary until a new corporate sponsor could be found.

Astros team owner Drayton McLane Jr. said he was glad to "put this issue behind us." McLane estimated it would be a few months before one of seven other Houston companies won the naming rights to the two-year-old stadium. The terminated deal with Enron, which had been a thirty-year agreement for $100 million, ended with a $2.1 million buyback by the Astros. The team didn't want fans to be "reminded on a daily basis of this continuing tragedy."

Rumors—and overwhelming fear—spread across the city as speculation grew over which seven companies were vying over the naming rights. We knew Arthur Andersen Park was not likely, but beyond that it could have been anything. Waste Management Field (a.k.a. The Dump) would make eating hotdogs a little upsetting. El Paso Park would definitely confuse a few people on their way to the game.

But the worst case—the nightmare scenario—was that naming rights would be sold to create Gallery Furniture Stadium. For as long as I can remember, while growing up in Houston, the yelping and shrieking of Gallery Furniture owner Jim "Mattress Mac" McIngvale has invaded our living rooms. While talking at a thousand words a second, Mattress Mac would screech about his low-priced sofas and recliners (the kind that can be plugged into the wall, with refrigerated compartments for cold beverages under the armrests). Recently, the company sponsored a college football bowl game, called the Galleryfurniture.com Bowl, which quickly became the laughing stock of sports commercialization. If Gallery Furniture were to successfully acquire the naming rights to the Astros Field, several hundred thousand Houstonians would undoubtedly flee to a new life in Canada.

As the stadium waited for a new corporate name, *thousands* of Enron logos were removed from the stadium, as "Enron Field" slipped into history.

Across town at the new football stadium, Ken Lay had surrendered his ownership stake in Houston's new NFL football franchise, the Houston Texans. Team owner Bob McNair purchased Lay's minority stake in the team for an undisclosed amount. In the press release, McNair stated, "Ken Lay has requested that I purchase his interest in the Texans. I have consummated this transaction . . . and Ken no longer owns any interest in the Texans."

Among the remaining owners of the team: former Enron vice chairman Joe Sutton.

As Enron faded away from the Houston sports scene, Enron logos were also being removed from a local Boys & Girls Club near downtown. The center, which included a gymnasium and computer room, was taking down the Enron logos. The bankruptcy preempted a $2.4 million donation from Enron that would have supported the center for ten years. Fortunately, a local businessman stepped up and made a new donation, keeping the center active under a non-Enron name.

To the other extreme, the Smithsonian's National Museum of American History in Washington, D.C., was starting a collection of Enron memorabilia. The Smithsonian started the collection with a coffee mug and a copy of the *Code of Ethics* manual (just like the one I left behind at my desk).

A Smithsonian spokeswoman said the museum, which holds more than 140 million artifacts, would consider acquiring the enormous Crooked E statues that sat in front of the Death Star once Enron had changed its name.

An Enron spokesperson responded to the idea of selling the logo statues, saying that Enron "had some casual interest in the signs, and a good number of tourists who stop for a family picture." The spokesperson added, "But are we tossing and turning about eBay-ers with hacksaws? No."

At first-day orientation, every new Enron employee was given a *Code of Ethics* booklet, but that was the regular employee version.

There was another version, made specifically for "Executives and Management." Here are some highlights from this sixty-four-page, pocket-size booklet:

From the section titled "Principles of Human Rights": "We are committed to operating safely and conducting business worldwide in compliance with all applicable environmental, health, and safety laws and regulations and strive to improve the lives of the people in the regions in which we operate."

From the section titled "Securities Trades by Company Personnel": "No director, officer, or employee of Enron Corp. . . . shall, directly or indirectly, trade in the securities of [publicly traded Enron companies] while in the possession of material non-public information." The booklet then offers some examples of such material non-public information that shouldn't be traded on: "projections of future earnings or losses; news of a pending or proposed merger, acquisition, or tender offer; changes in management; impending bankruptcy or financial liquidity problems; and the gain or loss of a substantial customer or supplier."

From the section titled "Business Ethics": "No bribes, bonuses, kickbacks, lavish entertainment, or gifts will be given or received in exchange for special position, price, or privilege."

"Relations with [Enron's] many publics—customers, stockholders, governments, employees, suppliers, press, and bankers—will be conducted in honesty, candor, and fairness."

From the section titled "Governmental Affairs and Political Contributions": "[Enron] employs governmental relations and public policy personnel who are assigned the responsibility of fulfilling its corporate public affairs responsibility, communicating with public bodies and officials pertaining to [Enron's] position on public policy questions, and maintaining the goodwill and understanding of public officials."

From the section beginning on page 57, which *should have been* titled "The Andy Fastow Rule": "No full-time officer or employee should: Own an interest in or participate, directly or indirectly, in the profits of any other entity which does business with or is a competitor of [Enron], unless such ownership has been previously disclosed in writing to the Chairman of the Board or Chief Executive Officer of Enron Corp. and such officer has determined that such interest or participation does not adversely affect the best interests of [Enron]."

All employees were required by Enron to sign a statement of compliance.

One of my favorite publications since business school has been *Business 2.0,* a magazine always on the leading edge of changing markets and new technology. Of course, being on that leading edge often meant that *Business 2.0* took the leading step into a cow patty—first with some of the e-stupidity of the late '90s, and then with Enron.

In an editor's note in early 2002, the magazine acknowledged that they had been En-wronged:

> *It's worth pointing out that, yes, we celebrated Enron's achievements before the bankruptcy and scandal. We had no idea that Enron was, well, a fraud. We—along with regulatory agencies, Wall Street, and pretty much the entirety of American journalism— just plain got suckered. And for that we apologize.*

Suckered indeed. For example, *Business 2.0* had Enron's cutting-edge, digital-revolution-leading CEO Jeff Skilling on the cover of their August 2001 issue. The issue hit newsstands *less than a week* before Skilling resigned.

Apology accepted.

In an attempt to avenge their suckered Enron past, they covered their March 2002 issue with a photograph of Ken Lay sporting a five-inch nose. When I first saw the Kenocchio cover, I laughed so hard I nearly popped a blood vessel.

The following month, *Business 2.0* offered "The 101 Dumbest Moments in Business." Enron scored sixteen spots on the list, which included a self-inflicted jab at the magazine itself for the timing of the Skilling cover. Linda Lay's tearful *Today Show* appearance, the name "Enron Field," Lehman's Strong Buy rating, and the many antics of Lay and Skilling were among the Enron entries.

Also on the list, at #76, was Enron's payment of $55 million in retention bonuses just before the bankruptcy. I wasn't surprised to see it there, but I was surprised to see so many other similar entries that occurred in 2001:

- After filing for bankruptcy, Polaroid paid $19 million in retention bonuses to its top forty-five executives.
- Global Crossing founder Gary Winnick cashed out $734 million in stock while leading the company to bankruptcy.
- Pacific Gas & Electric, after filing for bankruptcy caused by the California energy crisis, paid its executives retention bonuses of $17.5 million.
- Webvan CEO George Shaheen led the company's stock into a 99 percent free fall in less than two years. Then he quit, earning himself an annual pension of $375,000 (which couldn't actually be paid because Webvan went bankrupt a few months later).

I didn't get it—what the hell was going on? Since when did *filing for bankruptcy* become such a lucrative exit strategy?

Here's a news flash on retention bonuses: How about if *keeping their jobs* could be considered compensation enough; or, if you do need to keep critical people around by paying bonuses, make the amounts somewhere between "reasonable" and "excessive," instead of past the point of *ridiculous.*"

The two issues of *Business 2.0* sparked my decision to save some of my own Enron memorabilia. I figured someday I could look back on Kenocchio and the list of Enron's dumb moments and have a good laugh; plus, if the Smithsonian was starting a collection . . .

My collection included anything leftover from the eBay sales (like that cherished baseball), my Enron coffee mug, my security badge, some leftover business cards, plus a few interesting documents from my time at Enron:

- My offer letter from Enron: *"We take great pleasure in offering you employment with Enron North America, the leading provider of worldwide energy solutions. We are confident that a career with Enron can provide you with the professional challenges, satisfactions, and rewards you are seeking."*

- Enron's October 2001 presentation (after the devastating third-quarter earnings release) to Wall Street analysts, which was the last earnings presentation before bankruptcy: *"Conclusion: continued strong operating performance; increased transparency of financial and operating results; active management of non-core businesses. Enron's diversified franchise provides solid platform for sustainable growth."*

- A memo from Ken Lay that came with the *Code of Ethics*, dated July 1, 2000: *"As officers and employees of Enron Corp. . . . we are responsible for conducting the business affairs of the Company in accordance with all applicable laws and in a moral and honest manner. . . . An employee shall not conduct himself or herself in a manner, which directly or indirectly would be detrimental to the best interests of the Company or in a manner, which would bring the employee financial gain separately derived as a direct consequence of his or her employment with the Company. . . . We want to be proud of Enron and to know that it enjoys a reputation for fairness and honesty and that it is respected. . . . **Let's keep that reputation high.**"*

• • •

I decided to stuff my Enron collection into a box and forget about it. In a way, I was relieved they weren't paying me anymore. Cin-

gular Wireless had finally cut off my Enron mobile phone, and
Enron had also stopped paying for my Internet service.

Maybe I could finally put the Enron mess behind me.

Almost a year after my Enron job interview with McLainey, I met
with him again. Duffy was there as well, and the three of us sat
around and talked Enron over some margaritas.

Our vision of packaging up our team and our business plan and
selling it to the highest bidder was all but dead. Ultimately, the
businesses we were dealing with wanted to avoid anything Enron;
in fact, they wanted to distance themselves from Enron. At the
time of this meeting, we were each exclusively focused on our
individual futures, no longer our future as a business team.

So when we talked Enron, we were finally talking Enron in
the past tense.

McLainey was surprisingly calm about the whole thing. He
wasn't bitter at all. "I'd just like to see them get due process . . .
then whatever happens happens," he said of Enron executives
facing investigations.

Duffy disagreed, and smiled as he shared a more direct craving
for justice. "I would like it if they all got hit with conspiracy of
fraud charges. . . . I'd like to see them lose every penny."

As we discussed the hearings, the players, and the potential
outcomes, I couldn't help but think about the thousands of Enron
employees just like Duffy and McLainey. We all joined Enron for
the same reasons, and we all got screwed by Enron for the same
reasons, but unlike me, these two guys had kids to support and had
just relocated their lives to Houston on behalf of Enron. I had it
easy. I was lucky.

Then McLainey pointed out that he'd had some luck as well:
"And by *God's grace*! . . . we got PAID for an extra two months!"

Later in the month of March 2002, McLainey would get a new job in Denver, Colorado—an engineering job completely unrelated to Enron's business. McLainey and his wife would pack their two little girls—plus Pumpkin the hamster and Squiggles and Zippy, the two lizards—into the minivan for a drive to the next city. It was a drive from humid and hot to cold and snowy; a drive from sea level to a mile high; a drive from bankruptcy to fresh opportunity. He would say good-bye to Houston, and he hoped it was for the last time.

Also late in March, Duffy landed a consulting job in Houston. Unlike McLainey's job, Duffy's new opportunity was *closely* related to what we did at Enron. I was refreshed to hear the news, as it somewhat validated the work we had done. We had so many great ideas, I was happy to hear that Duffy would be keeping them alive.

Since his new consulting practice was a reincarnation of our old group, Duffy later offered me a job. I was flattered, but respectfully declined.

As Mr. Blue had suggested, I needed a break from corporate America.

Liz Perry landed a new job in sales. When Liz and I met for lunch she was only in her first week. She explained to me what she was selling, but I honestly didn't get it—some industrial system or equipment or something.

Whatever it was, she was happy to be employed. Enron's accidental paychecks had bridged the gap for her and her husband, and the new job meant they could keep their house and continue feeding their fat-ass dog.

I asked about her new work environment, how it compared to Enron.

"I like it. It's nice to have some freedom [being out on sales calls]; not as intense; not as high-pressure." She explained that she didn't miss the PRC process, the arrogant fraternity culture, or the Building Guy in the elevators.

She continued, "But I do miss that feeling—that feeling that I'm part of an amazing company, a company that everyone is in awe of."

"Do people at your new job care that you came from Enron?"

Liz responded, "They're not bothered by it, if that's what you mean . . . but they do tease me about it. Like, they call me 'Miss Enron,' and whenever there's math involved, they say, 'How would you know, you're doing Enron math.' "

I laughed—not because the teasing was funny, but because the teasing was so low-level compared to Enron teasing.

And if anyone could deal with the "boys will be boys" behavior at a company, it was Liz Perry. She was the perfect example of an emerging truth among ex-employees: If you could handle Enron, you can handle anything.

I never met up with Lazarri after the bankruptcy, but I heard from other members on our old team that he was still job searching. I found it hard to believe, especially with all the firms in New York and twenty-seven trading firms in Houston grabbing ex-Enron talent.

Then it became clear that maybe his old Enron attitude was getting in the way of his next job. Those who had spoken to Lazarri quoted him, in reference to his failed job search, as saying, "Those fuckers are just scared of me . . . afraid I'll just go in and make them look bad."

Make them look bad? Quite possible.

As I pulled up to the Japanese restaurant, I thought about rice.

No, not *cooked* rice.

I was thinking about Enron's core values (RICE) of Respect, Integrity, Communication, and Excellence. I was amazed at how well Enron had drilled the value acronym into our heads—yet had failed *miserably* in the practice of those values.

The restaurant was Café Japon, a sushi place near the Houston neighborhood of River Oaks. I was there to meet Waterston. He was late, and I was early.

As I waited by the hostess stand, I noticed an awkward buzz throughout the restaurant. I scanned the restaurant, and then I saw him.

Andy Fastow.

I had seen him on CNN just days before, raising his right hand and announcing he would "respectfully decline to answer questions."

I had a few questions for him myself, but I just stood there and stared.

He had a fish-eating grin on his face. I watched as he and his wife finished their meal, paid the bill by credit card, and got up to leave. Fastow looked relaxed and *happy*. It even seemed like he enjoyed the fact that everyone in the restaurant was staring at him.

As he passed me, we locked eyes. Perhaps he knew my face from around Enron, or perhaps he was reading my mind. In either case, we stared at each other for several slow-motion seconds.

Then he was gone.

For *days* I would continue to come up with the perfect thing to say to him, all kinds of good stuff. But at that moment, without preparation, nothing sounded right in my head.

When Waterston showed up about thirty seconds after Fastow left, I told him, "You just missed Andy."

He froze. "Really!" I could see him thinking about what *he* would have said . . . or not said.

I asked, "What would have happened if you arrived a minute sooner and seen him?" I expected a graphic description of hand-to-hand combat, possibly involving chopsticks and ear holes.

"Nothing." Waterston said it like it was hard to say, like he was trying *hard* not to be angry about Enron.

I responded, "Oh, c'mon? Really."

"Really . . . I would have said 'Hello,' it would have been awkward, but . . . " Then he cut to the chase: "I'm not angry at anyone; I'm not angry about Enron. I worked hard, got paid a lot of money, and now it's time for something else."

I admired what he was saying, but found it hard to believe.

"You don't believe me?" he asked.

I didn't believe him because, out of everyone I knew at Enron, he had the most to lose. Waterston was in the pole position at Enron. He was considered a genius, and respected for his brilliance. The prime of his Enron career had been right in front of him, and bankruptcy took it away.

I responded, "Yeah, I believe you."

Knowing I wasn't convinced, he added, "Enron was finished last August—don't you remember when I first suggested we start looking for new jobs? Anyway, it's over now . . . it's time to move on to bigger and better things."

As I scanned the sushi menu, I noticed something interesting. The "Enron Roll" was not only the gaudiest and most overpacked sushi roll on the menu, it was also the most expensive.

baked with green onion 6.50
VOLCANO ROLL (6 PIECES)
Baked white tuna and broccoli 6.50
SILKWORM ROLL
Shrimp, enoki mushroom and avocado 6.50
ENRON ROLL (8 PIECES)
Spicy salmon with green onion tri-color tobiko, spicy
spouts, shrimps and avocado 7.95

SUSHI ROLLS
(All 6 pieces except where noted)

California Roll	Crabmeat With Avocado and Cucumber . $3.50
Hamachi Tataki Maki	Baked Yellowtail with Green Onion $3.50
Tekka Maki	Tuna roll $3.50
Futomaki	Big Roll with Egg, Crab, Spinach

From the menu at Café Japan, near River Oaks in Houston.

The Enron Roll had three types of caviar spread over a cut roll of shrimp and spicy salmon . . . and it tasted like fish shit.

Waterston didn't really care what happened to the Enron executives, like Fastow, who would be defending themselves for years to come.

"I think the damage to their reputations, and the years of legal battles, is punishment enough," he said.

He was more concerned about the long-term effects of the Enron failure on markets and the business environment.

Waterston explained, "[Enron had] come so far with deregulation and had developed markets that didn't exist before. I don't want to see this thing slow that down. I don't want to see the markets flip over to *reregulation*."

We agreed that Enron, for all the negative that came out in the end, delivered positive ideas and fantastically forward thinking to the world.

Oops. I'm starting to sound like Jeff Skilling.

After our brief sushi meal, Waterston had to run off to a job interview. I stayed behind for a moment to ask the waitress a question:

"Excuse me . . . the Enron Roll? Where did that come from?"

In the best English she could muster, "Oh, they use that name to sell more rolls—but now customer ask to remove it—so it go away very soon."

"Hey Bickers," I said when he answered the phone.

He sounded relieved it was me. "Dude . . . how's the job search?" He was dealing with other energy companies in trouble, as they were "pulling an Enron."

I skipped the job question. "Guess who I saw at a sushi restaurant today."

"Uhh . . . a sushi chef?"

"Fastow . . . with a big, red-carpet grin on his face."

Bickers's response was slightly different from Waterston's. "Holy shit! That bastard—did you kick his ass?"

"Why—so I can go to jail with him?"

After talking more about the Fastow encounter, Bickers and I flashed back through all the peculiar events of the past year.

Then he said it again. "Dude . . . you ought to write a book about this shit."

"Whatever, Bickers. That's the second time you've said that. I don't have *a clue* how to write a book."

As Enron's existence—the name, the sponsorships, the logos, the sushi roll—became part of the past, the sequel to its story was shaping up. This sequel had the makings of a gut-wrenching courtroom drama, one I would most certainly enjoy.

The legal cases against Enron and Andersen executives seemed fairly clear early on, as did their defense positions.

Lay, Skilling, Fastow, Kopper, and the Andersen shredding team faced the greatest legal threat.

Lay was in charge; therefore, he had some responsibility even though he may have averted his eyes. A jury in a Lay case would probably be given "ostrich instruction," meaning that a judge would tell them not to let a defendant off the hook simply because he intentionally kept his head in the sand. Lay might have *knowingly chosen not to know things,* a defensive action that won't protect him if prosecutors offer proof of intent and recklessness.

Skilling, by speaking at hearings and facing the music out loud, put himself at risk for perjury charges if anything he said is found inconsistent with the truth. McMahon and Mintz delivered some examples of possible inconsistencies, with many more to come.

Fastow and Kopper, who will likely go with the "I just did what I was told" defense, could get hit with mail- and wire-fraud charges, which would apply to things like deceptive SEC filings, press releases, and investor communications . . . and hiding the truth about the money they made from the partnerships.

The Andersen shredding team was facing obstruction-of-justice charges. The big problem for prosecutors: How do you prove the relevance of a document that no longer exists?

And if prosecutors could prove a RICO violation, then more serious charges and jail time could be inflicted upon *several* executives. The RICO Act (Racketeer Influenced and Corrupt Organizations Act of 1970) would apply if investigators could show that certain violations were committed (and covered up) by multiple parties working together.

Convictions under the RICO Act (which could create the *new* Enron acronym of "Respect, Integrity, Communication, and Organized crime") were the legal result most ex-employees I talked to were hoping for. It was the result most likely to include jail time.

Whatever the legal outcomes, it was well understood during the months following bankruptcy that the proceedings would provide years and years of perverse entertainment.

These were not going to be quick and dirty cases. Defendants' attorneys would stretch the legal fight out as long as possible, fearing "premature adjudication."

Soon after I ran into Fastow, other ex-employees told me they bumped into Ken Lay at the George Bush Intercontinental Airport in Houston. Instead of being at the hangar for Enron Airlines— walking down the steps of the Gulfstream V with an entourage of pilots, baggage handlers, and security personnel—Lay was standing there by himself, waiting for his luggage just like everybody else. He wasn't hiding from the crowd of Houstonians that stared at him. He wasn't wearing dark sunglasses and didn't have a hat pulled tightly over his head.

Lay had just flown to Houston from Colorado, leaving his wife, Linda, back at one of their mountain keeps, in the state where their other mountain homes were up for sale.

He had just flown commercial.

Many people—mostly ex-employees I have spoken to—have expressed how sorry they feel for Ken Lay. They explain that he is a kind, decent man with great character; a man who was sucker punched by his "lieutenants." They say he deserves recognition for building the Enron that others destroyed.

Others say that he is an evil man, and they draw comparisons between Lay and the Roman emperor Nero or other twisted leaders of kingdoms past. They describe him as the embodiment of greed, or as the symbol of everything wrong with capitalism.

Personally, I couldn't care less.

The judgment of what Ken Lay is—or was—simply doesn't fall

under my jurisdiction. Judges, juries, professors, history books, and the heavenly forces can make that call. All I can think is what I know.

Ken Lay merged a pair of dusty old pipeline companies, and in fifteen years built a globally dominant and impenetrable corporate force. He assembled a team of the most influential, clever, and ruthless executives ever to occupy a single glass tower. He then used that power and those people to change government, to change industries, to change markets, and to change the way the world does business. These changes were designed to feed and nurture his Enron Empire . . .

. . . until it grew into a monster he could no longer control.

But even with Enron six feet under, and with Ken Lay flying commercial airlines again, the legend doesn't end.

Because the monster Ken Lay created has a ghost, one that will haunt the business world forever.

If an investor is worried about the next Enron, they need look no further than a company's board of directors. The directors are the watchdogs for the investor—with the pure and simple task of maximizing shareholder value. The question shouldn't be, "Do I trust this company?" because a "company" is nothing more than an officially authorized illusion. A company is not a person; therefore, it should not be judged as having human characteristics. A company is not trustworthy, loyal, naughty, or nice. For those who argue that companies are "controlled" by people, I refer them to Exhibit X: Enron. The people there were "controlled" by the company.

The question of trust should be asked on an individual level, not trust in the company but trust in its leaders. Am I talking about CEOs and CFOs and the rest of the C-level managers? No.

Let me now refer you to Exhibits Y and Z: Skilling and Fastow. The question—and the responsibility—of investor trust should be aimed aggressively at the independent members of the board of directors. Unlike management, they have an agenda strictly in line with shareholders. After all, directors are most often *elected* by the shareholders. The members of the C-level gang, on the other hand, have peripheral agendas, some that can be potentially lethal to the stock price and the stability of the company.

The days of quick and simple board meetings are over. Enron's collapse is an alarm bell for board members to start *earning* their $300,000 per year, instead of just sitting on their hands (sometimes in a blacked-out room), listening to "reports" from management and agreeing to whatever recommendations that individual directors or executives make. Board members have a fiduciary responsibility to act in the best interest of—and *to protect*—the shareholders, even if it means *grilling* one another, arguing with the leaders, and breaking down political (and social) barriers within the company.

People have asked me who I blame the most for the Enron mess, and now you know my answer.

As an investor, I have three things to point out to the independent board members of every company I own stock in (and some companies I don't own stock in):

1. There are a lot of crooks out there.

Studies by the FBI and Bureau of Justice Statistics in 1999 (the last year available) show that white-collar crime is alive and well in the United States. In that year, more than 487,000 arrests were made in the crime categories of fraud, embezzlement, forgery, and counterfeiting.

Also in 1999, federal courts convicted over 12,000 individuals of committing crimes in those same categories. For cases related to financial fraud and institutional matters, the Department of Justice ordered $491 million in restitution payments.

In 2001, the SEC ordered the surrender of $522 million in illegally obtained trading profits. Over the five-year period from 1997 to 2001, the SEC initiated an annual average of 495 enforcement actions (including civil, administrative, and contempt) against individuals and companies that broke securities laws.

White-collar crime isn't just for breakfast anymore. Pay attention to what your senior managers are doing and what they may be hiding.

2. Risk has gotten riskier.

Risk is the possibility of loss. It sounds so simple, yet the business world is facing possibilities that are becoming increasingly complex.

Risk management is not about *avoiding* risks—risk management is about managing risk (Surprise!). Board members need to be aware of what these risks are and, more important, how the CEO and others are managing them.

Risks facing businesses have always been bucketed into a few basic categories: market risks (such as foreign-currency-exchange risk, interest-rate risk, commodity-price risk, and equity-price risk); business risks (such as competitor risk, technology risk, and supply/demand risk); and operational risk (such as natural-disaster risk, quality-control risk, and management-error risk).

Let's see, I left out liquidity risk, regulatory risk, environmental risk, industry-consolidation risk, international-expansion risk, insurance risk, bankruptcy risk, credit risk, payroll risk, legal risk, model risk, Internet-hacker risk, computer-virus risk, terrorist risk, fraudulent-behavior risk, you-could-go-to-prison risk, you-just-lied-to-the-shareholders risk, the CEO-said-

"asshole"-risk, *Wall Street Journal* risk (credit Andy Fastow with that one), and many, many, many more.

My point: Perhaps the board, and the board's committees, should raise more questions about the risks a company is (or is not) dealing with.

3. Ethical Behavior = Higher Returns.

As proven by Enron, dirty deeds at work inside a company can cut a stock in half in just a few stock-market minutes (see above: *Wall Street Journal* risk). Sudden surprises that sink well below the ethical waterline can do much more harm to the stock price than would consistent, clear doses of the unshredded truth. Especially when those sudden surprises are first revealed by news organizations like the *Journal*.

Deliberately misleading stock analysts, masking true financial conditions, spewing positive propaganda around failing projects, silently delivering flawed products—these efforts to conceal reality will indeed support a short-term gain, but ultimately the truth will wipe out investor confidence and the many price multiples that are tied to it.

In business schools, unsexy values often take a backseat to the glorified priority of "maximizing shareholder wealth." After 2001, those unsexy values (respect, integrity . . .) may have earned their place among the *critical components* of maximizing shareholder wealth.

Enron actually had those values well defined in its own *Code of Ethics* handbook, but it appears the only time the board of directors ever paid attention to that handbook was when they were *officially agreeing to disregard it.*

• • •

Tuesday—March 26, 2002
ENRNQ opening price: two dimes
ENRNQ closing price: four nickels
ENRNQ trading volume: a few million

I looked in the mirror.

What I saw—exactly a year after the day I joined Enron—was someone who desperately needed to shave.

I looked in the mirror, again.

I saw an unemployed guy, but a *much smarter* unemployed guy; smarter because I worked at Enron and Enron *made people smarter;* smarter because I learned that nothing in life is risk-free; smarter because I realized that people—not corporate identities—are the real substance of the business world.

I was smarter because the guy in the mirror was not the next Mr. Blue. I was smarter because my wife, my family, my friends, my dog, and my cat were much more important than bonuses, stock options, and an office on the fiftieth floor.

Was I stupid to believe in Enron? No way—Enron was thousands of people with thousands of spectacular, positive ideas.

Was I stupid to see Enron as a pot of gold? Absolutely.

Was I *greedy?*

I took the accidental paychecks, I got my free computer, and I sold my Enron stuff on eBay. Was that greed? Or did Enron really owe me? They *did* lay me off, and they *did* cancel the severance plan just the day before—after fifteen years with it. Plus, I lost thousands of dollars on ENE stock in 2001.

Was I greedy, or was I just trying to get back some of what I lost?

By any definition, "greed" is an *excessive* desire, but I was never exactly clear where that "excessive" line should be drawn. When

does desire—for money or material goods or whatever—
become excessive?

We live in a world in which desire builds things, invents things,
cures things, and discovers things. But when does this desire
become gratuitous? Is it excessive to want a better life—to want
more adventure, a bigger house, a nicer car, fancier clothes, or premium dog food?

I don't think it's that simple. I think greed—or excessive
desire—is defined by the means, not the end. It's the *behavior* that
should be tested for excessiveness. *Greedy* is a term that applies to
someone who lies, cheats, and steals in the name of possessing
more than they need or even deserve. Financial success alone
doesn't equal greed, but being a *scumbag* with financial success—
that's where the line should be drawn.

So were Enron executives greedy because they had eight-digit
bank accounts? No. Were they greedy if those millions were generated by fraud or at the expense of others? Absolutely! And the
Enron culture of bonus-driven behavior that twisted the truth and
devastated thousands of people . . . Greed, Incorporated!

A year after starting at Enron I looked in the mirror, and I was
thankful that *I could stand to look in the mirror.* I thought others might
be having a hard time with that.

The time had come for me to turn toward the future. I walked
away from the mirror and thought of what that future might be. A
break from corporate America? A book? Several people had suggested I write one, and I got those extra paychecks as if even Enron
somehow supported the idea. Plus, writing a book would put an
end to my futile job search.

Whatever. I needed to put Enron behind . . .

. . . And then I remembered my Enron e-mail. The paychecks
had stopped, the parking garage wouldn't let me in, my security

badge was useless, the mobile phone . . . all of these things had come to an end.

But what about my Enron e-mail? I hadn't checked it since the paychecks stopped. As a source of curiosity and idle amusement, I checked to see if my password had expired. Why did I care? I didn't, really.

I sat down at my computer and went to the e-mail login site. After three unsuccessful attempts, the Enron server gave me a plain white screen.

And on that screen was a message. It was a message that finally put an end to my Enron journey.

"Error: Access is Denied."

List of Sources

While much of the information contained in *Anatomy of Greed* originates from the personal experience and opinions of many individuals directly associated with Enron, including my own, I have also relied upon a variety of external sources, which are listed below. In addition to those listed, I accumulated internal Enron materials during and after my employment with the company. I also interviewed more than one hundred former and current Enron employees, retirees, shareholders, customers, partners, and competitors.

The following sources were invaluable to me in gathering and corroborating the facts contained in *Anatomy of Greed* (the names of reporters who deserve special recognition are listed below the name of their publications):

1400smith.com (http://www.1400smith.com)

Asia Times (http://www.atimes.com)

Associated Press (http://wire.ap.org/APpackages/enron_flash)

BBC News (http://news.bbc.co.uk/hi/english/in_depth/business/2002/enron)

BigCharts.com (http://bigcharts.marketwatch.com)

Business 2.0 (http://www.business2.com)

BusinessWeek and **BusinessWeek Online** (http://www.businessweek.com)

Businesswire.com (http://www.businesswire.com)

CBS Marketwatch (http://www.marketwatch.com)

Center for Responsive Politics (http://www.opensecrets.org)

CFO Magazine (http://www.cfo.com)

CNBC TV (http://moneycentral.msn.com/cnbc/tv)

CNN and **CNNfn** (http://money.cnn.com)

CorpWatch.org (http://www.corpwatch.org)

CowParade Holdings Corporation (http://www.cowparade.net)

CSPAN, Televised Enron Hearings (http://www.c-span.org/enron)

Daily Camera (http://www.thedailycamera.com)

The Daily Enron (http://www.thedailyenron.com)
Denver Post (http://www.denverpost.com)
Engineering News-Record (http://www.enr.com)
Enron Ex-Employee Relief Fund (http://www.eerfa.com)
Enron Press Room (http://www.enron.com/corp/pressroom)
EnronX.org (http://www.enronx.org)
Fast Company (http://www.fastcompany.com)
    Chuck Salter
Federal Bureau of Investigations (http://www.fbi.gov)
Federal Election Committee (http://www.fec.gov)
Financial Times (http://specials.ft.com/enron)
FindLaw Investigations: Enron (http://news.findlaw.com/legalnews/lit/enron)
Fortune.com and **Fortune Magazine** (http://www.fortune.com)
    Bethany McLean
    Patricia Sellers
Harris County Public Records (http://www.co.harris.tx.us)
HarvardWatch (http://www.harvardwatch.org)
House Energy and Commerce Committee (http://energycommerce.house.gov)
Houston Astros (http://houston.astros.mlb.com)
Houston Business Journal (http://houston.bizjournals.com)
    Jennifer Darwin
    Monica Perrin
Houston Chronicle (http://www.chron.com)
    Alan Bernstein
    Mary Flood
    Tom Fowler
    Laura Goldberg
    David Ivanovich
    Bill Murphy
    Mike Tolson
    Allan Turner
Information for Former Enron Employees (http://www.enron.com/corp/alumni)
Kaplan Fox & Kilsheimer LLP (http://www.kaplanfox.com)
KHOU TV 11—Houston CBS Affiliate
KPRC TV 2—Houston NBC Affiliate

KRIV TV 26—Houston Fox Affiliate
KTRK TV 13—Houston ABC Affiliate
Laydoff.com (http://www.laydoff.com)
Los Angeles Times (http://www.latimes.com)

    Lisa Girion

    Jeff Leeds

    Thomas Mulligan

    Lee Romney

    David Streitfeld

Milberg Weiss Bershad Hynes & Lerach LLP (http://www.milberg.com)
Moles.org (http://www.moles.org)
MSNBC.com and MSNBC TV (http://www.msnbc.com)
National Transportation Safety Board (http://www.ntsb.gov)
National White Collar Crime Center (http://www.ifccfbi.gov)
New York Stock Exchange (http://www.nyse.com)
New York Times (http://www.nytimes.com)

    Reed Abelson

    Neela Banerjee

    Shaila K. Dewan

    Kurt Eichenwald

    Nathan Glater

    Stephen Labaton

    Mireya Navarro

    Richard A. Oppel, Jr.

    John Schwartz

OddTodd.com (http://www.oddtodd.com)
PBS.org (http://www.pbs.org)
Platts (http://www.platts.com)
Powers Report (Report of the Special Investigation Committee—Enron Board)
Reuters (http://www.reuters.com)
Risk Waters Group—WTC Appeal (http://www.riskwaters.com/wtcappeal)
Salon.com (http://www.salon.com)
Scoop—New Zealand (http://www.scoop.co.nz)
Security and Exchange Commission (http://www.sec.gov)
Senate Commerce Committee (http://commerce.senate.gov)

Severed Enron Employees Coalition (http://www.theseec.org)

Shredco, Inc. (http://www.shredcoinc.com)

Swoon.com (http://www.swoon.com)

Texans for Public Justice (http://www.tpj.org)

TheStreet.com (http://www.thestreet.com)

    Peter Eavis

    Christopher Edmonds

Time Magazine (http://www.time.com)

U.S. Department of Justice (Sourcebook of Criminal Justice Statistics)

United States Bankruptcy Court—Southern District of New York

United States District Court—Southern District of Texas

USA Today (http://www.usatoday.com)

    Greg Farrell

Wall Street Journal (http://online.wsj.com/public/us)

    Susanne Craig

    John R. Emshwiller

    Jason Leopold

    Jathon Sapsford

    Rebecca Smith

    Jonathan Weil

Washington Post (http://www.washingtonpost.com)

    Peter Behr

    Paul Duggan

    Jennifer Frey

    Carrie Johnson

    Lois Romano

    Hanna Rosin

    Susan Schmidt

    Joe Stephens

Yahoo! Finance (http://biz.yahoo.com)

Acknowledgments

The Author wishes to thank Peter Cox of ILRM for backing a bitty first-time writer from across the Atlantic; Philip Turner, genius Executive Editor at Carroll & Graf; the legendary Herman Graf for applying his supreme wisdom and vision to the idea; and Jody Hotchkiss of HAA for that Hollywood thing. Many thanks to Steve Salbu, Dean of the Texas MBA program, for somehow squeezing "write Cruver's intro" into his chaotic schedule.

This book simply wouldn't exist without the help of other Enronians, who not only rode on this roller coaster with me, but also provided and/or confirmed much of the material: the real Bickers, Duffy, McLainey, Middleton, Perry, Waterston, the "Blue" men of Rudi Lechner's, and hundreds of other former and current Enron employees. Thank you all, and best of luck in your post-Enron adventures!

Finally, a special thanks to the people who supported me throughout the writing process, including the helpful citizens of Telluride, Colorado, and Venice Beach, California; my family and friends (even those who tried to talk me out of this); and Mom, for baking a huge dish of lasagna that fed me through chapters 7 and 8.

About the Author

Brian Cruver was born in 1971, and grew up in Sugar Land, Texas, before heading to Los Angeles to attend the University of Southern California, where he graduated with a degree in communications. He later returned to his home state, where he earned an MBA from the University of Texas at Austin, in 1999. With a diverse background that includes consulting, corporate finance, and strategic planning, Cruver ultimately landed his dream job at Enron Corp. in Houston in March 2001. *Anatomy of Greed* is the story of Cruver's extraordinary journey as an Enron employee during the months leading up to the company's collapse, until he was among the masses laid off the day after the bankruptcy filing. After being mysteriously left on the Enron payroll, and with a hard-won perspective on corporate America, Cruver decided to write *Anatomy of Greed,* his first book. Cruver and his wife currently live in Houston.